ADVANCE PRAISE

MW00573069

Jared Ball's carefully constructed narrativ[...] cal and evidentiary sources to provide a concise explanation of the mixtape movement. Simultaneously, he uses this history to illuminate how the media promotes ideological interests, and how those interests serve not simply the corporate bottom line, but the much larger political objective of assigning each of us our "place" in society. *I Mix What I Like!* serves as both an example of emancipatory journalism and a model for emancipated thinking, without which we will be consigned to struggling for a kinder, gentler subjugation rather than true human liberation.—Natsu Taylor Saito / Author of *Meeting the Enemy: American Exceptionalism and International Law*

Jared Ball is one of the most important activist intellectuals in the United States. His book is powerful and provocative.... Unlike President Obama, Professor Jared Ball is committed to revolutionary change in America. His book provides an insightful analysis and critique of culture, media, and African American politics.—Ollie Johnson / Department of Africana Studies / Wayne State University

Dr. Ball has created a twenty-first century Black radical manifesto that samples and remixes the best of the radical and anti-imperialist tradition. *I Mix What I Like!* recognizes the colonized nature of contemporary Hip Hop and the colonized context of the people from which Hip Hop emerged. In the tradition of Noam Chomsky and Public Enemy, Jared Ball brings the noise to the status quo and lays out his vision of Mixtape emancipatory journalism as the liberatory mass medium for today and the future. I strongly recommend this work for all those interested in reflecting upon the theory and practice of struggling for social justice in today's America.—Dedrick Muhammad / NAACP / Author of *Understanding Racial Inequality in the Obama Era*

One way to prevent the appropriation of a revolutionary culture—one that expresses the desires and visions of the oppressed to fight for liberation and self-determination—is to smuggle the word as if it is a liberatory tool, replicating the clandestine, anti-colonial and resistant drum of the maroon. Jared Ball's concept of "mixtape radio" follows that tradition with an irreverence that we so sorely need.—Claude Marks / Freedom Archives

Jared Ball's work conveys the ultimate reality about hip hop: that there is no nation space in hip hop but that which exists for revolutionary music for the Africans and African and Indigenous oriented colonial Spanish speaking peoples (misnomered latinos). The strength of the colonial argument presented places whites as settlers in hip hop. Load the audio clip and bust a shot for freedom!—Mark A. Bolden / The Fanon Project

Dr. Jared Ball's impressive book is a bold undertaking in which he critiques and ultimately distances himself from the prevailing assumptive logic found within pop academic circles. To be sure, Mixtape Radio does not offer itself as a panacea for the oppressive structures he addresses. The revolutionary power of this book lies in its capacity to interrogate staid constructs of thought and re-pose vital questions pertaining to "emancipatory journalism." For the power to pose the question is the greatest power of all.—Frank B. Wilderson, III / Author of *Incognegro: A Memoir of Exile and Apartheid*

I Mix What I Like! is a brave and necessary book that focuses the conversation about hip hop (and politics) beyond the limitations of 90% of published materials on the subject. Once again, walking the walk, Jared Ball offers a provocative, though not surprising, piece of work that shifts the debate into a much-needed direction.—Shaheen Ariefdien / Former member of the pioneering South African hip-hop group Prophets of da City

Like a classic—cassette recorded—Stretch Armstrong and Bobbito Show, circa early 90's New York City, Jared Ball's manifesto is a raw, uncut, ground breaking contribution to a new frontier of critical thinking and critique within Hip Hop discourse. Too many, are stuck on 'repeat' and 'ain't sayin nothin'! Love it or hate it, Jared Ball's work is necessary and vital for the cultivation of tradition and responsibility. Strong arm the system, grind mode heavy, "Let's Get Free!"—Carlos REC McBride M. Ed. / TRGGR MEDIA Group

Here, Jared Ball takes us back to the value of polemic and the revolutionary new knowledge-base of worldwide anti-colonialism before it was driven underground by counter-revolutionary repression. *I Mix What I Like!* is terribly thoughtful, terribly original—a joy for the "wonder-ground," and a political-intellectual terror for the overlords.—Greg Thomas / Author of *The Sexual Demon of Colonial Power* and *Hip-Hop Revolution in the Flesh*

Jared Ball is determined to rescue hip hop and left activism from increasingly subversive corporate control. This book is a manifesto that needs to be read, argued about, and yelled from the rooftops. Let the bricks fly!—Todd Steven Burroughs / co-author of *Civil Rights Chronicle*

The Funkinest Journalist breaks it all down for all servants of Soul/Funk music and Art in the 21st Century. His Mixtape Manifesto explains what we are up against battling corporate empires that control the coveted consumer-merchant access points, and offers us an option to distribute, connect, and popularize our culture.—Head Roc / "The Mayor of D.C. Hip-Hop"

I MIX WHAT I LIKE!

A MIXTAPE MANIFESTO

I MIX WHAT I LIKE!

A MIXTAPE MANIFESTO

BY JARED A. BALL

AK PRESS
EDINBURGH • OAKLAND • BALTIMORE

I Mix What I Like! A Mixtape Manifesto

By Jared A. Ball

© 2011 Jared A. Ball

This edition © 2011 AK Press (Oakland, Edinburgh, Baltimore)

ISBN: 978–1–84935–057–0

Library of Congress Control Number: 2011920475

AK PRESS	AK PRESS
674–A 23rd Street	PO Box 12766
Oakland, CA 94612	Edinburgh, EH8 9YE
USA	Scotland
www.akpress.org	www.akuk.com
akpress@akpress.org	ak@akedin.demon.co.uk

The above addresses would be delighted to provide you with the latest AK Press distribution catalog, which features the several thousand books, pamphlets, zines, audio and video products, and stylish apparel published and/or distributed by AK Press. Alternatively, visit our web site for the complete catalog, latest news, and secure ordering.

Visit us at www.akpress.org *and* www.revolutionbythebook.akpress.org.

Printed in Canada on acid-free, recycled paper with union labor.
Cover illustration by Joe Widener | Layout and Interior by JW & KK.

Por mis niñas Maisi y Marley.
No hay razon mas grande para luchar.

TABLE OF CONTENTS

ACKNOWLEDGMENTS

Much love and thanks to my wife Yari and my mother Arnette. Thank you to my godfather Tom Porter and to my entire extended blood and political family.* Thank you to the D.C. hip-hop community for your inspiration and support. Thank you to the many great elders and ancestors whose work is and is not mentioned here. Thanks to my many comrades and colleagues, with a special shout out to Organized Community of United People—no longer together but always with me. Thank you to the Malcolm X Grassroots Movement and to The Fanon Project. Thanks also to the many mixtape DJs and vendors who have sustained us for decades. Many thanks also to the low-power radio community, to Radio CPR-istas, and specifically to the inspiration of The Black Liberation Radio and Human Rights Radio networks. And special thanks to Mbanna Kantako. Thanks also to the D.C. Indymedia community. And many more hugs and pounds to Badia Albanna, Ciatta Zinna Baysah, Gabriel "Asheru" Benn, Mark Bolden, Mark Bowen, Todd Burroughs, Rosa Clemente, DaveyD, Bruce Dixon, DJ Earth 1NE, Glen Ford, Kymone Freeman, Suzette Gardner, Adanna Johnson, DJ 2-Tone Jones, Maleena Lawrence, Claude Marks, Parrish McLeary, Mazi Mutafa, Jason "Haysoos" Nichols, Dre Oba, Saswat Pattanayak, DJ RBI, Head-Roc, DJ Soyo, DJ Underdog, and Geoff White.

And a special thank you to all the political prisoners, past and present, whose support networks will be the only financial beneficiaries of this book.

A PREFATORY "NOTE TO THE READER"

I pledge allegiance to the mixtape DJs of the world!
—DJ Jazzy Joyce

DJs, producers, journalists, mixtapers of the world unite!
—The Funkinest Journalist

What does not kill us is an opportunity to organize!
—Parisa Norouzi

I Mix What I Like! is titled as an homage to the collection of articles, *I Write What I Like,* written under the pseudonym "Frank Talk" by Steven Bantu Biko.[1] Just as Biko sought to use his brand of alternative journalism to encourage a Black Consciousness among his South African audience—a consciousness meant to inspire a colonized population into spirited rebellion against an unjust regime—so too does the following suggest that the same journalistic purpose be put to the hip-hop mixtape.[2] That is, despite tremendous shifts in image and application, African America (and by extension the rest of the country and world) continues to suffer a process of colonization subsumed within a media environment more pervasive and all-encompassing than any other known in world history and against which alternative forms of journalism and media production must be employed. What follows is an argument in support of the underappreciated mixtape as a tool that can serve that specific purpose.

This process of colonization is predatory and is essentially "an entire conquest of land and people."[3] It distorts communication, dislocates victims from their cultural origins, and creates an ever-evolving and all-encompassing environment that inhibits the very establishment of a "political vocabulary" necessary for its identification.[4] One prominent form of this linguistic assault is the strict ordering of the most popular component of hip-hop—its speech element: rap music. It is the cultural equivalent to the assault elsewhere on the language of "neo-colonialism and imperialism" which, as accurate descriptors of current conditions, are "replaced by the language of post-coloniality and multi-culturalism (not to mention post-modernism)." This shift is made possible by, and is indeed necessary to, the "white power" that "continues to rule with an iron (if largely unnamed) fist. This is the power of white colonial rule, politically, economically, culturally, etc. past and present."[5]

As a particular assault on the linguistic element (though similar effort is waged against all other elements—indeed all other people—as well) colonialism aggresses upon the very "function of speech within African culture" and, therefore, also speaks directly to an expanded role of the theft of soul. The tradition of "Divine" or "Good Speech," what ancient Africans recognized as the role of the word, was at its essence a reference to the "ancestral transmission" or that which "links the human community to God."[6] Interruptions, distortions, or hostile manipulation of a people's linguistic expression is not only considered a part of the United Nations' definition of "cultural genocide," but, as seen by many African traditions, it is a preventative measure against divine metamorphosis. Colonialism requires an assault on the immaterial culture of a people in order to protect an assault on their material resources; the management of consciousness is a permanent concern for those in power, and there is no end to the need for or attempts at its management.

This predation—the act of the predator that has always included a theft or distortion of cultural expression as part of a project of colonial domination—has quite a long history, which even when quickly considered makes today's occurrence seem as if it is, inevitable.[7] For instance, one satisfactory point of departure could very well be the archetypal form of cultural domination: the theft of "the soul of the world" where African metaphysical astrology was reduced to Western religion.[8] Such theft forced even Sigmund Freud to finally overcome his fear and publish conclusions he had long before reached: "that the man Moses, the liberator and lawgiver of the Jewish people, was not a Jew, but an Egyptian… he was an Egyptian whom a people needed to make into a Jew."[9] Even earlier, Gerald Massey had determined that this theft had culminated in a Christianity that he assumed to be "the work of virtual forgers who obtained possession of sacerdotal authority upon pretenses entirely false."[10] But it was the enslavement and colonization—the theft of land, body, and spirit—that became that archetypal theft originating in the reduction of people to their specific, limited, and necessary function within developing empire(s). So, as Volney lamented in the early nineteenth century, a "race of men [is] now rejected from society for their *sable skin and frizzled hair*, founded on the study of the laws of nature, those civil and religious systems which still govern the universe."[11]

Today, those of "sable skin" continue to form part of a "race of [wo]men now rejected from society" despite having largely built it. This colonial or "social pyramid," that is, the hierarchical ordering of a society that is decidedly undemocratic and imperial, can and must be perceived so that it can be consciously organized out of existence.[12] This is the essence of this work. The choice of "colonialism" as name for these current conditions is explained further below but is simply meant to draw focus away from foolishly, even dangerously, insufficient descriptions of "failed democracy," or "an imperfect America," or any manner of description which at all denies the violently intentional inequalities against which are demanded wildly different arguments and suggested solutions. And, more specifically, conveying some degree of understanding of this colonial structure and how it defines the function of mass communication is essential to an argument that is itself almost cowardly or safely couched within a media analysis and journalistic response.

In the "Note to the Reader" that stands as preface to his now-classic work *Black Reconstruction*, W.E.B. DuBois makes clear the fact that one's ability to truly hear unconventional ideas requires first a recognition that a people's observable conditions are the result of imposed processes rather than their own inherent flaws. In his case, DuBois sought to demonstrate the processes by which Black America was forced "back into slavery" after the Civil War, whereas here the argument is that mass media function in support of a continuing colonialism, that is, in support of the continued expropriation of labor and wealth, and the spirit and culture of African America and, by extension and connected to, the rest of the world.

In this case, arguing that the rap music mixtape be fashioned as a radical form of journalism requires that we understand the colonial pyramid and the power it represents and protects and in whose service the mass media operates, intended, as it is, to create the societal fish who cannot then discover water because "a pervasive medium, a pervasive environment is always beyond perception."[13] Such an argument is intentionally in discord with conventional wisdom full of hope in the appearance of new technology and new appearances in leadership, most of which discount or diminish the intentional design of inequality or the necessity for those apparent shifts. Communities whose position within the pyramid are predetermined to be at the bottom may benefit from considering how low-tech media options connected to localized political organizing outside a non-profit industrial complex may further and invigorate their efforts.[14] But it is first this initial understanding that there is no inherent or natural tendency among the world's Black people to the lower rungs of the global pyramid that must take precedence for the following argument to even begin to resonate with the reader.[15] So, therefore, the intent here is to speak locally to a global issue and to then echo the sentiment of DuBois who wrote,

> [i]t would be only fair to the reader to say frankly in advance that the attitude of any person toward this story will be distinctly influenced by his theories of the Negro race. If [s/]he believes that the Negro in America and in general is an average and ordinary human being, who under given environment develops like other human beings, then [s/]he will read this story and judge it by the facts adduced. If, however, [s/]he regards the Negro as a distinctly inferior creation, who can never successfully take part in modern civilization and whose emancipation and enfranchisement were gestures against nature, then [s/]he will need something more than the sort of facts that I have set down. *But this latter person, I am not trying to convince.* I am simply pointing out these two points of view, so obvious to Americans, and then without further ado, I am assuming the truth of the first. In fine, I am going to tell this story as though Negroes were ordinary human beings, realizing that this attitude will from the first seriously curtail my audience.[16]

And more recently Slavoj Žižek has revisited this very point.

> Things look bad for great Causes today, in a "postmodern" era when, although the ideological scene is fragmented into a panoply of positions which struggle for hegemony, there is an underlying consensus: the era of big explanations is over, we need "weak thought," opposed to all foundationalism, a thought

attentive to the rhizomatic texture of reality; in politics too, we should no longer aim at all-explaining
systems and global emancipatory projects; the violent
imposition of grand solutions should leave room for
forms of specific resistance and intervention.... If the
reader feels a minimum of sympathy with these lines,
she should stop reading and cast aside this volume.[17]

Amen. Rather, Amen-Ra![18]

INTRODUCTION

People will not challenge us. They must treat us with silence.... So watch who people quote when it comes to Black scholarship. If they're quoted forget them.... If they are considered the most "compelling," the most "brilliant," what you see then is someone that does not help us. It is the invisible. It is the ones that we know. The ones that do not receive grants, the ones that are not lauded or called "super heroes" in each other's books. Or worse still the ones who are not considered the best by White scholars who stand over our archives like vultures keeping our history hostage and asking as the price of admission that you trade your soul for access to the things that your Ancestors inscribed. Those people that write on the backs of books that "this is the finest new scholar," that is the person that you should never quote. Rather, buy all their books. Read them for the sources. Get the sources yourself because what they have contributed is not a frame for interpreting but rather they have just given you a roadmap to the things that you need to reclaim.
—Greg Kemathi Carr

To talk about the subject I am going to talk around the subject.
—John Henrik Clarke

Complacency is a far more dangerous attitude than outrage.
—Naomi Littlebear

My approach was and remains unabashedly confrontational.
—Ward Churchill

In the late 1990s and early 2000s in northwest Washington, D.C., Cornelius Mays, aka "Big Man" or "Big Daddy," would sell, along with various articles of small clothing items, toiletries, oils, incense, etc., mixtape compact discs (CDs). From his van and portable tabletop he would post up on various corners most days of the week and, as he said, "provide a service" for those who "cannot afford store-bought music." At about $3 to $5 per mixtape CD, it was true that those willing to sacrifice some of the improved packaging of the standard music store CD could purchase copies of the latest rap, R&B, and reggae bootlegs and artist/DJ unofficial "for promotional use only" mixtapes. "I move about two hundred CDs a week if the police ain't harassing me," Mays said. And the police would often enough make sweeps of street vendors, looking primarily for those who, like Mays, could be said to be engaging in copyright infringement for selling bootlegs, or unlicensed copyright protected materials (CDs, DVDs, etc.).

The overt claim from law enforcement is that the unlicensed sale of music hurts artists and that much larger piracy operations are even used to fund terrorism.[19] While the latter claim can hardly be put to Mays, he did suffer enough police harassment, ostensibly to protect artists' ability to earn a living, that he eventually gave up that wing of his business. "When people claim that I am taking money from artists," Mays would say, "I remind them that [many of them] went broke long before I got into this business."[20] There would also seem to be a covert purpose here in the repression of mixtape vending or the criminalization of copyright infringement. First, artists do not, in most cases, own their own music, so bootlegging their music has less of a direct impact on them than some might suggest. Plus, with the increasing prevalence of "360 deals" (in which the corporations who own the artists' music gain percentages of everything the artist does that "uses the artist's brand or music"), it is the fundamental relationship that these corporations have with art and artists that is the real culprit in any exploitation that occurs.[21]

Second, the issue moves beyond the sale of music. What is ultimately at stake is the regulation of communication and the management of populations who have been targeted for subservience. Communities set to be ruled or colonized are not to be allowed a free flow of communication or cultural exchange. The very existence of a music industry that then lobbies Congress for further funding to better police its product speaks to an arrangement of colonial rule; of dominant, top-down management of distribution; of popularity and, therefore, of the *ideas* that will or may dominate a community. Should networks of unsanctioned communication occur, space will then exist for unsanctioned ideas to be exchanged, which may then inform or encourage unsanctioned behavior. Lockdowns on street-vending and mixtapes is analogous to protection of digital spectrum or terrestrial airwaves. They are the equivalent of the big-business giveaways of that spectrum and those airwaves, the assault on low-power/ pirate radio operators, or, historically, the assaults on alternative media-makers and journalists whose work has been seen as unpatriotic, heretical, or dangerous to the sanctity of existing power. —"State run radio"

Power is ultimately at issue, and control over media, primarily at the point of distribution or promotion, is essential. But as important as this fact is, "most ignore the basic relationship of the media to power. And power, whatever its nature, today includes a crucial media component."[22] Management, even at the level of mixtapes within America's internal colonies, must be maintained lest there be some upsurge in critical consciousness and activity. Management of media and communication is today a corporate and military operation where even advertisements are seen as "a vast military operation openly and brazenly intended to conquer the human spirit."[23] When media, along with "government, corporate or military power remain out of the control of ordinary citizens, no matter how profitable or efficient that may appear when 'packaged' for the public's consumption, it is tyranny—whether it appears 'friendly,' 'patriotic,' 'lawful and orderly,' or 'economically necessary.'" And, "media ownership remains the private domain of a privileged few in corporate America."[24] —Lupe SRR

Under the guise of a specific explanation of FreeMix Radio and the expansion of the more general concept of "mixtape radio" as a tool of "emancipatory journalism," this manifesto is meant to join existing explicit calls for organized (media) action in "defense of lost causes"—specifically the colonialism that continues to engulf African America and by extension the world.[25] The prescient warning (as it should be considered at this point) from Kwame Ture that "Black visibility is not Black power"[26] needs the deepest reconsideration at a time when the hypervisibility of Blackness in every realm of this society masks, but fails to deny, the fact that this same community exists far more as a colony than a citizenry.[27] As has been said quite rightly, "we are in no post-colonial moment," and are certainly "not completely free."[28] And why? Because, as Robin D.G. Kelley reminds us, "virtually every radical movement failed because the basic power relations they sought to change remain pretty much intact. And yet it is precisely [their] alternative visions and dreams that inspire new generations to continue struggle for change."[29] We are *not* post-colonial, post-modern, nor post-racial. What we are is a threat to power, as those who hold it are intimately aware. Their response to that threat includes, but is certainly not limited to, permanent assaults on our consciousness at any and every turn. "Capitalism," Kwame Ture still resonates, "makes us think we are thinking when we are merely reacting to stimuli."[30]

In one sense, we react to proclamations that change and progress have occurred with little real thought. We even allow these claims to stand in defiance against the conditions we see or experience. The claims are ideological. Acceptable boundaries of thought, expression, and certainly action are protected to assure that no unsanctioned change actually takes place. Consider, for example, the statement against clemency for Stanley "Tookie" Williams offered by Arnold Schwarzenegger, the governor of California in 2005. It was a statement in defense of colonialism and a justification of *only* the terror and violence of the state. Schwarzenegger took time to make the specific argument that reverence for representatives of certain kinds of thought and behavior should be punishable by death. It is as clear a public statement in defense of the current order that we are likely to see. As final proof against the "redemption" of Williams the governor wrote that

> [t]he dedication of Williams' book *Life in Prison* casts significant doubt on his personal redemption. This book was published in 1998, several years after Williams' claimed redemptive experience. Specifically, the book is dedicated to "Nelson Mandela, Angela Davis, Malcolm X, Assata Shakur, Geronimo Ji Jaga Pratt, Ramona Africa, John Africa, Leonard Peltier, Dhoruba Al-Mujahid, George Jackson, Mumia Abu-Jamal, and the countless other men, women, and youths who have to endure the hellish oppression of living behind bars." The mix of individuals on this list is curious. Most have violent pasts and some have been convicted of committing heinous murders, including the killing of law enforcement. But the inclusion of George Jackson on this list defies reason and is a significant indicator that Williams is not reformed and that he still sees violence and lawlessness as a legitimate means to address societal problems.[31]

Defining what these women and men represent ideologically or their alleged actions as deserving imprisonment or worse is itself subjective or ideological. And this statement should be read as explicit proof of the continuity of the struggle in which these women and men—the listed, the *condemned*—were, and are still, engaged. It is proof that their analyses and actions are themselves criminal and deserving of the most violent state repression. It is also proof that there is a penalty, even that of losing one's life, for simply and openly identifying with these people. In other words, it is not proof of Williams' lack of redemption but rather final proof of the absence of redemption, progress, or change in the state. It is final proof that this absence of state redemption is the presence of its continuing purpose and the continuity of a justifying worldview.

Mass media, the function of which is always the maintenance or expansion of that national ideology, are today more pervasive, more powerful, and more tightly controlled than at any other point in world history. In the United States, a continuing—as all processes are—colonialism has at its service this media technology, system of control, and academic scholarship, which, for the most part, mask colonialism's existence and the function that media play in its maintenance. Media, when put in the proper context of colonialism, can be seen as purveyors of "psychic violence," torture, or terrorism.[32] If terror and torture may be defined as that which distorts the target's ability to accurately interpret reality, to communicate with the outside world, or to fully locate one's own individual or collective identity, then certainly mass media perform this function.[33] Popular mass media that targets Black America (among others) fragments[34] the population via specific multi-genre productions, channeling, and monopolized ownership that consistently present the most limited ranges of Blackness[35] and provide little to none of what can be considered news or change-encouraging information (news),[36] or cultural expression.[37]

The argument that the rap music mixtape be fashioned into a form of mass media that can help disseminate those visions and dreams of fallen struggles (and call for their re-emergence) is born of the recognition of the primacy of colonialism, the need for anti-colonial struggle, and the notion expressed above that popular scholarship, media, and, therefore, ideas are fashioned in such a way as to discourage such perspective and activity. It is the intentional construction of a popular understanding of the world that produces conventional wisdoms or the common sense that is often "more common than sense."[38] This requires the prevalence of a different kind of journalism and scholarship, as our current ones far too rarely offer insight into the continued systemic, predetermined nature of a system that results in a "continued agony" among those within the lowest rungs.[39] Duty to popularity, to funding, or to tenure forces much of that work to be mildly biting in its critique while always reverting back to the safe and acceptable "solutions" of simply encouraging more thought on inequality, suggestions of individual uplift, or at most appeals to governing bodies in the hope of impacting legal policies.

This is a manifesto that centers African America *as* African America[40] and as such sees the Black American struggle as distinct but ultimately connected to that of the African world and with all those on the lower rungs of a global colonial pyramid.[41] An explicit argument for a reconstruction—more an updating—of that colonial pyramid so as to re-center *colonialism* as *the* continuing problem with its function being carried out through the mechanism of the state and its attendant institutions, mass media supreme among them.

Internal Colonialism Theory (ICT), a re-emerging theoretical approach, forms the foundation of this argument and it is to be hoped that it can become a valued contribution to that theory's multi-varied and growing body of work.[42] This theory will be discussed in greater detail below but in sum argues that Black or African America exists today more as an internal colony (or colonies) held within the United States. Rather than citizens, more "citizen-subjects," these communities experience a form of colonialism (domestic, internal, and/or neo) in which they are cordoned off and ruled, even if by proxy, from more dominant, distant, and White populations.[43] This colonialism can be summarized, as it once was by Jack O'Dell, as occurring where an alien population arrives to conquer indigenous ones or may also emerge as a people are "uprooted by the colonial power from their traditional territory and colonized in a new territorial environment so that the very environment itself is 'alien' to them."

Each occurred as part of the development of the project of the United States of America. And for our immediate purposes, a theory of colonization clarifies succinctly our concerns that in "*defining the colonial problem it is the role of the institutional mechanisms of colonial domination which are decisive.* Territory is merely the stage upon which these historically developed mechanisms of super-exploitation are organized into a system of oppression."[44] Such an approach, it is hoped, will aid the work of others who have attempted to return African America to a place within an international anti-colonial struggle so as to help fill a void wherein exists "postcolonial theorists [who] tend not to consider the experiences of African Americans when exploring matters of imperialism."[45]

The colonialism described herein related to African America and the United States is naturally a subset of a larger imperial process or what is often referred to openly as "empire."[46] Accepting this, then, it stands to reason that discussions that proceed on the basis of people as "free citizens," as opposed to *subjects* of empire, are inherently doomed. Discussions of subjects should proceed in terms of the colonialism that binds them. After all, empires are not composed of free citizens in democracies. Empires are composed of subjects within *colonies*, including those held domestically or internally. Theoretically, this approach is important for those interested in the development of practical responses designed to upset these relationships. Limitations imposed by false (faulty) notions of "citizenship," "democracy," "freedom," "progress," or even the suggestion that there is a "postcolonial" moment, render similarly limited analyses and prescriptions regarding response.[47]

Returning to a focus on colonialism allows for apparently foolish suggestions (i.e. the use of the hip-hop mixtape as a method of practicing a form of journalism called "emancipatory" that will inspire new movements whose aggression will replace this with a new society) to be reconsidered, thereby performing the important role of expanding debate.[48] If given time and appropriate attention, something as simple as a mixtape can, perhaps unexpectedly, reveal the nature of today's mass media and their relationship to, and function in support of, colonialism at home and imperialism abroad.

FreeMix Radio is a rap music mixtape freely distributed in and around Washington, D.C.[49] In this incarnation, the compact disc becomes an "airwave" or conduit through which forms of the music can be blended with journalism, speeches, interviews, and audio clips from any number of sources and then disseminated with the intent of being an underground press for the twenty-first century. The goal of this "new" press is to support and indeed foment social and political reorganization itself designed to bring about revolutionary change in the United States and the world. Each edition of the mixtape attempts to bridge the gap between the tradition of rap-music mixes and the tradition of street-corner oration, politically radical press, journalism, media-making, and specifically radio, whose relationship to Black America has been most solid, important, and remains today more interwoven into that community than any other form of mass media.[50] While all communities, of course, enjoy media that target them, none enjoy the kind of close-knit relationship held between Black America and Black radio.[51]

The suggestion that there is a need for a more critical or radical practice of journalism—emancipatory journalism/emancipatory media—or
that a low-tech mixtape be considered as space for this to occur has a
legacy to which it can easily be connected and a rationale which, with
equal ease, demonstrates that necessity once all is considered through a
non-conventional view of history and contemporary reality.[52] This is not
meant to suggest that the mixtape itself has been exempt from the process
within colonization that has been the case with all media technology and
the cultural expression of colonized people.[53] On the contrary, the mixtape—rap music's original mass medium[54]—has gone from the underground distribution network used by DJs to spread house (or street) party
mixes to a corporate-driven, track-listed "exclusive" prerelease mechanism
stripped of any originality in purpose, function, or content.[55]

However, unlike other popular forms of mass media today, the mixtape remains among the most viable spaces for the practice of emancipatory journalism and inclusion of dissident music or cultural expression.
With few exceptions, the intentionally designed structure of commercial
radio exempts that space for any such content. Low-power radio that
might serve as such a space has limitations of legality, which itself extends
as a problem to station location or housing, as well as cost prohibitions
placed on broadcast technology. Further are concerns of overall reach
where many low-power stations have a limited broadcast range of no more
than a few miles.[56] Beyond that, low-power FM simply does not have the
kind of cultural normalcy that exists between the mixtape and the hip-
hop or Black/Brown communities. Certainly there are legendary efforts
at micro-radio from within these communities. However, none match the
legacy of the mixtape which, to this day, remains a far more popular and
recognizable communicative form among hip-hop's progenitors.

And the Internet, contrary to popular sentiment, suffers existing gaps
in access for Black, Latino, and poor people,[57] coupled with heightening
attacks on Internet neutrality[58] and the establishment of higher broadcasting fees for those on the web.[59] This mass medium is no guaranteed
safe-haven for freedom of expression. Similarly, the Internet has not itself
proven to break any historical trends regarding media technology and
overthrows of power, nor has it been shown to alter which sources of
music and news are most popular. None of the most visited websites or
those that dominate popular "news" coverage would surprise those familiar with the current prevailing mass media corporate consolidation.[60]
Just as Huey Newton noted, in helping us establish what should be "*Our*

Newton's Laws," advances in technology are born out of the exploitation of labor and then used to further suppress workers.[61] It is the "abundance of bounty from robbery [that] has built a monster of technology."[62] Mixtapes, to the contrary, despite being products of modern mass-media technology, have a method and a network of distribution that is bottom-up as opposed to top-down, making them still more suited to the kinds of journalism being advocated here. And while they do face some levels of cost prohibition regarding production and distribution, mixtapes offer communities on the other side of that "digital divide" a reach that is equal to and more legal than low-power or "pirated" forms of radio.[63]

colonial pyramid

Highly disagree context 2011

Colonial Pyramid
of petty tyrants

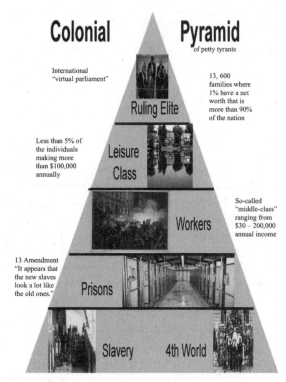

International "virtual parliament"

Ruling Elite

13, 600 families where 1% have a net worth that is more than 90% of the nation

Less than 5% of the individuals making more than $100,000 annually

Leisure Class

So-called "middle-class" ranging from $30 – 200,000 annual income

Workers

13 Amendment "It appears that the new slaves look a lot like the old ones."

Prisons

Slavery   4th World

A modern day system of economics which remains based on the theft of land and natural resources from Indigenous lands, that community's maintenance on reservations and the imprisonment, poverty, "ghettoization" of Black or African people.

CHAPTER ONE

THE COLONIZED RHYTHM NATION

> *In the fifteenth and sixteenth centuries, Europe not only*
> *began to colonize most of the world, but also instituted a*
> *systematic colonization of information about the world.*
> —John Henrik Clarke

> *By nineteenth century's end, the Western European will to*
> *know had consolidated in the expansionist exploration*
> *and attempted colonization of the globe.*
> —Gloria Sandoval

> *The ghetto might as well be the Gaza Strip.*
> —Black Thought

The United States is often referred to as an "empire," just as an ever-expanding community engaged in various aspects of its elements is often referred to as a "hip-hop nation."[64] But too rarely are the two concepts appropriately related. That is, if this nation is indeed an empire, it then proceeds from and is itself engaged in imperialism, or "the practice, the theory, and the attitudes of a dominating metropolitan center ruling a distant territory." Empire is also a "relationship, formal or informal, in which one state controls the effective political sovereignty of another political society," and this can be arrived at "by force, by political collaboration, by economic, social, or cultural dependence. Imperialism is simply the process or policy of establishing or maintaining an empire."[65] And as an empire, its relationship to its own citizens and certainly other nations is one of colonialism. Empires create colonies, externally and internally as well. Within the U.S., whether Indigenous, Black, or Latino or the more popular, politically safer, and less racially-specific "hip-hop nation," all exist more as internal colonies as opposed to free and equal citizens. And therefore, interpreting them as such, while challenging to conventional wisdom, is far more appropriate.

Consider, for instance, the previous point made by Jack O'Dell that, in "*defining the colonial problem it is the role of the institutional mechanisms of colonial domination which are decisive.* Territory is merely the stage upon which these historically developed mechanisms of super-exploitation are organized into a system of oppression," and is, of course, a logical conclusion of empire. Empires do not deal with equally sovereign nations or citizens.[66] Empires reduce nations (those both exterior and interior to themselves) to satellite client-states, which do not contain equally free sovereign people but at best "citizen-subjects" who, even when born into a "first world" setting, are met by the "intersections of race, culture, sex, gender, class, and social powers [that] are already locating in order to provide a particular space to hold [them]." This allows for appearances of "freedom" where "good citizens" unconsciously "replicate the social order and its hierarchizations, *usually* without the necessary imposition of directly brutal state force."[67]

This is a national or colonial equivalent to Marshall McLuhan's claim that "we don't know who invented water but we know it was not the fish. An all-pervasive medium, a pervasive environment, is always beyond perception."[68] So regardless of whether we embark upon an analysis of rap music, or the entire "hip-hop nation," as being "located within a continuum of black cultural movements including the Harlem Renaissance of the 1920s and the Black Arts Movement of the 1960s" or "through an evolution of African American musical production, with the blues, jazz, and R&B as its predecessors" or "mapped diasporically as a point of convergence for African polyrhythms, Brazilian capoeira, and Jamaican sound systems," what cannot be avoided in any case is that it emerged as part of a pre-existing, and global, imperial process of colonization that had long been in full swing.[69] The hip-hop nation is a colonized extension of a predating and continuing colonialism that engulfs its progenitors and governs still the process and necessity of the theft of soul or the grossest forms of distortion of communication.

When, not long ago, Derrick Bell described the impact of current U.S. public policy on African America as the equivalent of "weekly, random round-ups of several hundred" Black people who are then "taken to a secluded place and shot"[70] he was describing the end results of a public policy designed, as said by Ronald Walters, to protect a "*white nationalism*"[71] which can also be read as a protection of an imperial, colonizing settler population. That is, these policies that determine to whom goes the wealth or benefits produced by the nation are intentionally and permanently managed so as to result in the grossest forms of unequal distribution. In the end, the United States sees its own version of Memmi's "colonial pyramid of petty tyrants"[72] where this kind of maldistribution of material goods and positive treatment goes overwhelmingly to the top ten percent of the top ten percent, or to no more than 13,600 families.[73]

Similarly, James Cone has recently described these same policies in terms of a prison industrial complex and the very continued existence of ghettoes which he suggests act as institutionalized mass lynching, or crucifixion, meant to instill social order and control via terror.[74] This massive industry of incarceration, primarily of Black and Brown people, is also described as an extension of a still legal slavery[75] and the "political economy of the black ghetto" still requires that spatially, ethnically, and racially distinct populations produce wealth for some other *and dominant* society.[76] In fact, so long has this been going on and with so little change (Black people in the United States still have the same one percent of the nation's wealth held in 1865[77]) that even prior to this most recent economic crisis the economic conditions faced by African America had been described as a "permanent recession."[78]

These conditions result from Said's "legacy of connections," which were determined in a process of European expansion that saw as necessary the enslavement of African people and the establishment of settler and satellite colonies around the globe of which the United States and its internally-held colonies of Indigenous, African, and Latin American populations still find themselves.[79] And while African America has a long and re-emergent history of being described as suffering some form or another of internal/domestic/semi-colonialism rarely is this analysis brought to bear directly on this hip-hop nation as a method of analysis.

Even in its imperfection, an analysis that extends from such colonial analogies or from the notion of hip-hop as a "nation" is quite helpful. So it is true that the African and Latin American progenitors of hip-hop do not have "in common a single history, language, culture, territory and economy," nor do they have the requisite political control to be considered a "nation-state."[80] However, this hip-hop nation did develop certain tenets of nationhood, namely a shared sense of "culture, where culture in turn means a system of ideas and signs and associations and ways of behaving and communicating," and perhaps more importantly, where "they

recognize each other as belonging to the same nation. In other words, nations maketh [wo]man; nations are the artefacts of [people's] convictions
and loyalties and solidarities. A mere category of persons (say, occupants
of a given territory, or speakers of a given language, for example) becomes
a nation if and when the members of the category firmly recognize certain
mutual rights and duties to each other in virtue of their shared membership of it." It is "their recognition of each other as fellows of this kind
which turns them into a nation, and not the other shared attributes, whatever they might be, which separate that category from non-members."[81]

Taken "anthropologically," this hip-hop nation has become "a basic operator in a widespread system of social classification." The widespread acknowledgment of hip-hop's elements shows that there are
"establish[ed] grounds for authority and legitimacy through the categories they set down."[82] And while not constituting the aspect of "nation"
that is a "modern territorial state," hip-hop does consist of the prereq-
uisite basics of a "nationalism" necessary for the later development of a
nation proper.[83] It now even has its own *Gospel of Hip-Hop* (2009), its
own myth of origin (thinking back to Freud's discussion of the purpose
behind how Moses was reconceived), and a call for a new hip-hop identity as part of a "new civilization."[84] And ultimately, hip-hop does exhibit
a nationalism that Marimba Ani says "refers to the commitment on the
part of the members of a culture to its political defense, its survival, and
its perpetuation."[85] So there is a degree, a minimum achieved, to place
hip-hop nationalism within a broader context of imperialism and colo-
ny-formation. In other words, even if hip-hop is de-raced or somehow
(as some prefer) removed from its particular African diasporic origins
and racial, political, social context, its study must still contain the fundamentals of colonialism or anti-colonial theory. Empires and imperialism
are as transnational as any hip-hop nation and, therefore, so too is the
colonization of that nationhood.

As an expression in content and form of colonized people, hip-hop
is permanently and globally seen as a problem. Its colonized status travels
with it. And, therefore, its tendency to be a mouthpiece internationally
for those suffering various forms of empire creates for this international
hip-hop nation a constant hostility.[86] In the U.S., Charise Cheney describes similar, and what should be seen as obvious and natural, emergent
trends of "rap nationalism" and "Black nationalism." In each case these
were and still are "imagined communities" where "'nationalists' are a nation within a nation, or more accurately a nation without a nation."[87]

But as is the case everywhere, and where this becomes an international and ever-present problem for empire, Cheney's "imagined political community"[88] develops what Eure and Spady call a "Hip-Hop Nation Language," which spreads like a "fever" on the waves of "revolution," which Max Roach would say can always be "heard in the drums."[89] "Revolution, Revolution… Rap music is the voice of black people. Not just black people because you're black and you rap, but black people live in adverse situations like we find ourselves in here in America. And speaking out against that."[90] But this was prior to the mid-1990s and the massive move of the corporate elite to subsume this national tendency within its own imperial designs. On its own, the hip-hop nation was largely headed toward non-alignment:

> Think of how many wars, conflicts, disturbances (racial, ethnic, religious, territorial) occurred between 1970–1990. Palestine-Israel conflict, Guinea-Bissau, Korea, China, Senegal, South Africa—everywhere. Is it unreasonable to witness domestic violence when so much international violence is occurring, not to mention the proliferation of bloodshed on the domestic front?[91]

But empire is hostile to revolutionary nationalism. Imperialism requires a constant creation and re-creation of both the colonized and colonizer and a permanent re-inscription of the rightfulness of the settler.[92] The very purpose of popular culture and media within a colony is that it "reminds the settler of the reality of colonial power and, by its very existence, dispenses safety, serenity."[93] It simply cannot coexist with a popular "Nation Language," which belies the nature of hip-hop as "metonym" for the potentially threatening "black working class."[94] Then, as now, this Nation Language had to be assaulted, has to be constantly re-assaulted, via established corporate structures. Hip-Hop Nation Language, as explained, is threatening in its conscious reference to a history, identity, and world that crashes through those established specifically for the colonized. It is

> the language which is influenced very strongly by the African model, the African aspect of our New World/Caribbean [Black American] heritage. English

it may be in some of its lexical features. But, in its contours, its rhythm and timbre, its sound explosions, it is not English.... It is what I call, as I say, Nation Language... *a howl, or a shout or a machine gun or the wind or a wave.*[95]

And in his own more recent "discussion" with hip-hop, MK Asante, Jr. further demonstrates a kind of "Nation Language" simply not suited to sustaining empire. A language of Pan-Africanness, or that which validates any pre-coloniality must be discouraged if the colonized are to accept their state as natural or deserved. So, Asante says, "Hip-Hop... thanks for your time":

> *So, can you tell me where you're from?*
>
> Originally, of course, I'm from Africa. The Mother-land. I mean, it ain't hard to tell—just peep my first name...
>
> *'Hip?' I didn't know that was African....*
>
> The word 'hip' comes out of the Wolof Language, spoken by the Wolof people in Senegal, Gambia, and Mauritania. In Wolof, there's a verb, '*hipi*,' which means 'to open one's eyes and see.' So, *hipi* is a term of enlightenment. My first name means 'to see or to be enlightened,' ya dig...
>
> *Definitely, definitely, I can dig it...*
>
> That's Wolof too.
>
> *What—dig?*
>
> Un-hunh, it comes from the Wolof word '*dega*,' which means 'to understand.' So, you know, there's nothing new under the sun. It all goes back. Whether we know it or not, it's all rooted in Africa.... That's why my godfather named himself Afrika Bambaataa and

called his crew the Zulu Nation. That's *hipi, dega?*...
and remember to tell the people: I am their weapon!
Peace.[96]

Media, as the "fourth arm" of the military are manipulated to "secure
ideological victories" over the colonies through the application of propaganda.[97] Popularity in all forms, images, framing of news, manicured
forms of cultural expression or pop culture, are all managed to justify
the rightfulness of the settler in her or his civilizing mission, as well as
to demonstrate the rightfulness of the colonized as existing as such. The
kinds of expression represented in Hip-Hop Nation Language are simply
at odds with that mission. After all, imperialism is not simply an issue of
accumulating wealth; it is an issue of defining wealth, determining who
shall have it, and assuring that those who do are not openly, publicly, or
popularly known and criticized for it. Hip-Hop Nation Language, as that
which represents a more immediate example of the kinds of "oppositional
consciousness" that threatens empire,[98] represents also a response from
the "new interpreters" of the colonizer's "transmitted text," which must
now make a "new claim to validity" upon being confronted with an expression that resists "the systematic distortions of communication which
legitimate domination."[99]

The dominant "transmitted text" of hip-hop, that of African and Latin American people, is one that explains the necessity of their condition
as a colony and, therefore, cannot tolerate popular images of these communities that distort their "distortions." Stereotypes, as Walter Lippmann
famously described, are the "core of *our* personal tradition, the defenses
of our position in society."[100] Here was the point of Freud, Massey, and
Volney, and of the role of popular culture within imperial projects. The
very sanity and preservation of the psyche of empire requires established
mythology both of empire and its subjects. Or, as James Baldwin said, the
"root of the American Negro problem is the necessity of the American
white man to find a way of living with the Negro in order to be able to
live with himself." This required that an image of Black people be recast
as one that did not require "the impossible... for Americans to accept the
black man as one of themselves, for to do so was to jeopardize their status
as white men."[101]

It is not the perfection of Internal Colonialism Theory as a model
or analytic frame that compels. It is an attempt to address what appears
to remain a serious void in public and popular discussions of hip-hop,

the removal from them of "any historical context regarding the overall exploitation of black artists over the last one hundred years." Norman Kelley's particular criticism of the Marxist/Frankfurt School of "cultural industries" and "commodification" is that they ignore Harold Cruse-styled concerns over a cultural control and the development of "a black economy." Internal Colonialism Theory synthesizes concerns over race, class, and culture and addresses Kelley's concerns that the role of Black music in U.S. political economy is under-appreciated. Colonies are essential to the political economy of the colonizing "mother country." The natural resources of the colonized become invaluable contributions to the broader imperial project and, therefore, it stands to reason that Black music—as a raw-material natural resource—has always been and continues to be a powerful component of the larger political economy. So Kelley is absolutely correct in his description of "America's colonized Rhythm Nation," which works Black people under "plantation-like conditions" for a hip-hop industry that produces "aggregate worldwide revenues" of at least $40 billion per year.[102] These conditions exist because the fundamental relationship remains fully intact. It is not simply a matter of analogy.

As a theoretical approach to the study of African America, Internal Colonialism Theory (ICT) has a long history even as it garners new attention among scholars today.[103] It is by no means monolithic. There is no singular universal theory of colonialism as it relates to any of those most analyzed in such a manner (Native Americans, Indigenous People, Chicanos, Latinos, or African Americans). That internal debate, essential and fascinating as it may continue to be, will not be taken up here. However, a form of that theoretical approach is applied herein and will be given some context and justification below. Similarly, "colonialism" is used interchangeably with more historically specific terms such as "domestic" or "neocolonialism." This is not to dismiss important differences; rather it is to simplify the larger discussion and debate around the continued process of colonization and what that means regarding U.S. mass media, popular culture, and the role of the mixtape as journalistic response. In its simplest form the point is to draw attention to how Black American internal colonization "parallels in all important respects external colonisation, characterized as it is by settlement; extension of political control; relations of superordination/subordination implied or actual use of coercion."[104]

That said, it is important to offer some of the background and justification for the application of ICT or the study of colonialism regarding twenty-first century African America. Variations of this approach have long been associated with understanding and developing appropriate responses to the conditions of Black people in the United States. *At least* as early as Martin Delaney in 1852, this concept of African America being a "nation within a nation" has been considered.

> There have in all ages, in almost every nation, exist-
> ed a *nation within a nation*—a people who although
> forming a part and parcel of the population, yet were
> from force of circumstances, known by the peculiar
> position they occupied, forming in restricted part of
> the body politic of such nations, is also true... such
> then is the condition of various classes in Europe; yes,
> nations, for centuries within nations, even without the
> hope of redemption among those who oppress them.
> And however unfavorable their condition, there is
> none more so than that of the colored people of the
> United States.[105]

Its continued use and current re-emergence speaks to the fundamentally unchanged relationship Black people continue to have as a nation within a nation, as well as the role of the state itself in global geopolitics. ICT remains the best-suited theoretical approach today and speaks to an argument that anti-colonial media—in this case the mixtape—need to be developed in support of political organization against such conditions.

As shown in the model above, it is the colonization, as opposed to citizenship, of Black America that forms the center of this examination and explanation. Such an approach is helpful beyond African America and, in fact, helps extend a more complex understanding of this nation as a legitimate empire[106]—a singular dominant global power making all nation-states less relevant as individual sovereign entities and more so as all comprising worldwide communities currently existing in a "reactionary intercommunal" relationship.[107] That is, while traditional colonialism, much like its brother-in-arms, capitalism, has been reinvented,[108] it remains that its framework best defines the continued nature of the relationship between labor, capital, race, and gender.

Huey Newton was right to question all models of colonialism (neo, internal, etc.)—even the concept of "the nation" itself—given that "[t]he people and the economy are so integrated into the imperialist empire that it's impossible to 'decolonize,' to return to the former conditions of

existence."[109] It is also true, given the Western imperial design of each
and every single one, that no currently constituted state can decolonize to
one that is authentic or indigenous. All states are composed of formerly
separate and sovereign groups (or groups conquered and reorganized under a previous order). All countries today are the byproduct, directly or
indirectly, of European imperialism, and to that extent are inauthentic to
the people now therein contained. However, he was equally right that the
singular nature of U.S. empire—though now in decline—does maintain
a colonial relationship between itself and all other peoples.[110] It is this
relationship and its definition of institutional functions and roles that are
essential here.

To that end we can again take from Newton what has elsewhere been
described as "*Our* Newton's Laws."[111] These laws are the political extension of the laws of motion attributed to Sir Isaac Newton. He once gave
name to pre-existing universal laws of motion that can be summarized
as (1) nothing changes course without force; (2) the size of what is to be
changed determines the force required to change it, and; (3) change comes
to all involved in achieving it. And, of course, there is a political equivalent
here. *Our* Newton's Laws applied to the specific context of media technology
and their function within a colony first conclude that advances in technology are "gained through expropriation from the people, including slavery
proper but also chattel slavery followed by wage slavery. With this expropriation, a reservoir of information was created so that Americans could produce
the kinds of experimental agencies and universities that created the information explosion," which in turn is used to further the exploitation of
those same laborers.[112]

More specifically, the point becomes that advances in media technology by no means represent the requisite force needed for there to be
radical changes in social relationships. Revolution was not simply await-
ing the arrival of the Internet, Twitter, or Facebook any more than a gun
improperly used or directed can be expected to hit the right target.[113] The
transformations required to bring about the progressive societal changes
that many claim to desire require political organization and indigenous,
culturally-relevant media practices and journalism as a whole. Our currently constructed media environment is massive, which means the media produced in support of grassroots political organization must be at
least as strong. In fact, part of Newton's analysis regarding the issue of
colonization and decolonization was specific to this point. As Besenia
Rodriguez explains,

Departing from Lenin's notion of imperialism as the
highest stage of capitalism, Newton argued that capitalism, when traversing national boundaries to exploit
the "wealth and labor of other territories," transformed both the capitalist nation and the subjugated
territory. "The rapid development of technology led
to a shift in the relationships within and between nations. *The "swiftness with which their 'message' can be
sent to these territories has transformed the previous situation*," Newton argued. Beyond becoming a colony or
a neo-colony, these territories, unable to "protect their
boundaries... political structure and... cultural institutions," are no longer nations, just as the U.S. is no
longer a nation but an empire whose power transcends
geographical boundaries.[114]

Extending *Our* Newton's Laws to mass media, we must also conclude
that this media strength has to include, if not be solely culled from, existing low-tech and practical networks of community-based media and
journalistic practice themselves tied to political organization. In this case
the mixtape can serve just that function.

So, again, Newton's critique of models of colonialism should not be
mistaken to mean that more conventional approaches are themselves appropriate. In fact, his preference for Intercommunalism—or the concept
of there being no sovereign nations, only global populations all working
in various ways in service of a single empire—can only be understood
by first understanding the fundamentals of colonization. An inability to
decolonize to a previously existing indigenous grouping does not deny or
alter the colonial relationship held between, in this case, African America
and the United States or between the United States and all other nations
and people. This led Newton to appreciate tendencies among oppressed
people to seek "nationhood because they have not exploited anyone.
The nationalism of which they speak is simply their rightful claim to autonomy, self-determination, and a liberated base from which to fight the
international bourgeoisie."[115] This can and must be applied to African
America and to Latin America, as well as anything which is considered as
a hip-hop nation.

Colonialism as a model of analysis remains as imperfect today as
when it was more in vogue. But even in its imperfection it reveals more

accuracy and honesty about that relationship and what is needed to improve it than more traditional notions of pluralism, democracy, and "progress." As those who convened in April of 2009 to pay tribute to Robert Allen's *Black Awakening in Capitalist America* demonstrated, the application of a model of colonialism, internal colonialism, or neocolonialism is by no means monolithic.[116] There are many variations of such an analysis and what is described here is but one form. However, in that discussion, in those differences, is found more fruitful analyses and praxis than those that ignore, dismiss, or diminish the continuing colonialism engulfing the world.

By colonialism we mean a relationship between two (or more) racially, ethnically, culturally, and spatially distinct and defined groups between which there is an absolute *im*balance of power, whereby one determines the "social, political, and economic" condition of the other.[117] And what continues to confound scholars, activists, and their audiences is that trying to understand anything related in this case to African America, mass media, or even hip-hop without understanding colonialism is like "trying to understand the tides without considering the influence of the moon."[118]

A continued colonialism is precisely how the regions of the world replete with natural resources can at the same time be the poorest financially. More specific to the argument here is that this is precisely how a Black America can produce wealth for the primary stockholders in major corporations without at all eradicating gross poverty and gaps in access to material resources within Black America. A multi-billion dollar a year hip-hop industry has not done away with a single project or ghetto, and has done nothing to correct a system of education or expand the political strength of its progenitors.[119] However, and unfortunately, this is scientifically inevitable as a result of a continuing process of colonial exploitation, a political relationship that has seen no fundamental change since it was inscribed prior to this even becoming the geopolitical entity known as the United States of America.[120]

This relationship is *necessary* to maintaining those in power. It is the epitome of that which has been described as the dialectic between the development and advancement of one group that *requires* the equal underdevelopment and devolution of the other.[121] Before dealing with the ideology of mass media within a colony and, therefore, the placement of hip-hop cultural expression, the mixtape, or the notion of the mixtape as emancipatory journalism (or even just what precisely that is!), the central concept of colonialism demands some discussion.

One fundamental problem when attempting to reconceive African America as an internal colony is the continued standard for Black
America being plantation or chattel enslavement. Because pre-Columbian
Africanity is consistently (and foolishly) left out of most discussions, the
paradoxically correct standard of chattel enslavement in the end confuses
contemporary reality. The paradox, of course, is that were North American enslavement put in its proper context, African America would be
naturally connected to that longest strand of human history, making such
enslavement part of a continuum of African history rather than some sort
of a disconnected "beginning." Of course, this would then challenge ideas
of African people being "slaves," which suggests some sort of "natural"
condition. It would demand, instead, that they be seen as an enslaved
people with a history that predates that condition. From that it follows
that contemporary Black America could be seen less as "equal and free"
than as people potentially less free now than at many prior moments in
their history.

However, because this standard of plantation enslavement (then
sharecropping, lynching, Jim/Jane Crow, segregation, mass incarceration,
etc.) remains, it furthers misconceptions of progress or acceptability. With
this being the standard, everything seems like progress (and of course is!).
Against this, Malcolm X cautioned in his statement about a knife being
plunged "nine inches in your back… if it is then pulled out six inches you
don't thank them!" This standard continues to create difficulty in identifying a need for struggle and the methods that struggle should use. And
these seem—again placing African America within a global context of
anti-colonial struggles—to be similar to issues faced by those in other set-
tings. In Brazil, for instance, while these efforts are obviously not entirely
successful, there does appear to be a continuity in strategies used by those
in power to deny genuine freedom to Africans there. This system includes
"a denial of racial discrimination, a proliferation of negative stereotypes
of Blacks, and an imposition of illegitimacy on anyone who challenge[s]
the *de facto* unequal racial status quo."[122] Such tactics, while not perfectly
successful in preventing political struggles, should not be denied in their
attempt or existence. Even an emphasis on the agency of the colonized
should not ignore the attempts to blunt that potential power by those
whose own power is threatened by it.

Frantz Fanon perfectly summarized a definition of colonialism
when he said that "it is the entire conquest of land and people. That
is all."[123] That is, when considering hip-hop, mixtapes, or anything

produced primarily by and originally for African America and Latinos (or Spanish-speaking Africans colonized slightly south of us), we must remember that these populations only exist in response to the prior need of Western Europe to colonize the land and people of the "Fourth World."[124] And it remains the process of predation whereby the predator needs to confuse the primary fact that it requires a host, a geopolitical entity—a country or nation—that can and must only be subsumed beneath its own definition, its "constructed deception,"[125] and very real function; that of a colony.[126]

Rap music, and its original mass medium of the mixtape, come at the latter part of a long process of conquest of people and land. First, there is the physical theft of land and removal of resistance. Second, the attendant "psychic violence" waged against the surviving population.[127] It was Predator's original Shock Doctrine[128] via the creation of popular imagery further supported by the development of colonial "education" via Native Residential Schools whose task—modeled after the development of Black Industrial Education where schools were established to "replace the stability lost by the demise of the plantation"[129]—was to "kill the Indian and save the man."[130] Today, this "psychic violence" or terror is waged via incredibly powerful media technology that magnifies colonized images of oppressed people through advertising, careful selection, and promotion (through massive repetition) of playlist song and video, or ultimately an entire media structure designed specifically to maintain societal order within the colony and to assure the sustained placement of the U.S. as a singular global empire. The result continues to be an audience predominantly incapable of interpreting our reality, organizing to change it, or with an outlet to promote the need and existence of that resistance.

DEFINING COLONIALISM: A BRIEF HISTORY

Defining colonialism, or what it means to be a colony, and its relationship to power has never been easy and is no more so today. DuBois raised this concern when he asked, "What then are colonies?" Explaining the difficulty in defining them he went on:

> Leaving analogies, in this case none too good, we look to facts, and find them also elusive. It is difficult to define a colony precisely. There are the dry bones of statistics; but the essential facts are neither well measured nor logically articulated. After all, an imperial

> power is not interested primarily in censuses, health
> surveys, or historical research. Consequently we know
> only approximately, and with wide margins of error,
> the colonial population, the number of the sick and
> the dead, and just what happened before the colony
> was conquered.[131]

DuBois would eventually conclude, "using the term 'colonial' in a much broader sense than is usually given it," that Black America did comprise a relative nation within a nation whose condition was that of a "semicolonial." Similar to the point here, DuBois also relocated African America back to its proper place among "the vast majority of the people in the world" who formed "quasi-colonies," thereby, demonstrating that "the future of colonies was of vast importance to the future of the world." And most important immediately is the continuity of colonialism and its central role today. "Colonies," DuBois continued, "are for the most part investments, the main object of which is profit for the investing [Mother] countries."[132]

DuBois' challenge remains posed. The continuity of colonialism and its absolute necessity in governing social relationships must be met with an equal measure of investigation, reporting, and politically-organized response even as it is obscured today at levels never before seen. The natural intellectual tendency of the colonial system certainly continues to function. The "dry bones of statistics" that demonstrate the reality of African America *devolving* in terms of health care, housing, income, and mass incarceration[133] or demonstrate the widening of overall gaps in wealth.[134] Or that Black America remains fixed in permanent poverty, which sees little change regardless of larger economic trends,[135] and has suffered the largest loss of potential wealth in the nation's history during the recent sub-prime housing scandals.[136] Or when it is mentioned that the state's response to the levees breaking in New Orleans challenged no historical precedent, or that the killings of Sean Bell, Deonte Rawlings, or Oscar Grant are part of a continuing *tradition* of police brutality.[137] When taken as a whole, we are left with an unending wave of propaganda[138] encouraging us to process all this through a perspective that assumes these to be accidents of democracy, or worse still the pathology of Black people.[139] It is, after all, the self-fulfilling prophecy of "victimization"[140] and "self-defeatism,"[141] as opposed to anything structural or predetermined that leads to such gross inequality or mistreatment, or so we are told.

This kind of structural inequality, predetermined and scientifically inevitable, is the result of a system itself born of a worldview. Kwame Nkrumah offers powerful explanations that help clarify the relationship described herein of an African American internal colony as part of an all-encompassing and global colonizing structure.[142] He distinguishes between the traditional external colonies held abroad by a separate mother country and an internal or "domestic" one: "Capitalism at home is domestic colonialism." Further, Nkrumah's explanation of the ideological extension of varying economic systems remains relevant; he points out that Marx and Engels discussed economics primarily because that was their way of explaining how these systems are about the "production and reproduction of real life." Economics, the study of how resources are withheld and allocated, how labor and lives are managed, is, according to Marx, Engels, and Nkrumah ultimately about social order and organization. "More than this," wrote Engels, "neither Marx nor I have ever asserted."[143] For Nkrumah, this also means explaining the social ordering function of economics and summarizing historical shifts in forms of exploitation—shifts that should not have ever been seen as anything but just that: *shifts*. He explains,

> Capitalism is a development by refinement from feudalism, just as feudalism is a development by refinement from slavery. The essence of reform is to combine a continuity of fundamental principle, with a tactical change in the manner of expression of the fundamental principle. Reform is not a change in the thought, but one in its manner of expression, not a change in what is said but one in idiom. In capitalism, feudalism suffers, or rather enjoys reform, and the fundamental principle of feudalism merely strikes new levels of subtlety. In slavery, it is thought that exploitation, the alienation of the fruits of the labour of others, requires a certain degree of political and forcible subjection. In feudalism, it is adequate to the same purpose. In capitalism, it is thought that a still lesser degree is adequate. In this way, psychological irritants to revolution are appeased, and exploitation finds a new lease of life, until the people should discover the *opposition* between reform and revolution.[144]

Applied today it must be understood that there remains a need to recognize that "continuity of fundamental principle" which "enjoys [the] reform" of civil rights, notions of "post-colonial," "post-modern," "post-racial," and even the election of a Black president.

Colonialism as a model for the study of Black America, while enjoying some isolated focus and re-analysis, is too often described without being named. [145] African America's rates of relative poverty, police brutality,[146] mass incarceration,[147] infant mortality,[148] and segregation (imposed separateness both spatial and social,[149] and cognitive and educational[150]) are consistently studied with voluminous published results. These studies have produced conclusions that acknowledge our national "parallel" to the 1968 claim that we are headed toward "two societies, one Black, one White, separate, hostile and unequal."[151] Today, we see an "economically enforced apartheid,"[152] which creates separate worlds where most experiences with the "other" are mediated almost entirely by mass media.[153] This mediation prevents many from recognizing the stark and horrific realities faced by those forced to comprise the bottom rungs of this pyramid. For instance, it has been said that the conditions faced by early White Americans in colonial Philadelphia were actually better than those faced by the colonized in today's South Bronx,[154] and Black people living in South Central Los Angeles today have higher rates of post-traumatic stress disorder than those living in Baghdad.[155]

Atop this base of the colonial pyramid exists a ruling elite, described historically as the "invisible government,"[156] the "higher circles,"[157] the "1% who control 90% of the nation's wealth,"[158] or the "top 1 percent [who by the mid-1990s] captured 70 percent of all earnings growth since the mid-seventies."[159] These are the "international trade regime" described in terms of global food scarcity,[160] or the leading families, those who are *Born Rich*,[161] whose "greatest source of wealth is inheritance,"[162] all of which culminates in a national economic "pyramid" whose top 10 percent can be "sliced off" to reveal an even tinier elite atop which rests the wealthiest 10 percent or 13,600 households.[163] And further we see that

> the world has divided into rich and poor as at no time in our history. The richest 2% own more than half the household wealth in the world. The richest 10% hold 85% of total global assets and the bottom half of humanity owns less than 1% of the wealth in the world. The three richest men in the world have more

money than the poorest 48 countries. Fact, while those responsible for the 2008 global financial crisis were bailed out and even rewarded by the G-20 government's gathering here, the International Labor Organization tells us that in 2009, 34 million people were added to the global unemployed, swelling those ranks to 239 million, the highest ever recorded. Another 200 million are at risk in precarious jobs and the World Bank tells us that at the end of 2010, another 64 million will have lost their jobs. By 2030, more than half the population of the megacities of the Global South will be slum-dwellers with no access to education, health care, water, or sanitation. Fact, global climate change is rapidly advancing, claiming at least 300,000 lives and $125 billion in damages every year. Called the silent crisis, climate change is melting glaciers, eroding soil, causing freak and increasingly wild storms, displacing untold millions from rural communities to live in desperate poverty in peri-urban centers. Almost every victim lives in the Global South in communities not responsible for greenhouse gas emissions and not represented here at the summit.... Fact, knowing there will not be enough food and water for all in the near future, wealthy countries and global investment pension and hedge funds are buying up land and water, fields and forests in the Global South, *creating a new wave of invasive colonialism that will have huge geopolitical ramifications.* Rich countries faced by food shortages have already bought up an area in Africa alone more than twice the size of the United Kingdom.[164]

This elite, whose "wealth translates into enormous power"[165] via interlocking networks with like-classed individuals, has amassed an international influence that has been described as a global "virtual parliament" able to rule the world through by-the-second investment in or disinvestment from any nation.[166] In the United States this concentration of wealth and power has resulted in an entrenched plutocracy[167] where such imbalances lead to concomitant imbalances in political power and to an "economic terrorism"[168] often serving—with little help from existing popular notions of liberalism, pluralism, or democracy and freedom—to obfuscate "one of the world's enduring covert partnerships," that of "power and money."[169] In the end this means that an overwhelming majority of the national population is held powerless over their own lives and possibilities. Improving or simply maintaining our position within the pyramid creates a permanent sense of unease or terror, the economic terrorism that ensures levels of permanent stress akin to war veterans suffering from post-traumatic stress disorder. Life within the nation, being colonized within the seat of empire, is not altogether different, it turns out, from the experience of fighting those colonized by empire in the exterior.

The nation-state itself, which many among the colonized fight to defend in those same wars, has too-long been seen as necessary to the establishment of such a pyramid and, as Joseph Salerno has written,

> the state throughout history has been essentially an organization of a segment of the population that *forsakes peaceful economic activity* to constitute itself a ruling class. This class makes its living parasitically by establishing a permanent hegemonic or 'political' relationship between itself and the productive members of the population.

Salerno goes on to further our own analogy by describing this "ruling class" as those who live off of the labor, wealth, and tax-producing elements of society as, in fact, "tax consumers." Those from whom this wealth is extracted he describes as subjects in colonies or tax-payers in democracies.[170] In other words, in a colony and a so-called "democracy," the result and relationships remain. Applied specifically to the United States this has been described in terms of a history of the development of a White Nationalism in which a sophisticated public "policy racism" has evolved, designed to protect those interests.[171] This, in turn, has prompted legal scholar and professor Derrick Bell to conclude that

> [i]f the nation's policies towards blacks were revised to require weekly, random round-ups of several hundred blacks who were then taken to a secluded place and shot, that policy would be more dramatic, but hardly different in result, than the policies now in effect, which most of us feel powerless to change.[172]

RACE AND RACISM WITHIN THE COLONY

Race remains a (the?) primary determinant of wealth, health care, standard of living, and education, while levels of proximity mean little in terms of genuine interaction or understanding between racialized groups. But it is the very limited realm of debate that prevents a more critical conception of reality today and keeps those involved within the very safe boundaries of maintaining the status quo or seeking reprieve within liberal-pluralist models (usually by suggesting we vote for a different democrat).[173] This "postmodern complacency" does encourage much of the popular scholarship on such subjects to adopt the "predominant ideology," which is dismissive of more heavy-handed criticism in favor of "softer" forms.[174] For what are we to do about a colonialism "which threatens to take in all thought about it?"[175]

The adoption of a model of colonialism "allows the application to the ghetto of theoretical tools of analysis in the study of developing nations."[176] Here it forcibly refocuses attention to the function of media as ideology, as cultural expression that is White supremacist—racist. As Fanon surmised, "a colonial country is a racist country.... The racist in a culture with racism is therefore *normal* [and] has achieved a perfect harmony of economic relations and ideology."[177] This also means that all that is produced by a racist culture, "whether they set out to attack it or to vulgarize it, *restore[s] racism*. This means that a social group, a country, a civilization, *cannot be unconsciously racist*."[178] This challenge from a model of colonialism is important because it demands that we shake off tendencies to find comfort zones within mainstream media. No amount of popular, sanctioned media is anti-colonial. They are all *consciously racist* products that operate as systemic defense mechanisms. Decolonization can only come with unsanctioned media. It is the softened media equivalent of Fanon's conclusions of literal violence. Here, the violent reclamation of media space or journalistic practice is the decolonizing activity. And it is a model of colonialism that, in fact, makes such action just within the context of international law. If, for instance, the United Nations ruled—as it did in 1987—that populations in "'the struggle for self-determination, freedom and independence' against 'colonial or racist regimes' or 'foreign occupiers'" can do nothing that falls "under the rubric of terrorism" then why not at least engage in mixtape radio or any other form of unsanctioned media work?[179]

This is important for at least two reasons. The first is that it, again, allows for African America to be placed back within a global context in such a way as to reconnect this community with others struggling against similar colonial oppression. Secondly, for the more specific purposes (later detailed) of situating a mixtape as part of an anti-colonial journalistic endeavor, this approach helps to explain the concept of emancipatory journalism and its relevance to twenty-first century Black America (and elsewhere). Another reason can be added as well. As mentioned above, such an approach helps to revive a lost tradition of a particular method of theorizing about Black America and points toward ways to radically improve the community. The ease with which Black people, hip-hop, media, and related topics are narrowly held within acceptable ranges of debate, most of which never appropriately address the situation, needs further challenge.[180]

Colonialism, or the process by which the land, labor, and cultural expression are all "mined," packaged, and marketed so as to extract resulting wealth from one community to build that of another, has long been held as a model of analysis for Black America.[181] Failure to apply such an approach often "allows for the false reading of the Western imperialist impulse as distinct from Black chattel slavery in America and Jim and Jane Crowism."[182] This reinforces a troubling lack of attention paid to the important fact that Black America, as a distinct African population, emerged (or was created) just as the peoples of the African continent and those throughout the Americas were themselves rearranged, named, and formed into European colonies. Similarly, the standard use of the term "colonial America" as a reference to this nation's origins encourages a disconnect between the "imperialism of Western societies" and the "American racial experience." "In emphasizing," as said Blauner, "the relations between the emerging nation of White settlers and the English mother country rather than the *consolidation of White European control*, the conventional usage [of the term "colonial"] separated the American experiences from the matrix of Western European expansion"[183] which itself has been described elsewhere in terms of tracing a "Cartography of Death."[184]

Similar dismissals of conventional interpretations of this nation's history support a model of colonialism. Just as imperialism and colonialism mean to establish dominance of an elite minority[185] over a conquered or controlled majority, so too are these the genuine origins of this country. The so-called "American Revolution" was more a supplanting of King George III of England with the eventual "King" George Washington (I); even as late as the 1960s it had been noted that "the American presidency has become very much more personal and monarchical than any

European monarch ever could be."[186] Eighteenth-century contemporaries noted only the semantic difference between European "nobles" and American "men denominated 'gentlemen'"[187] who had crafted a Constitution that was more a conspiracy to keep power among the tiniest and most elite "slaveholding interests in the South and moneyed interests of the North."[188] It must also be remembered, contrary to popular mythology,[189] that this nation and its non-democratic *republican* structure was developed to protect that tiniest faction of elite White men[190] against the "disease" of democracy or the "wicked projects" of cancellation of debt and egalitarian distribution of land.[191]

This "crisis of democracy," as it would become known by the 1960s, saw the kinds of ever-renewing energy among "women, youth, elderly, labor, minorities, and other parts of the underlying population" to "press their demands"[192] that continue to require various methods of suppression. This nation remains strictly a *Democracy for the Few*[193] who own society and govern our lives from their position as the "lords of capital,"[194] that "invisible government"[195] whose "hidden primar[ies] of the ruling class"[196] offer us the pre-determined victors of "quadrennial extravaganzas"[197] all arranged via *The Golden Rule: The Investment Theory of Politics*[198] to assure that this be nothing but *The Best Democracy Money Can Buy*.[199]

Deficiencies of democracy are more interpretable by models of colonialism precisely because of the focus on conquest and predation that they demand. Popular notions of democracy are antithetical to this, *or any state*, as they all comprise a continuing "Western colonial dynamic, however isolated... from the European center." The United States developed and remains grounded

> on the basis of Indian conquests and land seizures, on the enslavement of African peoples, and in terms of a westward expansion that involved war with Mexico and the incorporation of half that nation's territory. In the present period our economic and political power penetrates the entire non-Communist world, a new American empire, basing its control on neocolonial methods, having supplanted the hegemony of the European nations. *A focus on colonialism is essential for a theory that can integrate race and racial oppression into a larger view of American social structure.*[200]

The necessity and function of colonies as essential to the maintenance of power has to be considered in order to best understand the Black American condition, including impact on that community's cultural expression (hip-hop, mixtapes, journalism, etc.). In each case, as it is with African America, the colony is controlled from afar economically, socially, and politically[201] and supplies cheap natural resources[202] and labor[203] and mined cultural goods (e.g. blues,[204] jazz,[205] R&B, hip-hop,[206] etc.). The colonies are also used to expunge excess population whereby overpopulated European centers have sent overflow populations to settle other territories and seek out new wealth for the "Mother Country."[207] Colonies also serve as "a safety valve for modern society"[208] where societal ills (e.g. violence, drugs, prostitution, etc.) could be kept properly away from the civilized. Cecil Rhodes was perfectly clear when he noted in response to conditions among the poor in England, which had reached dangerous lows, that to save "40,000,000 inhabitants of the United Kingdom from bloody Civil War, we colonial statesmen must acquire new lands to settle the surplus population.... If you want to avoid civil war, you must become imperialists."[209]

However, interest in history aside, none of this has changed.[210] The advancement of colonialism into new phases, with new looks, had been foreseen even as the old form was in the throes of death (read: *transformation*).[211] Forms shifted. So says John Perkins that "modern-day conquistadors" serving new empire, went from doing so on behalf of Catholicism and "Caesar or King" to democracy and the "U.S. president." And all the while controlling African land and people—and the wealth and social control this generates—remains key: "if you ever intend to have children, and want them to live prosperous lives, you damn well better make sure that we control the African continent."[212] It varies only slightly in the U.S., but the function and relationship remain the same. Black people, as a community from which cheap labor and resources must be gleaned (in this case a cultural resource—hip-hop), must also always be maintained as a community in which this colonialism takes its most obvious shape. The existing distance, both social and cognitive, between Black and White America allows for the former to provide the latter with the necessary illusions[213] or the consensual hallucinations[214] required to maintain each in their varying positions within Memmi's pyramid of petty tyrants.[215]

COLONIAL ILLUSIONS AND DEPENDENCY

These illusions and hallucinations, in this case, refer to White America's inability to become "psychologically organized"[216] to struggle for

fundamental societal change (as opposed to reform), due in large part
to a belief that African America had its moment (in Civil Rights) and is
now relatively equal, or could be if not for the failings of Black people,
and are ultimately connected to—or the cause of—whatever perceived
injustice Whites feel regarding their own station in life. An extension of
Marx's explanation of the differences between colony and Motherland (or
in this case the difference between Black and White America) helps to also
explain, to some degree, how this illusion is maintained. Marx argued that
in the homeland (i.e., White America) there are more appropriate ratios
of space to population and capital investment to jobs and workers, meaning that more of those (percentage-wise) who need a job have one and are
then also *dependent* on that employer. Because of the induced hallucina-
tion this can appear as a "free contract" between employee and employer
when, in reality, this is imposed wage-servitude or slavery.[217]

But repression breeds its opposite. Within the colonies, rebellion or
resistance has great potential (hence also the reasoning for all the surveil-
lance, policing, and imprisonment). In the colonies, Marx continues, the
myth of a balanced ratio between workers and available jobs is destroyed.
The "beautiful illusion is torn aside."[218] Because the colony exists as an
over-populated, distant, under-funded community to which broader societal ills are exported and where capital investment and, therefore, jobs
are limited, there exists some potentially beneficial (and dangerous) *independence*. No capital investment, no jobs. No jobs, no dependence. No
dependence encourages alternative forms of earning and expression that
can and do occur. Herein has always lain the threat of the colonized.

Marx argues that this overflow of workers become themselves independent peasants and artisans who "disappear" from the pool of available cheap labor but not "into the workhouses."[219] "Think of the horror!"
Marx exclaims in jest. For, again, the outcome and the irony of this colonial situation is that the capitalist loses the home-court advantage, so
to speak. At home there is a close enough relationship between capital
investment, or the number of jobs available, and the needy labor pool.
Thus, the social control mechanism of dependence on the capitalist (colonizer) remains relatively hidden and runs smoothly. This balance is upset
in the colonies by higher numbers of unemployed and less capital investment, meaning that fewer job alternatives potentially develop among
those colonized. If you cannot or will not employ me why then should
I feel dependent upon you? The dependence on the capitalist (colonizer)
is weakened. Again, for Marx, whether in the imperial Mother Country

or colony, the same fundamental relationships exist between the wealthy elite and those whom they employ. The shape of or methods used to facilitate that relationship may shift from one location to another but only as those shifts are needed to maintain the elite as such.

What is also of prime importance to those interested in new media development or political organization is the "social relationship of dependence" described by Marx, wherein the worker (colonized) *must be dependent* on the capitalist (colonizer) in order to preserve the economic and *social* order. It is here that some attention must be placed on the issue of culture and the need to shape it for the purpose of maintaining that social order. If the colonized, as Marx explains, does not feel dependent on the capitalist for her or his income, the colonizer enters dangerous waters.

The danger is in how the colonized sustain themselves, with what methods and, in this case, how these efforts are communicated and with what impact. If money is ultimately only a surrogate for other forms of social control,[220] then a population able to derive financial sustenance from sources other than those provided by the colonizer is a population that may become unmanageable.[221] This is the underlying reason behind assaults on street-vendors, including mixtape vendors, who engage in the surreptitious acts of daring to earn money and disseminate ideas, breeding forms of dissident communication and culture all without dependence on or sanction from the colonizer. The ability of the colonizer to wage psychic violence requires the ability to maintain levels of poverty among the colonized while also maintaining order over their communicative potential.

The issue of culture will be discussed below but it is important to note here that the suggestion that the mixtape serve as a kind of underground press is an attempt to address the limits of Marx and to center the specific experience of the colonized. In one sense, this is important because a "rapidly advancing" domestic or neocolonial form of rule over African America—which is, as Allen describes, "a form of indirect rule, which means that there must be an agency in the indigenous population through which this rule is exercised"[222]—is cultural as well as political. That is, class divisions must be encouraged as a means of producing an acceptable political elite drawn from within the colony who look like the colonized, so as to weaken potential rebellion. But there must also be a popular cultural elite drawn from the colonized, who can perform the same function. This requires cultural dominance, the popularization of only certain forms of colonized culture, which support the larger project of the colonizers (who of course are in command of that popularization process).

This cultural focus, so well articulated historically by Fanon and Cabral, is also an attempt at moving beyond the limits of Marx, which, as Ayi Kwei Armah suggests, are found in his binding Eurocentricity and a lack of praxis. According to Armah, the flaws of applying or centering Marxist thought in the context of colonialism, from the perspective of the colonized, is that Marx's ideas may "constitute an interesting body of hypotheses, useful as probes, [but] not theories." What makes people revolutionary for Armah, unlike Marx and Engels, is that they become "participant[s], in actual praxis, in a movement that overturns an oppressive social system, replacing the oppressive rulers with the oppressed."[223] This, according to Armah, distinguishes Lenin, Mao, Giap, Ho, Fanon, and Cabral as revolutionaries.[224] For Fanon, the aspects of race and culture pointed toward key deficiencies in Marx. He writes, "[t]he cause is the consequence; you are rich because you are white, you are white because you are rich. This is why Marxist analysis should always be slightly stretched every time we have to do with the colonial problem."[225] The transformation of the mixtape into a tool of emancipatory journalism is an attempt to address this distinction, at least within the context of media and journalism.

In the end, and similar to the point made by DuBois, "the fact is that colonization is neither a series of chance occurrences nor the statistical result of thousands of individual undertakings." It is, continues Sartre, "a system" that arose out of the post-ninteenth century European need to replace, expand, and modernize (or make safer) the exploitation of body and land. And following Sartre, the intent here—through a discussion of media, hip-hop, and the emancipatory journalistic mixtape—is to demonstrate "the rigour of the colonial system, its internal necessity, how it was bound to lead us exactly where we are now, and how the purest of intentions, if conceived within this infernal circle, is corrupted at once."[226]

Colonialism and Mass Media

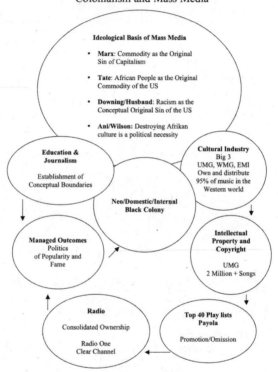

Ideological Basis of Mass Media

- **Marx**: Commodity as the Original Sin of Capitalism

- **Tate**: African People as the Original Commodity of the US

- **Downing/Husband**: Racism as the Conceptual Original Sin of the US

- **Ani/Wilson**: Destroying Afrikan culture is a political necessity

Education & Journalism

Establishment of Conceptual Boundaries

Neo/Domestic/Internal Black Colony

Cultural Industry
Big 3
UMG, WMG, EMI
Own and distribute 95% of music in the Western world

Managed Outcomes
Politics of Popularity and Fame

Intellectual Property and Copyright

UMG
2 Million + Songs

Radio

Consolidated Ownership

Radio One
Clear Channel

Top 40 Play lists
Payola

Promotion/Omission

CHAPTER TWO

MEDIA AS IDEOLOGY, CULTURE, AND COLONIALISM

When Goebbels, the brain child behind Nazi propaganda, heard culture
being discussed, he brought out his revolver. [He] had a clear idea of
the value of culture as a factor of resistance to foreign domination.
—Amilcar Cabral

It's the media causing mass hysteria in all
areas... barriers to emancipation...
—The Welfare Poets

Media are often ignorantly discussed as simply an industry or a collection of "organized technologies"[227] (i.e., radio, television, newspapers, etc.) "rather than as the complex *socio*technical institutions that they are."[228] More clarity as to their impact only becomes possible when media are more appropriately redefined along the lines of "the plural of medium" or the "range of possible channels of communication employed in discourse... [and discourse being] the way in which that functioning reflects and sustains power and those who wield it."[229] In other words, media are best understood as those channels through which ideology and culture are transmitted, such that they shape consciousness specifically (only!) to determine the behavior of the target population.[230] And, "in respect to culture, the mass media constitute a primary source of definitions and images of social reality and the most ubiquitous expression of shared identity."[231]

In fact, more than just the dissemination of ideology, media products *are* the ideology or worldview of those who create the notions that are then transmitted. Media are popularly disseminated ideology. Based on the current model, this ideology, broken into four primary components, consists of a need to (a) turn any and everything into a commodity, or something that can be bought, sold, or traded. This is what Marx called the "original sin" of commodity formation.[232] In the United States, the capture, purchase, and sale of African people became (b) the archetypal "original commodity-fetish" described by Greg Tate.[233] Black (Brown and Indigenous) people whose bodies and land have become the foundation of the nation's wealth continue to see what they produce (in this case the cultural expression of rap music) forced into those existing social relations. Black people have always been, and still remain, seen as producers of entertainment and wealth for White society. This in turn reifies the cyclical need to depict these African people as inferior and deserving of said treatment where (c) White supremacy becomes and is the national "conceptual original sin" of Downing and Husband.[234] Maintaining this necessitates, for political purposes, (d) the destruction among African people of an African consciousness. Or, in the words of Amos Wilson, it means keeping Black America "out of its mind."[235] Media play a primary role in helping to establish which forms of cultural expression will be popular and this in turn sets the boundaries for acceptable ranges of thought, cultural expression, and ultimately behavior. Because, in the end, Sonia Sanchez remains correct that "WITE AMURICA is the 'only original sin.'"[236]

Culture, or the ways in which people understand, interpret, and react to their environment, must be manipulated in order to achieve and maintain levels of compliance. Therefore, the cultural expression (in this case hip-hop) of a community must be managed so as to promote acceptable behavior (according to those who rule). If, as is assumed here, the term "culture" is understood to describe a "set of control mechanisms—plans, recipes, rules, instructions... for the governing of behavior,"[237] or as a "process which gives people a general design for living patterns for interpreting their reality,"[238] then clearly culture would be a primary target for the waging of psychic violence and terror. Words and musical sounds express and convey that which an individual or community has developed as their own "spiritual eyeglasses through which [people] come to view themselves in the universe."[239] But culture too is a "battleground" where the challenge is then to connect the cultural expression of a people "not only with pleasure and profit but also the imperial process of which they [are] manifestly and unconcealedly a part."[240]

So then, upon hearing a suggestion that the goal of the colonized *not* be to enter the mainstream, or "Eurostream,"[241] or that alternative media (i.e. mixtape radio) be developed for local communities with no design or goal of "mass" popularity often enough, the response is just as described by Fanon: one of confusion and disbelief. The idea's proponent is often met with invitations to adjust her language to accommodate what mainstream (even mainstream "progressive") media outlets would prefer. All too often, reflexive progressives express an empty hopefulness in sentiments that include "The Internet is a viable alternative;" "There is hope for change in appeals to the FCC or public policy-makers;" or "We must reform media policy before being able to use media for our causes." In other words, this progressive argument is that it is folly and the height of irresponsibility to abandon acceptable forms of struggle (media or otherwise) or to radically attempt to reclaim media space in low-tech, localized ways with differing style, content, or political foci. Or as Fanon put it, the decolonizing "native" is told to put her "trust in qualities which are well-tried, solid, and highly esteemed." But, as Fanon continues, when one who is bent on such decolonization

> hears a speech about Western culture he pulls out his knife—or at least he makes sure it is within reach. The violence with which the supremacy of White values is affirmed and the aggressiveness which has permeated the victory of these values over the ways of life and thought of the native mean that, in revenge, the native laughs in mockery when Western values are mentioned.... In the colonial context the settler only ends his work of breaking in the native when the latter admits loudly and intelligibly the supremacy of the White man's values. In the period of decolonization, the colonized masses mock at these very values, insult them, and vomit them up.[242]

This kind of necessary expulsion ("vomit") of Western or colonial values too has a long tradition of intellectual focus within African America. Afrocentricity or African-centered thought, one such tradition, while too often summarily dismissed (with little detail or academic rigor, which that wing of study in all its variation deserves[243]), remains relevant particularly when considering the cultural expression (hip-hop) of a domestically-held African colony. Returning to the model and the "Ideological Basis of Mass Media," one can see (beginning with the bottom or foundation) the African-centered recognition that destroying African culture is, as described by Amos Wilson, a "political necessity" where African America must be kept "out of our minds"[244] in order to be made to accept current conditions.

The composite culture of African Americans includes "residuals and fundamentals" of African culture but is also an "amalgamated product of the American experience,"[245] which is itself one of conflict, dominance, and an instrument of White power. So just as some have discussed mass media within the context of manufacturing consent[246] or public opinion[247] centering the experience of the African-descended origins of hip-hop requires that there be consideration of the *specific colonial experience* of Africans in the Americas[248] and the "socially manufactured" nature of culture as a means of shaping group or individual identity[249] in a manner that reflects that need to both create the colonized *and* the colonizer.[250]

This relationship of dependence is, of course, dialectical. Just as the dominant power or Mother Country needs the colonies to remain underdeveloped so as to assure its own development so too do those in power need to shape the image of those they rule, both to assure that the subjects remain dependent but also so as to recreate a mythological self-image that appears as divine or natural and which holds themselves as the only legitimate handlers of power. The underdevelopment of African America, as described by Manning Marable, is the "direct consequence of [a] *process*: chattel slavery, sharecropping, peonage, industrial labor at low wages and cultural chaos."[251] This, for Downing and Husband, is where their "conceptual original sin" can be seen; that is, as part of the need to set "race(s)" into "distinct categories defined by bi-polar extremes," which then generate a "mental economy" once these concepts are set to media.[252] In other words, people are defined by both who they are (or made to seem to be) and equally by who they are not. Just as "blackness" had to be constructed and revised over time so too has "whiteness" needed construction and consistent refashioning over time so as to maintain itself as distinct and superior.[253] In each case it is the colonizer being created through the creation of the colonized.[254]

This identity redefinition helps the process by which African people and thought can be made into commodities for the wealth accumulation of the colonizer. The fact of the sale or trade of any commodity comes only after establishing that such a transaction is intellectually and culturally acceptable. The struggle over this has long troubled colonized people and the indigenous, whose lands and people are turned into product. It is how a world can be forced to accept a multi-billion-dollar-a-year water industry when once this would have seemed an absurd concept.[255] Or how today those with money and access can enjoy the "chronic" of a higher quality bottled air, while the rest of the world is forced to breathe the schwag that is left behind. This requires shifts in people's consciousness before it can be adopted as the public policy described in its essence above.

So too is this the case with the remaining contemporary fundamentality of the purchase, sale, and distribution of both African body (mass incarceration and the prison-industrial complex) and intellectual and cultural production (blues, jazz, R&B, hip-hop).[256] Today the bottom rung of this nation's colonial pyramid of petty tyrants consists of Indigenous people, whose land and labor have been confiscated, and the modern-day enslavement of African and Latino (Spanish-speaking Africans) people via the prison-industrial complex (PIC) where annually billions of dollars are quite literally and figuratively mined from these communities.[257] This requires the development and promulgation of imagery that supports a (sub)conscious notion of acceptability.

This has tremendous historical precedent. The reshaping of the African Heru into the Greek Horus and then again into a very European blonde, blue-eyed Jesus is an early historical development of the practice of reshaping the image of the oppressed to facilitate their oppression.[258] Certainly the re-imaging of Indigenous people into "Redskins," "Chiefs," "Braves," and "savages" has long been connected to their genocidal removal.[259] And studies in media have long isolated the trend of just such an imaging of the "other," be they continental Africans,[260] Africans in America,[261] Arabs,[262] Latinos,[263] and so on. What is now occurring with the popularization of a narrowly constructed form of hip-hop is part of the colonizing process that supports the continued and necessary devolution of African America. This all helped provide a basis for the North American application of mass media that assisted the continuing "process [where] Whiteness and western-ness were normalized as unproblematic goals for all people of color."[264]

And, of course, as Charles Mills has powerfully identified, this is all part of a broader project born of a philosophical Racial Contract, which is the "political... form of domination... central to Western political theory" that protects "White supremacy [as] the unnamed political system that has made the modern world what it is today."[265] This contract categorizes as "other" the majority of the world whose absence of whiteness or Western origin reduces, even erases, their humanity. "Correspondingly," Mills continues, "the Racial Contract also explains the actual astonishing historical record of European atrocity against nonwhites, which quantitatively and qualitatively, in numbers and horrific detail, cumulatively

dwarfs all other kinds of ethnically/racially motivated massacres put together."[266] He goes on to briefly examine the track record (Englehardt's
"Cartography of Death"), which includes the "envious" competition
among the Spanish, Dutch, French, and English who would decimate
"95 percent of the indigenous population of the Americas... [initiate]
the slow-motion Holocaust of African slavery, which is now estimated by
some to have claimed thirty to sixty million lives in Africa, the Middle
Passage, and the 'seasoning' process... [engage in] the random killing of
stray Indians in America or Aborigines in Australia or Bushmen in South
Africa... forced labor of the colonial economies, such as the millions
(original estimates as high as ten million) who died in Belgian Congo...
[and] Native Americans [who] were occasionally skinned and made into
bridle reins, Tasmanians [who] were killed and used as dog meat, and in
World War II Jewish hair was made into cushions, and Japanese bones
were made by some Americans into letter openers."[267]

The popular imaging of people has long been part of an acculturation
process that justifies the material treatment of the victims. The process
is meant to both acculturate the colonized into accepting these views of
themselves and the colonizer into accepting the equally fraudulent sanctity of their self-concept and behavior. By limiting the types of cultural
expression and journalism accessible to Black people, the current levels
of worsening conditions are erased, made acceptable, or justified. Popular rap music, with its emphasis on commercialism, hypersexuality, and
self-directed violence is constructed as part of this population's experience with the imperial "Racial Contract" described by Mills. Black self-
reference as thugs, gangsters, pimps, hoes, and bitches who only desire
consumption of cars, clothes, and women is the Black American modern-
day form of the historical representation of targeted communities as "nits,
injuns, critters, varmints, animals, etc."[268] (to which we could add Arabs
as "sand-niggers"), all of whom are threats or obstacles to be removed or
colonized into "civility." However, modernized and on display within the
internal colonies of the U.S., these forms are performed by the colonized
themselves as opposed to being re-presented to the colonizer by the colonizer. Their cultural expression has unwittingly been imposed as a weapon
against the very people themselves.

This becomes, for Clovis Semmes, the "metaproblem" whereby cultural hegemony is "the systemic negation of one culture by another,"
and where "economic gain" through "exploitation [is] consummated."
Cultural dominance becomes the psychic struggle in which control over

image, language ("cognitive process"), historiography, and spirituality allows the dominant society to define relationships, where assimilation is seen as complete "cultural negation," which results in Black America's full acceptance of "European hegemonic consciousness."[269] For Fanon this is the social group being first "militarily and economically subjugated" and then held in that position through a "polydimensional method," which involves cultural manipulation in service of colonial power. The beauty of the process is its ability to "camouflage . . . the techniques by which man is exploited" or even that such an exploitation is taking place.[270] Consider how often artists express happiness at the opportunity to suffer through the arduousness of a recording contract. Forced into an initial desperation (various levels of poverty, etc.), they (we all) are simply happy to have work at all and the *chance* at fame and wealth. Just as we are all so starved and desperate that even the chance to blow what little we have on the lottery or various forms of casino gambling is a pleasure for which we are grateful. So thankful are most that few would even dare question the origins of that initial poverty or financial desperation.

However, colonialism demands "impositions of new institutions and ways of thought," for when "cultures are whole and vigorous, conquest, penetration and certain modes of control are more readily resisted."[271] For Cabral, it is "not possible to harmonize the economic and political domination of a people, whatever may be the degree of their social development, with the preservation of their cultural personality."[272] But it is Fanon whose summary most fits with the current discussion. For Fanon the colonial dynamic does not necessitate the "death of the native culture," but in a more ruthless and sinister fashion "the aim sought is rather a continued agony than a total disappearance of the pre-existing culture."[273] This is a crucial point. The culture of the colonized must survive in some form or fashion so as to create an appearance of validity or authenticity. Of course, once cultural expression is put to the machinery of capitalist production it loses, as bell hooks says, its "marginal location" and, therefore, is "authentic to what it is," a simple commodity controlled by others for their profit (socially, politically, *and* economically).[274] However, the cultural expression of the colonized must take on an apparent normalcy. It must appear as indigenous and inherent, innate as expressions should be. But it should support an image created by the colonizer—"the mythical portrait of the colonized"—so as always to sustain beliefs in a deserved and *perpetual* inequality.[275] Should it appear too abnormal it might be resisted. Fanon explains further:

This culture, once living and open to the future, becomes closed, fixed in the colonial status, caught in
the yoke of oppression. Both present and mummified,
*it testifies against its members. It defines them in fact
without appeal.* The cultural mummification leads to
a mummification of individual thinking. The apathy
so universally noted among colonial peoples is but the
logical consequence of this operation. The reproach
of inertia constantly directed at "the native" is utterly dishonest. As though it were possible for a man
to evolve otherwise than within the framework of a
culture that recognized him and that he decides to assume. Thus we witness the setting up of archaic, inert
institutions, functioning under the oppressor's super-
vision and patterned like a caricature of formerly fertile institutions.... *These bodies appear to embody respect
for the tradition*, the cultural specificities, the personality of the subjugated people. This pseudo-respect in
fact is tantamount to the most utter contempt, to the
most elaborate sadism. *The characteristic of a culture is
to be open, permeated by spontaneous, generous, fertile
lines of force.*[276]

Note, too, that from an opposite political pole comes the viewpoint
of the colonizer. Zbigniew Brzezinski has discussed this in terms of the
importance of cultural imperialism (or the "imposition of new systems of
thought" described above). In praise of British rule over southern Africa,
he too extolls the virtue of "cultural domination," which "had the effect
of reducing the need of relying on large military forced to maintain the
power of the imperial center." Updating his view for the U.S., Brzezinski
continues,

The American global system emphasizes the technique
of co-optation... to a much greater extent than the earlier imperial systems did. It likewise relies heavily on
the indirect exercise of influence on dependent foreign
elites, while drawing much benefit from the appeal of
its democratic principles and institutions. All of the
foregoing are reinforced by the massive but *intangible*

> *impact* of the *American domination of global communi-*
> *cations, popular entertainment, and mass culture* and by
> the potentially very tangible clout of America's techno-
> logical edge and military reach. *Cultural domination*
> *has been an underappreciated facet of American global*
> *power....* America's mass culture exercises a magnetic
> appeal, especially on the world's youth.... American
> television programs and films account for about three-
> fourths of the global market. American popular music
> is equally dominant, while American fads, eating hab-
> its, and even clothing are exceedingly imitated world-
> wide. The language of the internet is English, and an
> overwhelming proportion of the global computer chat-
> ter also originates from America, influencing the con-
> tent of global conversation.[277]

The colonial model of analysis assists in the proper placement of
hip-hop, and indeed *all* popular culture, in the context of larger political struggles, which continue amended only in form but not intent. This
centers the role that media play as conceptual managers in the service of
power and confirms *that there is, in fact, a continuing power struggle that*
necessitates such a function. It is the fact that much of this effort has been
designed to target the very notion of a power struggle that complicates
matters. Once the fundamentality of a struggle for power is accepted—
not dismissed as the fancies of ambition and business or ignoble politicians or laziness—but only in terms of a genuine need of some, an elite
minority, to control a massive population, then such an approach can
help expand the range of responses to accept such ideas as mixtape radio.

Those who argue against this and similar theories as being dismissive
of individual or communal agency often ignore, downplay, or miss the
point of the original intent in image and communication. Resistance or
acceptance of communicated ideas is irrelevant when compared to the
need of power to defend what Stuart Hall calls a "dominant cultural order" by setting "dominant [or preferred] meanings," which alone limit
interpretation or response.[278] The target is never the individuals who
might develop or who have already arrived at an "oppositional consciousness;"[279] the real targets are the others, those who are to be struggled
against if there is to be any real shift in power.[280] After all, this is the fear
to be protected against.

It is the ability to resist, the potential (with continued and historic demonstrations of the fact) to salvage culture and use it as a means of anti-colonial struggle, which demands such a powerful response from the colonizer's media. Colonialism as a model—certainly as applied here—does not devalue or omit agency. Instead, this approach encourages that agency be harnessed and developed into forms of political organization and media production (as well as analysis) that encourages movement or the use of existing technologies that, returning again to Newton, "would allow the people of the world to develop a culture that is essentially human.... The development of such a culture... would be revolutionary intercommunalism."[281] This reordering of the world is exactly what the function of media within colonialism is designed to prevent. In fact, the tendency to blame hip-hop or young people or newer generations for being lazy and unappreciative thrives largely because colonialism is not understood. This apathy is often the result of the inertia described above hurled upon the colonized. It is a predetermined outcome of the colonial process.

CHAPTER THREE

EDUCATION AND CONCEPTUAL BOUNDARIES

> *Schools and schooling in capitalist America are very little different from other institutions and their methodological processes in capitalist America. Institutions operate from a well-programmed blueprint, which is designed to serve the people in an unequal and hierarchical manner. To "serve the people" can be readily translated into "serve the devil." The heinous nature of capitalist America gives easy rise to a feeling of existing in a living hell for the majority of the exploited.*
> —Gloria Joseph

> *The tendency is here, born of slavery and quickened to renewed life by the crazy imperialism of the day, to regard human beings as among the material resources of a land to be trained with an eye single to future dividends.... [W]e daily hear that an education that encourages aspiration, that sets the loftiest ideals and seeks as an end culture and character rather than bread-winning, is the privilege of White men and the danger and delusion of black.*
> —W.E.B. DuBois

> *The social sciences were integral to the maintenance of bourgeois rule not only in the United States, but over America's expanding colonial empire in the South Pacific, the Caribbean and Latin America. The American colonial empire was also domestic in the colonization of the dark-skinned racial groups of the South and West, Indians, Mexicans and the largest "internal colony," Afro-Americans.*
> —James Turner and W. Eric Perkins

Though the present analysis is focused primarily on mass media and culture, and their political (colonizing) function, there are, of course, other social institutions playing this role. Related to FreeMix Radio or the mixtape radio concept are at least two other immediately important institutions. One is education, the other is journalism.[282] Their placement within the model is meant to demonstrate that these two also play a significant role in impacting or influencing the thought processes of the internally-held colony.[283] Education buttresses "the indoctrinating power of the 'media'" and serves as the "preconditioning" that "does not start with the mass production of radio and television and the centralization of their control. The people entered this stage as preconditioned receptacles of long standing."[284] This is necessary as it prevents the news or popular media in general from ever being that which jolts people into new forms of thought or behavior. With few exceptions, things like time constraints, standard and narrowly formed ideological ranges, and types of content are all carefully manipulated and manicured to prevent them from becoming a source of new ideas, consciousness, and, ultimately, behavior. In this form and functionality, "public opinions must be organized *for* the press if they are to be sound, not *by* the press."[285] However, most have not considered (or cared about) the specific examples of those colonized within the U.S. or specifically those who would go on to produce the cultural expression (hip-hop) now dominating the globe.[286] For the immediate purpose, the model turns its attention to education and journalism as part of that which creates these "preconditioned receptacles."

In order to establish this nation's version of the colonial pyramid of petty tyrants, through which Memmi meant to remind all where they stand in relation to and as a result of the condition (better or worse) of another, a system of education was developed for minorities which "represented classical colonialism."[287] This would help to develop the preconditioning necessary to the function of colonialism at both individual (e.g. employee and employer) and collective (e.g. colony and Mother Country or dominant society) levels. Education is required to establish social roles, places, and functions, and to organize and standardize the information or worldviews being disseminated; as such, the country's system of education emerged based on a nineteenth century need to solve the problems it faced, at the same time that it "became an uneasy mix of immigrants alongside colonized and dominated minority groups."[288] The founders or "architects" of this development, men like Dr. Benjamin Rush, established this education based on an ideology of racial dominance honed over centuries of enslavement, genocide, theft of land, ethnocentrism, and Manifest Destiny, where "Indians" were seen as "unclean and 'strangers to the obligations of both morality and decency'… not only 'too lazy to work but even to think.'" Black women and men were seen as no better and were, by Rush, "repeatedly proclaimed" as "diseased."[289]

In each case education reflected its colonizing purpose. What is routinely seen today as negative or deleterious imagery regarding these communities had its origin or became archetypal in the ideology of racial superiority seen as the foundation of the process of "educating" the people (or "serving the devil"). The dialectic of creating the colonized and colonizer re-inscribed itself through this process as people were made into the image their captors held of them, simultaneously cementing the equally false self-concept of the colonizer. This continues to be played out to this day as Black people (among others) continue to fulfill the popular cultural image of themselves set by those who rule, an image that defines them in opposition to an equally unreal definition of a mostly White, male, ruling class.[290]

Because of the post-Reconstruction need to "reduce black labor as nearly as possible to a condition of unlimited exploitation,"[291] meetings were held where the future of this population's education would be determined, with an eye toward assisting with that need.[292] The simple point of these meetings was to determine how those colonized would be maintained in modern forms of enslavement and further removed from their original or pre-existing (and, therefore, threatening) cultures. After all, "Blacks faced a neo-slave system when the Civil War ended. Cotton still had to be picked, tobacco fields needed to be tended, and menial labor was required for industries of the New South."[293] The system of enslavement ended for the safety of the enslavers,[294] but if the system of dominance by an economic elite was to continue, it needed amendment—not an end.[295] "Education" then, was necessary if the schoolhouse was going to "replace the stability lost by the demise of the institution of slavery."[296] And in the end, it was Northern industrialists and investment bankers who would determine the direction of Black and Southern education—and much of the colonized African world—Industrial Education for African descendants and Residential Schooling for the Indigenous.[297] All of this was intended to assure that, to the extent possible, a form of exploitation that was safer *for those in power* took hold among those colonized.

At the turn of the twentieth century, Northern industrial philanthropists united with Southern White school officials and established the General Education Board. Its purpose it was to install a system of industrial education. Its goal was to have education be part of what would

Jigga

"attach the Negro to the soil and prevent his exodus from the country to the city."[298] Among the greatest supporters of this effort was John D. Rockefeller who, by the end of the 1920s, would contribute nearly $130 million toward the cause.[299]

Again, image and education had long been a concern where it came to African people in the United States. The previously discussed problem of press defense of slavery and its promotion of slavery-supporting imagery of Black people must also be understood within the context of Black education. As Carter G. Woodson has explained, the shift in the ways that African people would be taught came about in the midst of the rise if industry. Before 1835, the Southern approach of minimum education was preferred. However, after the countless insurrections, most notably those of Gabriel Prosser (1800), Denmark Vesey (1822), and Nat Turner (1831), the trend shifted toward no education at all.[300] This would be maintained until post-plantation slavery would bring about a new need for industrial education.

nice

This education would not be dealt with haphazardly. "Ideology is not left to chance."[301] The manipulation of a community's governing ideas, its ideology, is essential to the process of colonialism. In any society, ideology plays what Kwame Nkrumah called a "solidarist" role. It organizes that group within the rubric of that society's "ruling group" who determine the "dominant ideology." Ideology, continuing with Nkrumah:

> seeks to unite the whole of society in which it finds itself… besides seeking to establish common attitudes and purposes for the society, the dominant ideology is that which in the light of circumstances decides what forms institutions shall take, and in what channels the common effort is to be directed.[302]

In this case, as it would be with all other societal institutions, the dominant ideological output must support the land and labor conquest of those involved. It must support the justification needed among the colonizing class just as it must support, among the colonized, a set of governing ideas that make their oppression seem natural, normal, and even their own fault.

A focus, if even an all-too-brief one, on ideology is also helpful when confronting the dismissive harangues of conspiracy theory. Chomsky is correct that these are attempts to "discourage institutional analysis." But equally important is the fact that at the level of ideology there is no need to claim or argue what are quite naturally the greater conspiracies of those that operate at *the unconscious levels of governing ideas.* Of course there are conspiracies, considering all that conspiracy requires is two or more people coordinating some form of unsanctioned act. More important are the individual acts committed unconsciously that have the same result. Whether the condition of people is the result of whispered back room arrangements or the unwitting cumulative acts of society's "middle-management," the resulting colonialism remains.[303]

Certainly this continues via school segregation in the twenty-first century, which rivals that of any other era,[304] and this schooling is connected to very different expectations for participation in society.[305] These are summarized more generally by people like John Taylor Gatto, who look at modern American education, its history, and political function. Changing the focus of discussions around the "problem" of education he asks, "What if there is no 'problem' with our schools?" Quoting Mencken, he describes the goal of education: "[to] reduce as many individuals as possible to the same safe level, to breed and train a standardized citizenry, to put down dissent and originality."[306] School then becomes a mechanism by which individuals are forced to assume fixed habits, so as to conform to a proper social role, and where grading and tracking serve to "tag" those who would or would not damage a strong "breeding stock." All of this is intended to determine who will be the "elite group of caretakers"[307] chosen to oversee society and who will be those they care for, not to mention how that "care" will be administered. Education is set to serve the greater and more fundamental colonizing function, as are journalism, media, and communication. Maintenance of order necessitates setting limits on acceptable ranges of thought and action.

And while our focus is the particular impact of this education on Black people, it is best understood within a broader array of concerns for the class represented by Rockefeller. The Rockefeller Foundation and Rockefeller-founded Chicago University would come to represent these needs. Out of its Chicago School of Economics would one day come the neo-liberal economics that continue to destroy much of the hemisphere. And out of the Rockefeller Foundation and the Chicago School would come much of the foundational communication studies research, itself grounded to functionalist social science. This was very much about the study of how communication could manipulate social relationships within a given society. It was funded and encouraged to the extent that those in power found it to be useful to maintaining themselves.[308] Rockefeller's goal (and those of both the U.S. government and other business elite) was to assist in the development of a field of study that could be used to determine the most effective ways of setting popular public opinion and to "suppress or distort *unauthorized communication among subject peoples*, including domestic U.S. dissenters who challenged the wisdom or morality of imperial policies."[309] There is little confusion within the current state of education and media regarding that which targets the predominantly Black and Latino poor. Both have long-since been established to result in compliant colonized populations.[310]

Here again we can find a response that assists in defining the tradition of aggressive reclamation of space for oppositional thought, education, or organization from which mixtape radio emerges. Attendant to this development of a system of education whose purpose was to extend and limit the effects of a change in enslavement was also the development of extra-institutional educational institutions for liberation. As Ahati Toure explains, "Afrikans were intent upon constructing the academic and research capacity to pursue their own in-depth teaching, research, and publication on the nature of the Afrikan global experience." This construction, he continues, "emerged [in the U.S.] from a tradition of Afrikan scholarship that functioned independently of the European academic structure" and "emphasized original research, publication, and teaching for principally Afrikan mass consumption."[311]

As early as 1828, activist autodidact study groups such as the Reading Room Society were established, the goals of which were to preserve, organize, study, teach, and disseminate through speeches and publications the history of African people. In 1896, Mary Church Terrell helped found the National Association of Colored Women and the following year saw the emergence of the American Negro Academy, which included the likes of Alexander Crummell and W.E.B. DuBois (to name but two). That same year, 1897, saw also the development of the ANA's sister organization, the American Negro Historical Society. It would be followed by Edward Bruce and Arturo Schomburg's Negro Society for Historical Research in 1911 and then the 1915 founding of Carter G. Woodson's Association for the Study of Negro Life and History. And shortly thereafter would come the Harlem History Club/Edward Blyden Society. All of these groups would inform the much more formal, not initially less radical, Black Studies Movement and the advent of Black and Africana Studies programs and departments within North American academia.[312]

These efforts to develop Black/African/Africana Studies programs and departments (what have been described as "street fighting disciplines"[313]) continue their engagement in an *Intellectual Warfare* (1999),[314] which forms part of a continuing tradition of Black (colonized) reclamation of autonomous spaces used for the dissemination of ideas, worldviews, histories, and journalism around which occurred the kinds of political organization that informed and evolved into mass social movements. It is to this history that the concept of mixtape radio or any twenty-first century media or journalism can and must be connected. Far from an original or disconnected argument or idea, mixtape radio does, in fact, have a lineage that it excavates at the same time that it inspires entirely new forms of resistance.

CHAPTER FOUR

JOURNALISM AND CONCEPTUAL BOUNDARIES

*The origin of the word "newspaper" is lost in the mists of time; the
word evidently had its origin in the diurna, which, of course, is the
etymological ancestor of "journal," and the word "journalist" seems
to have made its first appearance in seventeenth-century England as
a synonym for "writer" or "mercurist." The reference to the messenger
of the gods of Greece indicates the function of the journalist as the
agent of his employers, commissioned to transmit messages.*
—Herbert Altschull

*Who's got control of your mind, your worldview?
FBI, CIA, ATF, KKK, IRS, TNT, CBS, NBC...*
—Dead Prez

I turn on CBS and see B.S.
—Nas

Journalism, another function of the mixtape radio concept, continues
to play a similar role in limiting the consciousness and ultimately the
behavior of its targets. What we see, read, or hear is a carefully produced
product designed to encourage compliance among the population. From
the more or less innocuous signage telling us to stop or turn, to songs
instructing us to move this or shake that, to carefully crafted commer-
cials or news products, media are designed to encourage "preferred [or]
dominant" meanings[315] of the world in which we live so as to encourage acceptable ranges of behavior.[316] There is no news, only intentionally
imposed views of the world. What is called "news" has long-since been
determined to be biased politically,[317] outright racist,[318] and "for sale,"[319]
and demonstrating a strong class bias[320]—all the result of a consolidated
ownership structure itself bound to certain elite ideological principles,

all of which greatly limit journalists' knowledge of the world and their ability to report what little they do know.[321]

This is precisely why the Black press tradition would become what professor of media and journalism studies and veteran Black Press journalist Todd Steven Burroughs has described as both a "shield" to protect community consciousness and image, and a "bowl" from which African people could derive the nourishment required for that work.[322] It was a pre-emancipation[323] African America that began the Black press out of a need to defend against an image created in the mainstream White press that had cemented its pro-enslavement or colonization positions,[324] and had been so pro-lynching that some engaged in publicizing such terrorism in advance to help draw larger crowds,[325] or had just been generally racist and unsupportive of progressive societal advance.[326] It is why, for example, journalist David Walker wrote his *Appeal to the Colored People of the United States* (1830),[327] which as underground journalism also offered an "early assertion of an internal colonialism"[328] and encouraged violent revolt. The very possession of the text was a capital offense[329] and likely led to the author's own suspicious early death.[330] It is no coincidence that parallel to the development to the Black press was the establishment of a press arm to every radical or revolutionary organization. The need for the practice of journalism as part and parcel of a viable political struggle or movement has historically been taken for granted. In fact, the practice of emancipatory journalism pre-dates the advent of the specific phrase and the outlining of its ideological or philosophical foundation.[331]

Today the Black press has, in many ways, gone the way of Black political struggle. Expecting there to be a sanctioned press from among the colonized that poses journalistic challenges to established power is simply irrational. A colonized population facing the kinds of material deficiencies and hostility from the state described herein cannot be expected to achieve the financial, political, and social support from the dominant society necessary to sustain such mass media work. And to the extent that Black political struggle is not seen as legitimate by potential White allies (to be discussed below), the prospects for such a press are further weakened. This has led, in part, to the conclusion reached by George Curry, veteran journalist and former editor of *Emerge* magazine, who, when asked of the twenty-first century condition of the Black Press, responded:

> I think that the problem of Black media is the same as
> Black business, period. Whether you look at Motown,

> Johnson hair care products, whether you look at BET
> or whether you look at *Essence*, you see the same thing;
> that our major institutions are being bought off by
> conglomerates and then homogenized.[332]

His concerns over a lack of substance can be extended to any form
of popular media though the impact of that missing substance varies de-
pending on the pre-existing conditions and roles of the given community
vis-à-vis the dominant society. Todd Steven Burroughs sees the Black press
of today more as a mouthpiece of the Black *establishment*. He cautions
against seeing the Black press as providing a radical media solution to
the struggles facing the masses of that community. "As a 'Black mainstream' institution the Black press sees almost any mainstream advance
as a progressive one—certainly Barack Obama, but even, for example,
Condoleezza Rice and Colin Powell! The editorial and Op-Ed page might
even rail against them, but they'd *never* be called 'Enemies of the People'
the way, say, more radical papers such as *The Black Panther* or *Muhammad
Speaks* would have in decades past."[333] The implicit suggested remedy is
clear in the face of a tightly-controlled corporate and ideologically elite
media environment; the establishment of movement-based, organization-
ally-supported alternative or underground press and media.

The history of this kind of journalism, the reasons it was necessary for
similar manifestations to present themselves in the modern era, remains
well submerged beneath a contemporary media and press environment
wherein Blackness may at times seem ubiquitous, but it is so only insofar
as it parrots the mainstream (or "Euro-stream"[334]). Similarly, this history
and its contemporary equivalent are routinely ignored in existing "liberal"
or "progressive" media and media studies scholarship, or as often the journalism practice, too, remains solidly Eurocentric or White American in
its perspective and focus.[335] However, as will be discussed a bit later, there
did in fact (and does today) exist a press, journalism, or media justice
tradition that sought to make known many of the forces aligned against
oppressed communities.

In the "post-enslavement" era, the rise of mass media technology[336]
would be grafted onto this pre-existing need to manage the image of
a newly "freed" population.[337] From the rise of the sheet-music industry[338] to that of film,[339] phonograph/records,[340] radio,[341] television,[342] and
through to today's Internet ownership structures,[343] and the maintenance
of the Black image have remained the same. So too have these so-called

"advances" in technology exacerbated the already existing horrific relationship between African people and the West,[344] as well as the gaps in
wealth existing in the United States.[345] And in each case, with each new
mass medium, Black originators have had their art generate wealth and
political power (mostly through establishing popular image) that was
siphoned off as any other commodity would be mined from a colony
and taken to the Mother Country.[346] These origins, solidified in the post-
Reconstruction need to stem the advancements made post-enslavement,
remain to this day as cemented archetype.

As Reconstruction's gains were assaulted in a late nineteenth century White backlash via politics, economics, and violence,[347] so too would
that backlash incorporate media, journalism, and the imaging of Blackness as deserving of newer forms of enslavement.[348] Here the Black public
sphere[349] had to be reconstructed to suit the need of limiting discussion
(or its impact) so as to ascribe the necessary psychic violence required
for control. With so much mass media penetrating into separated Black
spaces (not to mention the early advantage of controlling education), an
infestation of thought and discussion occurs. The commercial radio playing in the barber shop or beauty salon allows for a colonizing elite to limit,
distort, or prohibit various forms of thought and discussion that might
otherwise take place there. It is no different from the historical shift in
image of a Black community diner—which in reality was a meeting place
of radical organizations—into a location for a situation comedy where
high-school hijinks occur.[350]

Rarely discussed in prevailing media (or hip-hop) scholarship is the
tradition[351] of underground, radical, or emancipatory journalism. Similarly, the context-building history of journalism's relationship to colonized
populations deserves more attention than it gets. If the African continent
is taken as just one example, there is an established history of journalism's
bias and use against African independence and those engaged in anti-
colonial struggle.[352] Neo-colonial "post-independence" has meant the extension of traditions of the press established in the colonial era,[353] which
continues to negatively impact the practice of journalists throughout the
African continent.[354] And in the United States (as is the case throughout
the West), the press is often described as seeking to discredit notions of or
tendencies toward African independence.[355]

Similarly, this historical pattern of media and journalism as mechanisms of colonization has been and continues to be challenged by Black
people seeking to maintain liberated spaces for much needed dialogue

and cultural exchange.[356] This is the tradition out of which the mixtape itself has emerged.[357] Unfortunately, however, resistance efforts were not able to overcome what has now been established as a U.S. popular culture founded specifically on the stolen artifacts of colonized and oppressed communities (*not* an "American" or even Western European, elite, WASP culture). The theft of cultural expression has also resulted in a theft of their function. That which can propel can also blunt. That which can encourage and support resistance may also work to prevent it, or worse, deny even the consideration of its necessity or legitimacy.

These approaches are, out of necessity, ignored or dismissed due to an absolute ignorance of African history in the diaspora or in the West. This limits debate and discussion and prevents essential points of history and current facts from being known, or organized or acted against. In other words, the negative imagery of Blackness is rooted in the origins of not only this nation's media system, but that of *any colonizer.* In fact, these systems of media and journalistic practice emerged out of the political and ideological mission of colonialism. Furthermore, ignoring the wonderful history of attempts at an underground press or guerrilla media suppresses attempts to address the ideological battles within media and journalism that would inevitably arise in such an investigation. The very ideological *function* of media and journalism is omitted. This forces journalists and students of journalism alike to be unaware that "they, too, promote ideology,"[358] or that they are involved in the process of promoting and disseminating an ideology of colonialism. Its overall negative impact on other communities, indeed the nation and world as a whole, cannot be understood without this basic fact. It is what has set in stone the relationship media have to society and particularly to Black people, all of which is carried out today through a system of mass media in general and the music (hip-hop) industry specifically.[359]

CHAPTER FIVE

REVISITING THE CORPORATION
AND CULTURAL INDUSTRY

*What they now call "corporate media" we used
to just call "the White media."*
—Glen Ford

*I'll never put my two guns down, because I need
them for the Industry Shakedown.*
—Bumpy Knuckles (aka Freddie Foxxx)

Often enough there are discussions of the corporate media, corporate
dominance, corporate greed, and so on, but precisely what a corporation *is* is frequently ignored. We have already looked at what culture is;
it's now time for us to examine how the cultural or ideological battle is
waged, and this is where the corporation comes in.

In the United States (as elsewhere) there exists a cultural industry
where this battle over symbols and meanings is waged. This industry, a
collective of companies whose function is the selection and arrangement
of that which will become the nation's popular cultural fare, consists of
corporations that have assumed the fourteenth amendment right to legal
personhood and have become extensions of a shift in need among the
ruling class to cloak this "power elite" and their "invisible class empire" in
anonymity.[360] Hiding behind boards of directors[361] and CEOs,[362] an elite
minority can maintain colonialism via indirect rule (neo-colonialism)
while remaining largely unknown. Corporations manage the interests of
those who own them, the so-called "corporate class,"[363] and are perfectly
amenable to the purposes of colonization as they themselves "produce
nothing. They are organizational devices for the exploitation of labor and
accumulation of capital,"[364] and as such must also be seen in terms of

their ability to organize and disseminate their ideology or to exert their will over the rest.

As should be common knowledge by now, the corporation today is the "dominant institution" whose power rivals that of historical dictators and the church.[365] If we return to the model of cultural domination, and examine the four major corporations,[366] the "musical OPEC," that own and disseminate "over 95 percent of all music CDs sold in the Western world,"[367] we have to understand this in terms of the ability of those running these corporations to influence the worldviews of their target audience. And, it is this worldview, one still based in the "conceptual original sins" reified through education and journalism, that necessitates the dissemination of the colonizer's view of the colonized so as to create and recreate both. The ability to determine which forms of cultural expression are widely disseminated and which are not is purely ideological and serves a colonizing purpose.

The details move and shift regularly. As the present study is being carried out, four major music industry corporations, themselves subsidiaries of larger conglomerates or private equity/hedge fund groups, control the popular hip-hop and R&B landscape: Sony, Universal Music Group (UMG), Warner Music Group (WMG) and EMI. While the collective market share of UMG and Sony alone is 58.6 percent of all music sales, that is nothing compared to the share they hold of national commercial radio air time.[368] During any given week, Sony and UMG by themselves own 80 to 95 percent of the top twenty songs played across national radio.[369] And even these already concentrated owners are further linked via board interlocks.[370] For example, the CEO of WMG, Edgar Bronfman, Jr.,[371] and the CEO of Sony, Howard Stringer, are both members of the board of directors of InterActive Corp. But even these kinds of interlocks are less meaningful when, as is demonstrated by the existence of a Business Roundtable, most leading corporations are aligned to assure the maintenance of their dominating existence.[372]

None of these corporations can be said to have a deep abiding concern for the world's majority. Their ability to dominate popular culture allows many of their other business interests and practices to chug along with little attention, scrutiny, or understanding. For example, UMG is in the first tier of a two tier "hierarchy" of media giants, *each of whom* "collect between $10 billion and $35 billion per year" in annual media-related revenue, and is part of a "global media system" whose desire is to expand even further its global reach and, therefore, impact.[373] Even as the world's largest music company, Universal Music Group only accounts for 14 percent of its parent company's (Vivendi) annual revenue.[374] The second largest music company, Sony Music, similarly accounts for only 6.1 percent of its parent company's (Sony) sales.[375] And the third leading music company, Warner Music Group, is owned collectively by three private equity groups who combined manage funds of more than $110 billion.[376] So while most focus only on the purely financial aspect of music sales, they miss the greater point that sales are less the issue than is the management of popularity. And, according to a recent report, the industry is predicting a sharp increase in music sales by 2014, as everyone adjusts to online sales, promotion, and distribution.[377]

An interesting exercise in tracing these boards of directors, interlocks, and corporate reach is to visit TheyRule.net[378] and play with their flash-driven website. Users can create maps showing individual companies and directors and the various other companies and directors to which they are connected through common directors. Warner Music CEO Edgar Bronfman, Jr., for instance, can be connected using this tool to the CEO of Viacom, Sumner Redstone, through Dell and Coca-Cola. And just as it works in government and private business, where often people leave government oversight committees to take top-level positions in firms over which they ostensibly had oversight, Bronfman—not so much in an oversight position but one of competition—had been a director on the board of Vivendi/Universal.[379] In the end, it is the collective interests of those implicated by their shared need to maintain varying degrees of dominance and complicity over those they intend to rule that are of primary concern. It is very much the concern herein that the twenty-year period between 1983 and 2003 witnessed all the media run by fifty corporations shift into the control of five men, giving them inordinate power never before seen in history. This is astonishing, for "no imperial ruler in past history had multiple media channels that included television and satellite channels that can permeate entire societies with controlled sights and sounds."[380]

The concern is not necessarily over the existence of these five men"who, as stated, are themselves representatives of power and not the final arbiters of control. That is, fifty corporations, or several hundred linked globally via boards of directors or racial and class-based interests, maintain a permanent coalescence as holders of power and managers of popular ideas. It then also remains necessary for this global minority to ensure that few, if any, questions are raised or raised to the level of an organized threat, which can only occur if people are aware and able to disseminate their own antithetical ideas. And it is toward this end that such large corporations (or as is the new trend, private equity groups[381] whose owners and directors are involved in any number of other national and international ventures) see a need for owning or managing, through advertising dollars,[382] the content of media companies. Their goal remains as described: to create a mass culture that is "identical... the people at the top are no longer interested in concealing monopoly; as its violence becomes more open, so its power grows.... [M]ovies and radio need no longer pretend to be art.... [It need only result in] imitation [that] becomes absolute... [and results in] obedience to the social hierarchy."[383]

CHAPTER SIX

THE POLITICS OF POPULAR CULTURE

> *It is very important to understand that music, like
> all art regardless of its form, is ideological.*
> —Thomas J. Porter

> *It is one of the great ironies of history that our people were stripped
> of their material cultural identities when they were shipped to the
> plantations of the Americas to be placed in no place while the stripped
> cultural artifacts were taken to Europe to be housed perhaps in the most
> elegantly built palaces, museums, basilicas, and university halls.*
> —Ayele Bekerie

There are a number of strategies for securing the obedience of the colonized through a manipulation of popular culture including the control of political media, the development of popular stereotypes,[384] and the use of the natural tendency to be creative as a semiotic weapon against a population. That is, the creation of popular culture—or the development of "image-making into a science" as Malcolm X once said—is part of establishing the "dominant ideology or 'mythology.'"[385] All popularity is fraudulent in that it cannot be what it claims to *represent*. It is, however, absolutely authentic to its *function* as myth. Thus, we might say that popular representations of Black people (African people), First Nations people, Latinos, and certainly women of all backgrounds are all incomplete, mythological creations designed to stand in for the more complex realities experienced by these people. Black people are not what is imaged in popular culture. The popular image is determined by the role they are meant to play in society (that of colonized people). Jesus is no more Heru than Obama is Black people or manhood. Mary is no more Aset than Oprah is Black people or womanhood. They do, however, do quite well in representing the appropriate societal function of the myths contained therein.[386] Just as Mary anglicizes an African archetype, so too do Oprah and Obama represent a colonized—therefore acceptable—myth of the Black woman and man. Oprah's popularity is as linked to her appeal among affluent White women as Obama's is linked to his appeal to affluent White men.[387]

This reoccurring mythological—or dominant ideological—trend can be, perhaps, understood as part of any group's need for that which will bind. Kwame Ture has spoken of the essentialness of myth for group cohesion just as Sigmund Freud, considered at times a founding father of mass communications research, suggested the same.[388] Freud's question in *Moses and Monotheism* (1939) concerned the potential destructive force, psychologically, of a community realizing its founding myth was false. Viewing media as his uncle saw myth, the leader in modern public relations (psychological warfare), Edward Bernays, defined propaganda as the "establish[ment] of reciprocal understanding between an individual and a group."[389] Mathematically speaking, reciprocity is measured by a coupling of numbers whose product is one. The universality of the sciences is demonstrated here, for the numbers demonstrate that a society's stability is determined by its uniformity of dominant thought. The purpose of myth is the production of one; a unity born of singularity or cohesion.

Freud's concerns with the potentially destructive effect of the collapse of the founding myth can be extrapolated to a system, one of colonialism, which requires the constant reproduction of both the colonized and the colonizer. In the context of the United States, this reproduction emerged with the sublimation of Africans into an African American colony, which coincided with the larger expansion of Western European power (or the "consolidation of White power") and the development of U.S. mass media technology,[390] itself intimately linked to the development of the popular mythology of African and, therefore, Black inferiority imaged for the world to see. This was natural to the process of enslavement and colonization and necessary to the maintenance of that power relationship.

Leon Wynter, for example, has traced the rise of American popular culture and its foundation in both Black cultural expression and, perhaps more importantly, White notions of Blackness.[391] Wynter explores the rise of American society within the context of a highly racially-stratified society in which "Whiteness" was slowly grafted to the national fabric as a method of developing and maintaining a White (Anglo-Saxon Protestant) elite. "Whiteness" had to be extended, sometimes with great pain and struggle, to the "heterogeneous, incoherent, distracted mass of European immigrants" as Thomas Jefferson called them.[392] But more important is Wynter's description of how this newly-shaped country also used popular culture and the dissemination of White "fantasies" of Blackness not simply to entertain but also to assure racial disharmony and the protection of a WASP (White Anglo-Saxon Protestant) elite.[393] He says that "from the start, pop culture has been constructed on the facts as well as White fantasies of nonWhites and their cultural forms."[394] In the words of those most interested in which myths would rule, "[n]o wonder then, that any disturbance of the stereotypes seems like an attack upon the foundations of the universe."[395] Wynter also accurately notes two other important aspects of the rise of American popular culture: first, the cultural expression of Black people has always been at the center of this development; and second, this centrality of Black cultural expression has continuously been marked by a fundamental "*pattern* of appropriation, exploitation, distortion, and ultimate marginalization of black and other non-White cultures in mainstream entertainment." And not only is it the case that this "remains the same today"; it also has "the same effect: the reaffirmation of White supremacy." Continuing with Wynter:

> In the beginning the cycle was simple, because it essentially turned in only one direction. Whites could only appropriate—literally—the identity of a mostly enslaved group of people in society, distort it to fit the limitations of their own creative imaginations (or constricting racial self-definitions) and the prevailing racist expectations in the market, and exploit it for gain without ever paying any social, political, or monetary tribute to the source.[396]

Just as "White males in blackface... created America's first culture industry—blackface minstrelsy"[397] so too would the origins of what Barlow calls "American popular music" begin "with songs in the blackface style," where the burnt-cork tradition of minstrelsy became this society's pop culture archetype.[398] While Wynter believes this relationship has become so complex that these origins are "barely recognizable," this view is hard to reconcile with the ubiquity of this tradition found in the mainstream just as its criticism is easily found if one seeks it.[399] These archetypes re-emerge as they must given the importance of this kind of stereotype to colonialism.

What Wynter describes as having undergone some kind of change has only solidified or improved in its method. Of course popular hip-hop (and all that cultural expression's forms: rap, DJing, graffiti, and dance, as well as dress and language) would eventually succumb to this tradition in the absence of a completed eradication of the original colonized status. Without recognizing this archetypal function of popular culture, the uninitiated will continue to be confused into misunderstanding what is happening or has happened to hip-hop, or what will happen to anything produced in the future by those who are colonized. The lens must be expanded to include this history so as to see the "truth that may slowly emerge, period after period, until it clearly forms itself into a truth impregnable, a fact nowhere stated as such in the mass of data covered."[400]

As the politics of popular culture emerged, so too would an industry managed by the corporate extensions of that power elite, which would later be called the "higher circles."[401] The "golden age" of the 1920s saw the rise of this technology and industry, where film would become instrumental as a purveyor of anti-African, Black-inferiority-laden imagery. Radio would emerge with its own specific style of the same and, the immediate focus here, so would the music industry, following the same cultural and business models, which pre- and post-date its arrival. In terms of music, the new technology of recording would evolve as the "stepchild of the sheet-music business,"[402] since now music could be recorded, records could be mass produced and shipped around the country and to the rest of the world, and all could be fashioned around the desires of those in power.

The business practices had more at stake than the simple extraction of material wealth and goods from the colony. This process also assured control over the popular form the colonized cultural expression would take. From the beginning, Black-owned independent recording companies had to struggle (often losing and going out of business) with the fact that even by the end of the 1920s most leading bluesmen were under contract to the recording company "giants" who were distributing "character songs" instead of "genuine blues," which would not have been as easily digested by White audiences.[403] It was, indeed, the very success of this model that formed the foundation of the music industry that would in turn expand the transformation of Black culture into a mass-produced commodity.[404] In fact, it was quickly recognized that the impression of blues as being "too black—that is, too independent of Euro-American cultural experience"— made it difficult, near impossible, "to gain a popular White following....

[B]lues has always been a separate, pure black vein that is *mined* and then alloyed with Euro-American additives to enter the mainstream."[405]

Wynter goes on to quote Ann Douglass, who suggests that, as the blues "became rooted in northern cities" (probably a result of the South-to-North Great Migration of African Americans during the 1920s–40s), "their rural and folk nature was altered, refined, Whitened. The songs were written down; lyrics cleaned up and elaborated, and the music was… Europeanized [to suit] conventional harmonies and turned into Tin Pan Alley Pop. Black blues and jazz musicians and singers who tended to stay closer to the original 'classic blues' format never sold with White audiences in the numbers their White imitators and peers did."[406] So today, when the appropriate comparisons are made between the blues and hip-hop,[407] Fanon's point can be better understood:

> Thus the blues—"the black slave lament"—was offered up for the admiration of the oppressors. This modicum of stylized oppression is the exploiter's and the racist's rightful due. Without oppression and without racism you have no blues. The end of racism would sound the knell of great Negro music.[408]

CHAPTER SEVEN

INTELLECTUAL PROPERTY, COPYRIGHT, AND THE OWNERSHIP OF THOUGHT

Personal is Political: My thoughts, my words, everything that I believe in my life, are not entirely original, definitely not entirely mine. Indeed, they are derived from, and hence belong to the entire world, past, present and its future. There is nothing so personal in my life that is not shaped by the political worldviews I have subscribed to or refuted. Hence, this blog is CopyLeft, not copyrighted. Feel free to distribute contents to fellow travelers for education, agitation, and organization towards an alternative world.
—Saswat Pattanayak, Saswat.com

The A&R is a house nigger. The label is the plantation.
Now switch that advance for your emancipation.
—Pharoahe Monch

The mechanisms involved in maintaining this cycle of appropriation and distortion may have become more sophisticated, but they remain intact nonetheless. In terms of the popularization of music, or the use of the music produced by the colonized to perform the archetypal role set for all popular culture, the model attempts to represent that process. The "Big Four" initiate that process by first corrupting or compromising the artist by contract.[409] In exchange for recoupable loans or "advances," these companies attain sole ownership over the art via copyright.[410] Copyright ownership becomes the functionary of that colonizing mission—copyright is thus a *form* of colonization, in this case. As has been said, "if you listen to commercial radio you will likely live and die without ever hearing an artist who owns his or her own music."[411] The goal, again, is to manage which artists and ideas become popular, so as to limit their "negative" impact on maintaining a colony. Once artists sign a contract allowing the corporation to record and distribute their music, in exchange for the promise of fame and wealth, they transfer ownership and rights over to that company. This means artists no longer have control over their art, nor over when or where it is played, or to whom the bulk of monetary gains go (and it is never them!). As was said of jazz, so it goes for hip-hop:

> In its relation with an underdeveloped country (colony), a more advanced industrial economy (metropolis, 'mother country') will use its superior technology to ensure that commodity exchange between the two redounds to the benefit of the latter at the expense (in the form of increasing impoverishment) of the former. The metropolis employs its ownership of capital to generate more capital—i.e., profits. The colony, possessing nothing to exchange save the labor power of its citizens and its natural resources, will have its capital slowly drained away to the metropolis.... Black musicians... labor not primarily for themselves, but to enrich those who own the 'means of production' enumerated above.[412]

This gives the exclusive rights of promotion or omission to the holders of copyright, which establishes them as the sole selectors of who will be popular and, therefore, the parameters of acceptable behavior for first achieving and then maintaining that popularity or "success."

Copyright, the subset of "intellectual property enterprises"[413] or "copyright industries,"[414] is of no small consequence, and though its function is greater than the wealth it generates as an industry, it does comprise more of the U.S. gross national product "than the airplane industry, more than the automobile industry and, yes, more than the agricultural industry."[415] The history of copyright, not coincidentally, begins in eighteenth century England, right in line with the development of modern capitalism. The first copyright law was passed in London on April 4, 1710. Since then, the purpose of copyright has become, ostensibly, the protection of an author's rights to his or her intellectual property exclusively for a term of twenty-one years, with the potential of an additional fourteen if she or he survived the initial term.[416]

Then, as now, this claim is made to suggest that the law is concerned with the interests of the artist and with encouraging them—by protecting what they produce as their own property—to create more to enhance the world.[417] However, this myth is easily dismissed. Most readers can probably identify at least two people they know who create art of one form or another with no expectation or desire for fame and wealth. Further, the intentionally created vicious cycle of cultural appropriation through ownership of copyright and the subsequent promotion of only that which is owned by elite corporations belies any real concerns about protecting artists and ensuring their continued artistic production. In fact, and if anything, the kind of oligarchic control of cultural expression through ownership of copyright is more about fostering "the erosion of national, regional, ethnic, and group autonomy, undermin[ing] democratic participation in cultural expression, and increas[ing] inequalities between people and nations."[418]

Quite accurately, copyright has been described as a "core media ownership policy," which is the equivalent to a "tax on knowledge" and a means of supporting "the interests of the largest media companies."[419] It was, in fact, the British model of copyright (the idea of which would be adopted in the United States, much like the model of indirect colonial rule) that claimed that, if the rights of producers of culture (authors, musicians, etc.) were protected, they would be encouraged to create more. There would be an incentive for them to produce what would generate substantial personal income while enriching the society at large. However, a problem emerged where copyright ownership moved from the specific artist to their contracted distributor, that is the largest media companies. "Copyrights are now a tradable commodity" (Marx's "original sin"), through which "[o]ur cultural heritage has been privatized," as recent laws extending copyright ownership indefinitely[420] have resulted in a corporate monopoly over the rights to cultural expression and ultimately a state of "corporate welfare" that has resulted in a decrease in the amount of artistic creation available to the public.[421] In other words, what we hear, see, and read is only a fraction of what is produced and is owned by an ever-shrinking number of companies.

Copyright, in terms of recorded music, generally operates on two levels. Whereas the individual artist may own the right to her or his own lyrics or music, rarely do they own the rights to the recorded copy of that song.[422] Ownership of copyright (sometimes referred to as publishing rights) is transferred to the record labels upon the artist signing a contract. This colonizes the artists on multiple levels. On the one hand they lose ownership of the recording, and on the other they are locked into what are often five or six album deals, and forced to appear for performances per company orders.[423] Because radio play is the great determinant of success[424] and radio play has been mostly determined by promotional payments (payola) made to radio stations,[425] an artist is entirely dependent upon the label to generate their success.

Further, if the first album does not sell well, the artist may be dropped or shelved by the label, with multiple albums still owed to the company. This means that artists' careers can be ended or permanently stalled simply by losing support from their label. Should they produce further albums anyway and one or all become successful—by fluke or belated promotion—it is their label that continues to benefit. Hip-hop artists rarely get through "half of their first contract... so the record company locks you up for a significant portion of your career."[426] To have that song promoted (i.e. played on radio and television) artists must relinquish their ownership of their copyrights or publishing. This is the most illuminating point made in *Takeover* (2001) during the "beef" between Jay-Z and Nas: "Yeah I sampled your voice. You was using it wrong. You made it a hot line. I made it a hot song. And you ain't get a coin Nigga you was getting' fucked. I know who I paid god, Serchlite Publishin'." Nas as an artist had no control over his song's rights, therefore, all monetary value for it went to a company.

There is a cultural effect here as well. Chuck D has talked about the change in the sound of hip-hop as the result of consolidated copyright ownership and changes in law and policing of sampling.[427] Sampling, where rap music producers extract pieces of existing songs for use in a newly produced track, has been forced to undergo a change since the mid-1990s explosion of the genre's popularity. Whereas artists in the early days of the art could freely take samples from a variety of songs all used to create a new sound, the new crackdown meant that rap music producers could no longer afford the enormous fees attached to the use of each sample. Tracks could no longer carry the same sound and producers were forced, by the cost of each individual sample, to reduce the number used, leading to the rise of today's heavily keyboard- and one-sample-based hip-hop production. What this illustrates is, again, the absolute normalcy of institutions within any societal setting operating to assure the survival of that society. In this case, colonialism requires that the colonized accept that their expression is severely limited and controlled. The ability to manipulate entire shifts within the genre of rap music, reshaped to suit the colonial will manipulated through the mechanism of copyright, demonstrates that colonialism's application is malleable, adjusting to currents needs and trends, preparing for their arrival and then forcing them into capitulation.

The importance of intellectual property law, as a function of colonialism, cannot be overstated. A consumer- and service-based society that produces fewer material goods by the day requires the transmutation of thought into commodity, both for the purposes of commercial exchange and for the constraint of ideas. Intellectual property, "the ownership and control of content through the mechanism of copyright," [428] and the ownership of thought function to maintain control of ideas. Once controlled, the profit derived from promotion, sale, and distribution is used to increase the social and political power of the owners, while decreasing that same potential power among the producers. This is the mechanism of the "consciousness industry," which is largely able to determine the ruling ideas that are, "in every epoch… the ideas of the ruling class." This is carried out "by the individuals who compose the dominant class [who] 'rule also as thinkers, as producers of ideas' and 'regulate the production and distribution of the ideas of their age'" or control the "means of mental production."[429]

This struggle is now shifting in response to the new technological challenges of the Internet, but the goals and efforts remain the same. The largest copyright holders in the world continue to find ways of maintaining control and, as is rapidly becoming clear, the new "borders" are not so much geographical as they are ideological. As one observer said:

> The copyright oligopoly's real desire is to create an international *police state* dedicated to the protection of their rights. That's the purpose of ACTA (Anti-Counterfeiting Trade Agreement), currently being negotiated very quietly by the leading industrial nations…. The proposed ACTA treaty would create international legislation turning *border guards* into copyright police, charged with checking laptops, iPods, and other devices for possibly infringing content, and given the authority to confiscate and destroy equipment without even requiring a complaint from a rights-holder. It's a horrific scenario. I'm not always a fan of the libertarian Cato Institute, but on this issue they are dead on.[430]

Ideas may only travel once sanctioned by the elite who own them. And even in an era of apparent change these issues prove themselves to be both serious to empire and, par for the course of colonialism, unchanging. The new Obama administration "Copyright Czar," Victoria Espinel, recently released the Joint Strategic Plan regarding enforcement of copyright infringement. The report suggests that "[s]trong intellectual property enforcement efforts should be focused on stopping those stealing *the work of others*, not those who are appropriately building upon it."[431] This is simply the cynical regurgitation of an upside down reality that denies the initial theft of artists' production by the corporate elite who now own the work, derive the most financial and ideological benefits from it, and who can now lobby for just these kinds of statements. The use of words like "czar," "strategic plan," and "enforcement" are clearly chosen—just as is the case with police and military operations—to recast their colonized targets as criminals and to draw attention away from their own initial and fundamental crimes.

This kind of linguistic deflection or the projection of evil-doing elsewhere has tremendous impact on many segments of society. Street vendors can be demonized, even from within their own communities, as deserving the harassment of law officials or scorn from the community because they are harming artists. Artists themselves, as has been the case with Mary J. Blige and Missy Elliott, may make well-promoted commercial appeals to the bootlegging "criminals" hurting these honest, innocent, and hard-working entertainers. Never do they encourage, certainly not so publicly, that the work of someone like Wendy Day be investigated so that artists can see how the real crime is the contract they sign with a label.[432] And there is also a confusion within academia and activism that is born both from this kind of industry messaging and also from an acceptance of a legitimacy of these laws and the ways in which we are encouraged to address, respond, or circumvent them.

To further summarize ways these issues are discussed, let us spend a moment examining a recent piece of scholarly work that attempts to address the situation.[433] *Stealing Empire*, a recent book by Adam Haupt, is of monumental importance to this discussion. Oppressed communities need an organized response to the fluidity of global capital that establishes Noam Chomsky's "virtual parliament," whereby an elite can determine international policy via their selective investment and reduce democracy or national sovereignty to idealist rubbish. Seemingly to the rescue comes Haupt, the Senior Lecturer for Film and Media Studies at the University of Cape Town, South Africa. In an attempt to stave off pessimism and inaction, he "examines the agency of marginalised subjects in the context of global capitalism and the information age."[434] This agency, that is, the power of the marginalized to challenge power, is found, says Haupt, in the reinterpretation and application of laws regarding the Internet, P2P (peer-to-peer) file-sharing, hip-hop sampling, and methods of distribution. In fact, he says, "these are possibilities for agency in Empire. Globalisation, commodification, legal frameworks, and news technologies can all be harnessed to serve the interests of the marginalised as well as the powerful."[435]

Stealing Empire describes Internet-based efforts at political and cultural response to the machinations of Empire that might otherwise render dim outlooks to the future. Haupt takes his readers into the Internet underworld of hackers who reinvent themselves as "hacktivist" Neos "hacking with an overt political stance,"[436] and where political radicals in hip-hop like Dead Prez and Immortal Technique can be found by an international audience in ways that subvert the power of Empire. In these Empire-free-zones, or at least Empire-lite spaces, the Internet and its open-source, community-commons capabilities are said to offer the necessary agency, even if that agency has "yet to be realized."[437] And so do we hear of the interesting work of political hacktivists and the work of subaltern and counterpublic hip-hop artists and collectives like Alkemy in South Africa and even get a nod to this author's preferences of mixtapes as alternative community-building, communicative networks. What some readers might find challenging, however, is just how these efforts have hurt, or can in the future really damage or destroy, that fundamental imperial relationship. Readers of other recent works on South Africa, for instance Frank Wilderson's *Incognegro: A Memoir of Exile and Apartheid* or John Pilger's *Freedom Next Time: Resisting the Empire*, would find it difficult to see how this Internet revolution is truly going to hamper neocolonial corporate power. But hope is a powerful commodity and is offered in heaps by Haupt in ways that may inspire critical rethinking of modern technology's impact and potential use.

Despite the author's best efforts, though, this is not the most intriguing or thought-provoking element of the book. There have been and will always be counterpublics, subaltern communities struggling against co-optation and cultural imperialism. The technology of the Internet does not change this. What is of most importance regarding Haupt's work is his centering of a concept of "empire." If for no other reason, *Stealing Empire's* value is in its centering of a global empire that Haupt defines as

> a form of supranational cooperation between the US
> and the former imperial powers of Western Europe
> that allows them to act in ways that benefit them eco-
> nomically, militarily, culturally and politically.[438]

Such a grounding already determines the direction and tone of the
book as being in diametric opposition to most hip-hop (and other) literature that often maintain a rather soft, safe, and illusory adherence to
founding myths of "democracy," "freedom," and "progress." His acceptance of this degree of international political, material, and cultural condition and his attempt to remain honest and true to it, demands that he engage to some degree the continuing debates of these and attendant issues.
Stealing Empire, again, for this reason alone deserves close, if not, repeated
reading and is essential to any contemporary discussion of hip-hop.

This, however, does not automatically save *Stealing Empire* from returning to what reads as safe and acceptable scholarly tropes, in this case,
the hope for legal, moral and non-violent progress, as well as, an almost
sycophantic or spiritual submission to the power of individual and communal agency. Ultimately, this means accepting the reality of a global
empire whose communicative reach is at once both powerful enough to
maintain it as such but which is filled with enough holes for the "power
of the multitude"[439] to use Empire's technology as a means of safely and,
of course, peacefully bringing it down. Therefore, while Haupt does so
well in incorporating existing popular criticism of international banking,
Western dominance of "former colonies" where "former colonial powers
in the northern hemisphere occupy positions of financial and cultural
dominance,"[440] he must return safely to the confines—that Linus security
blanket—of seeking out the "agency in the operation of Empire," which
offer "opportunities that globalization offers those who oppose the in-
equities produced by global capitalism."[441] After rightly acknowledging
the existence of global empire, including reference to work produced by
left-leaning economists like Joseph Stiglitz whose criticism of the International Monetary Fund (IMF) as a cause rather than cure of global poverty
is helpful, or Naomi Klein's similar criticism that such internationaliza-
tion of global empire reduces "representative democracy" to mean "voting
for politicians every few years who use that mandate to transfer national
powers to the WTO and the IMF."[442] Haupt must then dismiss, as "cynical," critics like Slavoj Žižek who asks, "Is the ultimate example of... the

vicious cycle of capitalist productivity, multiplying the very problems it pretends to solve, not *cyberspace*?"[443]

Such criticism must be dismissed, for it complicates claims of the mutual coexistence of empire and subversive, yet sanctioned, use of cultural and communication technology by the subjects of empire as viable methods of overthrow. This is a, and perhaps *the*, central theme of Haupt's work. Empire is real. However, it can be resisted—is resisted—by means of Internet usage, challenges to established functions of technology and hip-hop production, media, and legal policy. He argues that since empire is not bound to any particular nation-state, this allows for concepts of "reterritorialisation" and "deterritorialisation" to support that agency. If there is no "center of Empire," he explains, it is then difficult "to regulate or prohibit... communication because 'no one point is necessary for communication among others.'"[444] Interestingly, it is elsewhere that Žižek deals with just this kind of contradiction. In his own *In Defense of Lost Causes* (2008), Žižek takes to task those who would accept such notions of response to empire (as alluded to in his earlier quote) as a liberal desire for a "decaffeinated revolution."[445] In other words, to avoid the kind of grand and universal call that holds the empire accountable for its crimes (and thus overthrows it), we are encouraged to find acceptable loopholes, which can be accessed with sanction (Internet, P2P technology, media and trade policy, etc.) and used somehow to usher in its end.

In other words, Žižek represents an uncompromising, unsanctioned version of anti-imperial movement and Haupt more so the opposite. Rather than argue for "divine violence," the "softer" forms described by Žižek are, by Haupt, suggested.[446] In this case it is Haupt's focus on artists' ability to

> issue challenges to Empire (in its many forms) from diverse quarters and in a range of contexts—be it in oppositional practices, such as P2P file-sharing, sampling, culture jamming or subversive performance, or attempts at dialogue with producers of knowledge about legal reforms. These oppositional practices may very well be co-opted by dominant corporate media interests, but—as my discussion of the shift from sampling to the MP3 revolution indicates—there is little that media giants can do to predict what form challenges to their operation will assume in the future.[447]

Here is where Žižek finds contention with the prescriptive responses of Haupt and others, as do I. Though he does not accept what he refers to as a "technological determinist" label, Haupt does appear to suggest that Empire has made available technology and legal structures that can be used to overthrow or at least challenge Empire. His references to particular artistic expressions as examples of those kinds of challenges is an oft-repeated one, a "softer" critique of Empire, that does raise concerns. That is, while Downhillbattle.org—a media reform group mentioned in *Stealing Empire*—has declared "it seems safe to say that death has come to the corporate record labels"[448] as the result of tremendous drops in sales, what is not accounted for is the inability to gain popular culture status without them. In other words, it is the ability for corporations to determine popularity—not their ability to sell a certain amount of CDs to reach a certain amount of profit—that ultimately determines the status of Empire. Music labels, themselves offshoots of larger international conglomerates and private equity groups with wide-ranging sources of wealth, are less concerned with overall profits generated from music sales than they are in establishing a popular norm against which massive effort and organization is needed to overcome.

Similarly, it is difficult to accept that media conglomerates need to perfectly predict potential subversive capabilities of their subjects, as Haupt argues, in order to remain dominant. No amount of sampling or P2P file-sharing have wrested any power from the elite. So, again, here is not where *Stealing Empire* makes its mark. That mark is made by forcing the discussion, even where there is disagreement, to take place upon the foundation of an existing Empire bent on the appropriation of culture, land, resources, and labor. It does not require full agreement to appreciate that in the end Haupt's work does offer strategic use and potential for progressive re-appropriation of Empire's wares among those oppressed. Haupt is helpful in that he contextualizes the production of hip-hop and media within that pre-existing and determining Empire. His work, in what must be again described as a pleasant departure from most popular hip-hop/media studies work, is that he to some degree maintains what has been described as a "Fanonian tradition" that holds to a "'belief in the continued existence of the primary antagonism between coloniser and colonized.'"[449]

What those considered the cynics must then do is appropriate *Stealing Empire* for their discussions of how this work can support their political movements and encourage the strength required to not find agency within Empire but to have that agency accumulate into the death of Empire.

CHAPTER EIGHT

PAYOLA AND PLAYLISTS

Payola has replaced the ears and eyes of radio and video programmers.
I have seen the process grow first hand, the industry has followed
the nation, capitalism has replaced talent and creativity. Anyone
who tells you anything else is stating a bold-faced lie.
—Paul Porter

In the future, when social scientists study the mixtape
phenomenon, they will conclude—in fancy language—
that the mixtape was a form of "speech" particular to the
late twentieth century, soon replaced by the "playlist."
—Dean Wareham

The DJs don't really give a fuck about what you sayin' as
long as the payola payin' then somebody will play it.
—Hasan Salaam

"Most listeners don't know it," Eric Boehlert once said, "but virtually every song they hear on FM commercial radio has been paid for—indirectly—by five major record labels."[450] To further ensure that radio (as well as television and book publishing) continued to serve its colonial function, payola, the system of pay-for-play, was introduced. There is no need here to reprint the well-documented history of this practice. Payola, payment in exchange for promotion or popularity, has always existed[451] and remains perfectly legal if said arrangement is announced on air. Of course, this never actually happens. Such announcements run counter to radio's mythical existence as the media outlet that serves to provide "what the people want." Payola represents the very foundation or purpose of money: the socially constructed means of forcing compliance in trade and general behavior, which has its function—quite naturally—applied here to the music business.

Radio airtime is essential to sales and popularity, even though it's not a guarantee. Access to that airtime is expensive, sometimes as much as $5000 per song per station,[452] thus ensuring that only a small minority can afford to promote what they deem worthy of widespread attention. Record contracts offered to artists are designed to ensure some measure of control, guaranteeing some compensation to the artists for their contribution to an enhanced national and international culture. Contracts are the machinery of colonial extraction. They are the means by which the transfer from the colony to the Mother Country takes place. Artists are blinded by what appear to be huge sums of money, offered as part of a contract that ultimately trades the trinkets of immediate material goods or toys for the long-term ownership of the natural resource of art or cultural production. It is the "one more bale" sharecropping relationship re-inscribed in a contemporary setting. The more one works, the more one is in debt. Every song, video, tour, or appearance is designed to first repay the loans given in the form of an advance upon signing. The shibboleth of wealth promised in popular imaging is just that. African labor may be less necessary today but African cultural expression remains essential—embedded—in the function and purpose of North American popular culture.

Record contracts then, like sharecropping, bind artists to the very label (or land) they have committed to through the promise (rarely attained) of freedom, fame, and independence, once the debt is repaid. Contracts shackle artists to labels, shape their art, determine the amount or types of public appearances or performances[453] they will make, and, most importantly, allow an elite minority to determine what becomes popular. It is this purpose that payola invariably serves. The function of popular culture is far more important than individual record sales. As a conglomerate, the overall stability of an organization is not dependent on the financial or sales success of one record label. So while it is true that "airtime would by no means be sufficient for making a hit record, since many heavily promoted albums fail miserably,"[454] miserably failing albums that are still heavily promoted prevent the promotion and often the success of others. This is the primary and general function of promotion and the specific function of payola: to shape what is acceptable fare for consideration or the standard against which others are judged, or to shape the agenda for what is to be discussed or heard. It is just as important that people debate the quality of Lil' Wayne as it is that they do not have that same discussion about Godisheus.[455]

The use of Top 40 lists and shows such as MTV's *Total Request Live*, BET's *Top Video Countdown*, or even VH1's never-ending series of "Most this…" or "Best that…" serve as orchestrated funnels of culture that appear as if an independent, informed audience is selecting its favorite songs.[456] This, in practice, is how the necessary paucity of "cultural goods in circulation"[457] is developed and maintained. This limitation must occur so as to weaken any opportunity to expand what is discussed or considered that is essential to challenging existing power. This is how, as Melinda Newman of *Billboard* explains, "there are 30,000 albums released each year… [and] only 100 become hits."[458]

Payola is just one of the ways those in power determine national and international popularity through intentional magnification or projection of certain artists. Magnification is but one form of those colonized that is then projected far and wide for all to see. It establishes and maintains the preferred version of the projection against which all else is judged. The spatial separation, segregated living, and social lives—the difference—between settlers and the colonized allows for these projections to be determinant. Intentionally popularizing, in this case, one form of hip-hop or "blackness," African America can be completely understood with there never being any real contact. And, of course, this is preferable to all involved.[459]

There is yet another aspect that requires some attention. Radio, and specifically radio targeting the internally colonized African American population—the lineage from which FreeMix Radio and the mixtape radio concept emerges—developed in the U.S. adhering to all of the major ideological principles described above and squarely within the model. As such, the mechanisms of payola and playlists developed in similar patterns for similar reasons. Therefore, just as a "racial ventriloquism"[460] was established, allowing "Black sounding" White DJs on air to solidify that which would be the accepted form (while also setting standards of "authenticity" that must be adhered to by Black DJs), so too would payola and playlists serve the very politically-driven social role of maintaining "order." This established norm had long been set within the history of U.S. popular culture and the politics inherent to it. "Following a pattern established by minstrelsy and blackface actors on stage and screen, Whites played Negro roles in nearly all the early radio shows."[461] This method of maintaining social (racial) order carried over into the history and development of payola. The Top 40 playlist was installed to bring the graft upward from the lowly disc-jockey to station owners or program directors. The playlist would then be turned in for on-air hosts to simply talk up and play, the list having already been paid for and arranged. Yet this system of mechanized colonialism through payola also served to maintain that racial ventriloquism that required the separation of Black and White people so that one could be re-imaged and disseminated to the other in a form acceptable by the performer/shaper/owner. This adherence, or lack thereof, to social segregation—colonial maintenance—would prove to be the difference in how disc-jockeys engaged in payola practices would be treated.[462]

CHAPTER NINE

WASHINGTON, D.C.: A CASE STUDY IN THE COLONIZING FUNCTION OF RADIO

This is D.C. You might think that you own it. A piece of South Africa on the Potomac.... See you can't vote, but you got to pay taxes. Not a city or a state because they're scared of the Blacks. Fuck "Chocolate City," imagine a chocolate state with two chocolate senators in the debate.
—DJ Eurok

November of the year 2000, Washington Post Magazine, and learn about how Black housing in Southwest was demolished by the thousands to make way for a fresh new look to better the urban situation, the creation of a safe-haven't called gentrification. That's when they don't put money in your hood's education. And graduation drop-out rates suffer from inflation... facilities decrepit mold, in the ventilation. There's devastation clear and present at the food station. Rehabilitation is needed but the speed is hesitation. And the next thing you know for a pot of gold the result is a gymnasium. And now there's White folks in the cut walking with they pit-bulls lookin' like "nigga what?"
—Head-Roc

This is the bullshit, the extreme bullshit, the absolute bullshit. This is the bullshit of bullshit! This bullshit is so bullshit, I never want to hear this bullshit on the radios or in my children's ears 'cuz it's bullshit!... I present to you the bullshit.
—Jeru tha Damaja

Radio One is Black Power!
—Cathy Hughes (founder of Radio One)
(The absolute bullshit as delivered during her keynote speech to Morgan State University's 2007 graduating class)

Washington, D.C., the birthplace of FreeMix Radio, is often referred to *not* as a democracy but as "the nation's largest plantation,"[463] or as "America's last colony."[464] These, of course, are references to a majority Black city that has no voting representation in Congress; lacks internal control of its economy, its schools, and its law enforcement structure; suffers high-rates of gentrification; borrows policing techniques from the state of Israel; and has police officers who suggest that it is improper for African American residents to be in the increasingly affluent and White areas of the city.[465] However, were these analogies of enslavement and colonialism extended as the lens through which mass media in the city today are considered, then new analyses and responses might develop to grapple with some of the more difficult questions we need to ask. What would media in such a colony look or sound like? How would a community that perceives a need for liberation and, therefore, a desire to communicate that need, go about doing so and with what potential impact? If communicating liberation, however that is to be defined, is seen through the lens of anti-colonial struggle or as the practice of "revolutionary media"— that which is "illegal and subversive mass communication utilizing the press and broadcasting to overthrow government or wrest control from alien rulers"[466]—or as simply a way of communicating ideas that legally threaten the undesired genuine democratic restructuring of city governance, then how would such communication take place?

Payola and playlists, like the sale of advertisements, are a part of the mechanism that ensures radio serves its colonizing function. Here, again, is the importance of the initial development—and subsequent, continuing maintenance—of that racial ventriloquism. "Black" voices in radio remain in Fanon's "mummified" colonial form—a form more comforting to "The Whiteness at the Top."[467] Today's Black-targeted commercial radio extends from a pattern set forth in the medium's origins. White preferences for content (musical, news, or otherwise) and vocal style of the on-air personalities still dominate. This, of course, goes beyond the particular sound of the radio host or DJ and extends to the content of what she or he has to offer verbally or musically. The "ventriloquism" is both audible and ideological. What is said by the host or the music played must be consistent with the function of radio as defined by its owners and content managers (advertisers).

This point has been routinely driven home by media reform activists. For instance, Lisa Fager-Bediako has consistently raised questions about the focus of concern regarding hip-hop lyrics or imaging of women and others. As she argues, "We spend a lot of time going after the artists and blaming them for corrupting our kids… and we rarely hold feet to the fire those who are in key power positions who remain hidden behind the scenes but control what is heard or not heard on the airwaves day in and day out."[468] The extreme minority represented by the elite White men who own most of the media, the agencies or companies who pay to advertise, and the entertainment corporations who select which Black artists they will promote via payola or "legitimate" means, are rarely discussed.

Overall, radio finds itself confined to a position within a larger structure of mass media that are highly desired commodities because of their ability to ensure both financial profit and social order. The former is achieved through oligopoly, the latter through a uniformity of thought constructed and disseminated as such. Fragmentation, or the dispersal of audiences into "conceptual ghettoes"[469] to be fed specifically tailored media developed by the same ownership, allows for fewer people to be involved in the wider dissemination and penetration of audiences than ever before.[470] All of this has led to the conclusion reached by the Pew Research Center's Project for Excellence in Journalism that

> [n]ews consumers may have had more choices than ever for where to find news in 2007, but that does not mean they had more news to choose from. The news agenda for the year was, in fact, quite narrow, dominated by a few major general topic areas.[471]

In Washington, D.C., a similar trend has emerged with comparable results. Popular media are maintained to limit ranges of thought, and debate and news—particularly for the city's majority Black population—are both readily withheld and narrowly constructed. The largest media outlets in the city are, predictably, owned by the largest national media companies and conglomerates, as well as the wealthiest and most well-connected families. *The Washington Post* (owned by The Washington Post Company) may attempt to appear as a "family-owned" (read independent, professional, liberal) entity but its board of directors (which includes billionaire investor Warren Buffett[472]) and its obedience to the establishment[473] belie any such claim. *The Washington Times* was founded by Unification Church leader Sun Myung Moon, General Electric has WRC/NBC, Disney has WJLA/ABC, News Corp. has WTTG/Fox, Viacom has WUSA/CBS. In radio, Infinity Broadcasting owns D.C. radio stations WPGC 95.5 FM,

WPGC 1580 AM, WARW 94.7 FM, WHFS 99.1 FM, and WJFK 106.7 FM. And, of course, as is rampant in media (as well as in all business), "competitors" at times work with one another so News Corp.'s WDCA airs Viacom's United Paramount Network (UPN). Radio One, the nation's largest radio provider to African America owns WKYS 93.9 FM, WMMJ 102.3 FM, WOL 1450 AM, and WYCB 1340 AM. And not to be outdone or left behind, Clear Channel, the nation's largest radio station owner, has D.C.'s WASH 97.1 FM, WBIG 100.3 FM and WWDC 101.1 FM, among others. Adding to this is Clear Channel's dominance over the media landscape of the city's (and nation's) billboards, bus kiosk signage, and so on where D.C. has become one of its "branded cities" where "brandscaping" turns communal spaces into controlled environments where brands are "to be experienced" and unavoidably interwoven into people's daily lives.[474]

In fact, the deceptive Blackness and liberalness of the "Diamond District" serves, in microcosm, to perfectly represent a global (and certainly national) illusion of media liberalism that is thought to reflect the general attitudes of the people. Instead, as Thomas Franks explains, there exists in the city an "elaborate and heavily subsidized right-wing media machine" buttressed by a collage of think tanks, all of whom comprise an industry designed to project their agenda or "madness" onto the city and world.[475] Think tanks, institutions designed to transform the ideology of the tiniest segment of society into public policy—as demonstrated in the very book title of the Manhattan Institute's *Turning Intellect into Influence* (2004)—use their influence to, in part, adjust media content so as to project their interests to the detriment of the majority. These think tanks[476] use conferences, journals, press releases, and reports to generate the appearance of studied, reasoned analyses that result in the development of public policies designed to implement their will, under the guise of being in the interests of all. Their goal, so well defined by Amos Wilson, is to "organize, direct and regulate the activities, the production and consumption of the resources, internal and external social relations and institutions of society in order to defend and advance what it perceives as its overall interests." Their "intellectual output," continues Wilson, is "utilized to inform and shape the thoughts and behavior of the media and politicians."[477] It matters little that a community may still be predominantly Black, or poor, or lean politically to the left (at least!), or possess politics and worldviews that support who they might be. What matters is the inability of a *majority* population to project its

interests any farther than an extreme minority, well-funded and organized, will allow.

None of this is meant to suggest that alternatives do not exist. There
remain, for example, any number of smaller community and ethnic journals, magazines, and newspapers. There is *The Afro-American/Washington
Tribune* (Afro) newspaper, which overall has maintained four to five figure
circulation numbers in the face of a national drop in newspaper reader-
ship. There is WPFW 89.3 FM, the liberal Pacifica Network's affiliate and
a host of smaller "alternative" media outlets, including low-power FM and
even the author's own attempts at an underground press using the hip-
hop mixtape.[478] Yet, these sources are forced to struggle—to the extent
they reach or penetrate smaller audiences—against what is established
as the norm or dominant selection of stories, topics, and interpretations
all set by dominant media. So, as in all cases, these smaller outlets must
compete against a norm established to be that against which all else must
be measured. So, for example, even with recent drops in *Washington Post*
subscribers, their D.C.-area paid circulation is still 635,000[479] compared
to that of the *Afro-American*, which is now down to 12,500 with what are
said to be 100,000 loyal readers.[480]

Though broadcasting in FM stereo from a 50,000-watt tower, WP-
FW's impact is lessened by its lack of commercial advertising, and an
abundance of the marginalized whose disparate and eclectic—isolated—
voices fail to amass any powerful or collective movement. The power of
mass media's consolidated and fragmented ownership is in its ability to
tailor one message to the specific audiences it can then reach through
equally powerful advertising and promotion, the cost prohibitive nature
of which, and against which no community radio (such as WPFW) can
compete. Similarly, low-power FM with its limited signal (roughly three-
mile radii) or the low production count of mixtapes (no more than 3,000
per edition) demonstrate the historical pattern of uneven distributive or
promotional capacities. And while many claim the Internet to be the great
leveling medium, it too is limited in its capacity, as such, due to uneven
promotional revenues for varying websites (including those supported by
their parallel in other media, e.g., CNN can promote CNN.com) and its
general usage among individuals, which mimics preexisting interests and
political biases.

The emergence historically of a commercially-driven mass media in
which content is determined and managed by those who pay the advertising revenue sublimates particular ownership and ensures that media

will perform their colonizing function. It validates Marx's claim that "the ruling ideas of any epoch are the ideas of the ruling elite" and offers the deception that Noam Chomsky described in terms of violence and totalitarianism: "propaganda is to democracy what violence is to totalitarianism." So it is that the prideful "brandscaping" of Clear Channel is not simply about advertising for sales or products but for what advertising is known to be: the sale of people's consciousness—"The Higher Value of Eyeballs"[481]—from one to the next. In fact, this system of advertising driving or determining media content not only is a mechanism of negating the power of ownership but ensures that "the formal right to establish a free press exercised by dissidents [is kept] on the margins.... [T]he commercial system is such that these voices have no hope to expand beyond their metaphorical house arrest."[482] Advertising, product placement, and branding are processes of imposing ideology so as to encourage and ensure acceptable forms of behavior. All of this is, of course, buttressed by the ever-impending use of physical violence, should there be any breaks with so-called acceptable behavior—hence, the police brutality, mass incarceration, overt statements about where those colonized should or should not go,[483] the covert transportation,[484] and architectural impediments[485] to free form movement, including the recent police cordoning off of neighborhoods.[486] Washington, D.C. is a prime example of what Antonio Gramsci describes as a space within which "[e]verything which influences or is able to influence public opinion, directly or indirectly, belongs to [the ideological structure]: libraries, schools, associations, and clubs of various kinds, even architecture and the layout and names of streets."[487]

What this means is that those interested in communicating counter-hegemonic ideas, thus encouraging the development of Sandoval's "oppositional consciousness," which must precede oppositional political organization and activity, cannot expect to use mainstream media to that end. Washington, D.C. continues to provide an important example of what those around the country face.

Though its population dynamics are rapidly shifting, Washington, D.C. remains a predominantly Black city (57 percent) and is surrounded by Prince George's County, which, at 66 percent Black, is also the wealthiest Black community in the country.[488] Given these demographics and the very specific relationship between African America and radio, it is again this medium that must be considered most carefully. Black America's use of Black-targeted radio, with its roughly 80 to 90 percent household penetration rates, is greater than in any other targeted community.[489] And while, again, there exist various forms of media, radio remains the primary and most pervasive medium in African America.[490] Though Howard University's WHUR (96.3 FM) ranks first in city-wide ratings, it cannot be said to be so rated among Black youth, nor can it be said to have any more of an emancipatory content than the two stations that dominate among Black youth—a key demographic long sought after by activists to maintain or evolve radical politics, as well as by those seeking to blunt those same efforts.[491] For younger audiences, there are really only two radio stations: Viacom's WPGC (95.5 FM), ranked third in the city, and Radio One's WKYS (93.9 FM), ranked fifth.[492] Part of the overall problem, a problem to be developed more fully below, is summarized by Glen Ford and deserves to be quoted at length:

> In 1973, 21 reporters from three Black-oriented radio stations provided African Americans in Washington, DC a daily diet of news—*hard, factual information vital to the material and political fortunes of the local community.* The three stations—WOL-AM, WOOK-AM and WHUR-FM—their news staffs as fiercely competitive as their disc jockeys, vied for domination of the Black Washington market. Community activists and institutions demanded, expected, and received intense and sustained coverage of the fullest range of their activities. In scores of large, medium and even small cities across the nation, the early to mid-Seventies saw a flowering of Black radio news, a response to the voices of an awakened people. Black ownership had relatively little to do with the phenomenon. According to the National Association of Black-owned Broadcasters (NABOB), there were only 30 African-American owned broadcast facilities in the United States in 1976. Today, NABOB boasts 220 member stations—and local Black radio news is near extinction. With some notable exceptions, Black owners are as culpable as White corporations in the demise of Black radio news. In Washington, DC, the culprit is obvious. Black-oriented radio journalism in the nation's capitol has plummeted from 21 reporters at three stations, 30 years ago, to four reporters

at two stations, today. WPGC-FM (Infinity-Viacom)
fields one reporter, and Howard University's com-
mercially operated WHUR-FM employs three. Black
Washington's dominant radio influence is Radio
One, the 66-station chain founded by Cathy Liggins
Hughes, valued at $2 billion. Hughes employs not a
single newsperson at her four Washington stations—a
corporate policy reflected in most of the 22 cities in
which Radio One operates. The chain is the dominant
influence in at least 13 of these markets. (Radio One
also programs 5 channels of XM Satellite Radio, and
has launched a Black-oriented television venture with
Comcast, the cable giant.) While 1,200-station Clear
Channel deserves every lash of the whip as the Great
Homogenizer of American radio, the chain operates
only 49 stations programmed to Blacks, and is dominant in no large African American market. *The Queen
of Black broadcasting is Radio One [with well over 60
stations], and her dictum is, Let Them Eat Talk.*[493]

Ford touches on a number of serious concerns facing proponents of
progressive political struggle and certainly those seeking to expand the
reach of liberatory communication. First among them is that Radio One,
the leading provider of Black-targeted radio,[494] follows precisely the established model of dominant-society radio. Its FM stations follow the same
payola-based playlist format, assuring "homogenization" of the music and
a lack of investigative journalism or reporting. What Radio One offers, as
is the case with Washington, D.C.'s WOL and Baltimore's WOLB AM
stations, is Black-oriented talk radio, some of it nationally syndicated.
While the latter is not without benefit it does not replace news gathering,
particularly the kind Ford describes as being related and necessary to political movements. In response to these concerns are statements from Victor Starr, program director at Radio One's Baltimore FM station WERQ
92.3 ("92Q"), who dismisses the need to deliver news to the station's audience "in an information era" when one can easily go to CNN.com to get
the important news not covered in the two-minute segments 92Q offers
each hour—that is unless it is something on the order of "Anna Nicole's
death," in which case mention will be made.[495] Or from Lee Michaels,
at that time the program director of Radio One's XM169, "The Power,"

responded to these criticisms with the oft-repeated dictum that, "radio is business" and, therefore, Radio One need not and, indeed, *cannot* continue any tradition of Black progressivism in radio or that particular role for Black America. And in statements strikingly similar to the language of "media reform," Michaels too suggests that change can only come about if people appeal directly to the FCC.[496]

Yet it is precisely these disparate approaches—each calling for mass appeals to the FCC as the primary (only) mechanism for change, one from an ostensibly "outsider" media-reform movement, the other from one situated well within that institution—that demand attention be paid to the *systemic* nature of colonialism. The final mass media product, what hits the air to be heard or viewed by millions, is predetermined to be limited in scope, safe, and functionally supportive of that which determines its shape. In the end, neither race nor gender nor title ("owner" or "program director," for example) is of any real significance, and strategies for change that relegate all action to or overemphasize the importance of appeals to the FCC are the political equivalent of the hen's appeal to the fox or, better still, Malcolm X's popular expectation that a chicken would of course lay a chicken egg. Were it to lay a duck egg, he mused, it would be one "revolutionary chicken."

The Federal Communications Commission (FCC), whose nominal role is regulation of the public's airwaves, has, since its inception in 1934, never been able to ensure that Black image was ever anything other than an endless string of "Uncle Toms, Mammies and Aunt Jemimas."[497] Its five-member body, consisting of appointees of the president with the tie-breaker going to that president's party, along with its limited funding for in-depth study ensures its impotency as an agent for change. Its oversight of the initial multi-billion dollar give-away of the public's airwaves has been followed by decades of policy or inaction that has kept the control of those airwaves securely within the most elite segments of our society. "The function of the FCC, as one former chair informed William Kennard as he assumed the chair in 1997, 'is to referee fights between the wealthy and the super wealthy.'"[498] Its current project is to oversee the give-away of the digital spectrum, which is likely to result in the same fate for digital television and the Internet as traditional radio and network stations; it is, once again, the ongoing process of colonization.

In fact, this process is already visible where the Internet is concerned, and this is another strong indication that mixtapes and other "low-tech" media options are still as viable an tools for anti-colonial media work.

The Pew Research Center's State of the Media 2010 report shows that the top online news sites (measured by audience size) are the same *Washington Post*, *New York Times*, Fox News, *USA Today*, CBS, and MSNBC that dominate the traditional media world, with the addition of Yahoo and Google to their ranks.[499] Further, computer scientist Jaron Lanier, a seminal figure in the history of the Internet, said recently that the web, far from leveling the playing field, is the epitome of the "post-human society" where people must "feed the great machine," but only those who own or run that machine—not the people who create or who are themselves content—are to be paid. The rest of us are simply aggregated into "mobs" to be easily surveyed and marketed by the same major corporations who determine our news and popular culture.[500]

But perhaps most telling is the recent work of Matthew Hindman. By monitoring web traffic, which he defines as "visits" or a "request for pages or a series of pages with no more than thirty minutes of inactivity," he challenges the "Robin Hood assumption" of the Internet, which claims an equalizing effect of the mass medium. Many assume that the Internet allows everyone to exchange ideas and be heard equally without any real interruption of established power. But out of more than 800,000 websites, Hindman reduced the top news and media sites to only 300 and showed that among those only five by mid-2007 (Google, Yahoo, Yahoo Mail, Windows Live Mail, and MySpace) had 21 percent of all web traffic. The top 500 websites combined had 51 to 52 percent of that traffic meaning that roughly 750,000 websites are competing for the remaining 25 to 30 percent. Similarly, websites ranked first are more likely to stay there (60 percent) over the course of one year, whereas the fifth-ranked site is less likely (40 percent) and those ranked around 300 are more likely to change out and drop out by the day (80 percent). In other words, Hindman shows that there is only any real stability in web traffic for the top five websites. All the rest scramble for temporary attention but ultimately remain in relative obscurity. And certainly, even when, from time to time, a website has a tremendous uptick in traffic, it is never sustained to the point where they determine or alter a national, or even large community, agenda for discussion and the framing of information.

Further, as Hindman shows, in many ways the Internet is even more concentrated in audience than previous media forms, because the top news/media sites garner 30 percent of the web's audience while the top 12 newspapers hold only 20 percent of the total audience. So the more people move online and away from print media the *more* they are concentrated into the hands of fewer providers. Hindman also notes that the attempt to move online by major newspapers comes at the expense of local readers who are forced to find localized news in fewer and smaller outlets. Once online newspapers gear their product more toward a broad, and even international, audience, they forget about local needs.[501]

Finally, regarding the Internet, it is important to challenge the all-too-popular notion among grassroots artists that they are any more popular today than before due to this newer technology. At a recent panel convened on the subject by Words.Beats.Life., Inc. (a Washington, D.C.-based hip-hop nonprofit), the blogosphere was described by several hip-hop artists as a space for them to occupy that circumvented the music industry.[502] But, as Lanier has noted, while some may see levels of success they might not have otherwise experienced on the Internet, almost no one is making a career out of it. More importantly, very few artists are cracking the popular norm established by existing record label power. The Internet is not changing the agenda, is not making popular new forms or alternative forms of rap music, and certainly it has not resulted in an end to the material horrors of the community. Individual "success" here or there is no answer to the devolving conditions of the larger community.

In fact, it has been reported recently that the Internet is not even posing any immediate threat to existing "point-to-mass" terrestrial radio. Simply put, the Internet is a "one-to-one" communication technology where each individual listener comes at the cost of limited bandwidth. Radio, on the other hand, is a "one-to-many" technology, allowing a set cost for broadcasting that is relatively fixed regardless of how many people tune in. It continues to reach 90 percent of adults every week[503] and of listeners ages 12 and up Black Americans listen 21 percent more often than any other community.[504] The "titans of technology" have not quite figured out how to scale their economies so as to reach as many online as they do over the air.[505] No serious study of the politics of media can conclude that new technology will upset existing social relationships, and it appears again that advancing study of the Internet bears that out. Radio is, to those who own it, still safe and, therefore, still a problem for those interested in radical political and social change.

Since the 1996 Telecommunications Act further deregulated airwaves (paving the way also for corporations like Radio One to accumulate more stations), the situation has worsened as diversity of media content has lessened.[506] A 2007 study from the University of Chicago showed, among other results, that, overwhelmingly, Black youth did not like the hip-hop and R&B they heard on commercial radio,[507] and yet, as other studies conducted in part by this author show, the prevalence of that limited range of cultural expression (matched by almost zero news content) remains the norm. Colonialism and the media it produces do not require "liking." Colonialism only requires recognition of its norm and that it be the popular form of that which it claims to represent—be it music, news, a people's image, or whatever else.[508]

Radio and television monitoring projects conducted by this author's own classes at the University of Maryland at College Park (and continuing now at Morgan State University) with Lisa Fager-Bediako of Industry Ears and Chanelle Hardy, then with Consumers Union, resulted in dozens of FCC complaints being filed by students with no significant response or action.[509] However, with no expected structural change coming from student monitoring projects or letters to the FCC, the real value of these studies is their coerced focus on content, which results in higher levels of clarity among students as to what they are hearing and how that becomes what they hear.

Students, listening to one of the two dominant commercial radio stations (with an option to select any other commercial radio station as their second choice for monitoring), created pie-charts detailing what they heard, when they heard it, and for what duration. Students were asked to monitor programming, at one-hour intervals, between 5 AM and 10 AM and again 5 PM to 10 PM weekdays. These are the most popular and ad-saturated hours in radio. The results clearly demonstrate the aforementioned lack of news (most charts collected in the last run of this project contained no slots depicted as "news" and none that consisted of news departing from the variety described above by Victor Starr) and an adherence to the supremacy of advertising and major label-driven music. WPGC and WKYS, which dominate youth radio listening (ages 12 to 17), much like all dominant mainstream radio, have their content determined by a three-corporation "musical OPEC"[510] which is ultimately responsible for nearly everything we hear on radio (or see on music video channels). This leads to national airing of songs, or spins, which reach the tens of thousands in a month, 10,000 in one week, or once an hour, every hour, every day.

Student reports also demonstrated a concern facing those interested in counter-hegemonic or critical thought related to or in advocacy of societal change (liberation). Described by Noam Chomsky as "concision,"[511] the issue revolves around the amount of time allowed for substantive

discussion or the dissemination of ideas that might counter those promoted by power and, therefore, normalized. With so much of an hour
consumed by sanctioned, paid-for major label music, advertisements, and
"news," any time allowed (even hypothetically) would be greatly limited
so as to make the counter-normative ideas and attitudes presented seem
strange or delusional. With no time to make an unpopular argument,
the system resets or protects itself in perpetuity from becoming what it
has never been intended to be. Here, again, is the original intent behind
mass media: to reproduce that which already has been determined to be
accepted fare for the target audience, rather than to be a source of anything new, controversial, or system-changing. As legendary establishment
scholar Walter Lippmann has noted, with reference to "manufacturing
consent," public opinions "must be organized *for* the press if they are to
be sound, not *by* the press."[512]

This, of course, determines how much time every day will be spent
on airing songs and advertisments paid for by major corporations—time
that is expressly not available for other, non-commercial music, and certainly not for the kinds of information that might be useful to communities facing the worst of this nation's economic, social, cultural, and
racial policies. The radio that Dr. King applauded in 1967 for having
assisted the civil rights movement today exists, if at all, in a tremendously
weakened or limited capacity.[513] This issue is the subject of a recent documentary, *Disappearing Voices: The Decline of Black Radio* (2009). The film
traces the devolution of Black radio from a vibrant tool, which at one
time would allow "political and social activists [to] mobilize thousands
of people by simply putting the word out over the radio about a protest
or rally,"[514] to today where, as radio host and hip-hop historian DaveyD
has noted, no rally or political event is announced effectively to its target
audience in most major cities because Black-targeted radio is predominantly concerned with promoting "50 Cent" or some other apolitical
commercial artist.[515]

Iyanna Jones, executive producer of *Disappearing Voices* (2009), also
focuses on racism's contemporary damaging effects: much like the predetermination of Black economic and political poverty, the filmmakers
argue that a lack of Black radio profitability will lead to less openness
in those spaces for wider arrays (including radical ones) of Black radio
programming.[516] Arbitron skews ratings numbers so that there appear to
be no listeners and, therefore, no advertisers who are willing to spend the
necessary revenue to keep the stations going. In the end, Black radio is

forced to do more to appear like any other radio and this naturally means no news gathering and no critical or radical voices on the air.[517]

It is, therefore, a sad twist for an establishment newspaper such as *The Washington Post* to question the absence of critical voices on Black radio. Again, the colonized are blamed for their condition. The hypocracy has now become familiar: *The Post* is notorious for under-reporting of domestic political struggles and social movements and then having the gall to ask "Where Have All The Protests Gone?"[518] With respect to Black radio, the paper posed the question, "Where are the Petey Greens of today?"[519] in reference to the political activism and commentary of the popular 1960s Washington, D.C.-based DJ. It is particularly dispiriting to note that the question was raised—while praising the rise of Radio One and its adherence to the Black talk tradition with its inclusion of WOL AM talk radio—five days before the sudden dismissal of politically progressive hosts Ambrose I. Lane, Sr. and Mark Thompson (Matsimela Mapfumo) from the network. As *The Post* raised the question of the quality and power of Black talk radio, the genre's leading provider was undercutting its own potential for just that. Yet even if this were an attempt to move closer to the political middle where the most revenue is to be gained, it has apparently not been enough. Recent financial troubles at Radio One have led to the loss of further stations, its deal with XM satellite, and some top executives.[520]

Here, again, are the limiting effects of advertising revenue, which ultimately undercuts any individual owner's will and is assuredly connected to the recent trend in media purchasing by private equity groups (dubbed "the conglomerate of the 21st century: the private-equity media empire"), who are themselves involved in widely diverse international holdings.[521] So as more media become owned by fewer people, and they, themselves, become more invested in diverse businesses around the globe, the less room there is for dissident communication and the less recourse exists for audiences interested in challenging existing media practices. Whereas it may have at one point been politically savvy to boycott local media or their sponsors, this is less of an effective tool today given that the entity one is likely to protest is one of dozens held by its owners who are themselves beholden to advertisers involved in supplying revenue to any number of other outlets.

There is yet another effect resulting from such a media function: the encouraged apathy among colonized audiences. This apathy was described by Fanon as being so "universally noted among colonial peoples

[it] is but the logical consequence of this operation. The reproach of inertia constantly directed at 'the native' is utterly dishonest. As though it were possible for a man to evolve otherwise than within the framework of a culture that recognized him and that he decides to assume."[522] This inertia was made popular yet again, albeit unwittingly, when in January of 2007 Oprah Winfrey popularly stated that, "If you are a child in the United States, you can get an education. I became so frustrated with visiting inner-city schools that I just stopped going. The sense that you need to learn just isn't there. If you ask the kids what they want or need, they will say an iPod or some sneakers. In South Africa, they don't ask for money or toys. They ask for uniforms so they can go to school."[523] Aside from the anti-historical nature of the comment or her positioning as a "Black leader" despite being a "Neo-liberal Icon" with a primary audience of affluent White women,[524] Oprah's comments defy the reality of the media environment impacting these "inner-city" youths. Perhaps, to the extent that there is truth in these comments, she might investigate the content and messaging in her show or, more appropriately, explore the content and delivery mechanism of the media (and "education") directed at these unappreciative Black children. The desire for material goods that Winfrey laments is a likely result of the formulaic, massively repetitive, and news-less radio imposed upon that community—an imposition that, as previously noted, occurs regardless of a particular community's desire to hear it.

Few would argue that hip-hop has, by today, become one of the nation's (and world's) leading cultural products. It certainly remains so for young people and African America in general. *American Brandstand* is a marketing agency that has for several years tracked the prevalence of product brand names dropped in Billboard Top 20 rap music lyrics. When matched with the sheer volume of airplay or spins these songs get, there is little confusion as to why so many young people might, as Winfrey thoughtlessly lamented, be more focused on material goods than deeper intellectual pursuits. Perhaps were this matched with assessments of the modern "education" facing most African American students, the concern would shift from blame to radical change.[525]

For example, according to the 2005 *American Brandstand* report, Mercedes Benz topped the product placement "mentions" with 100 separate references in hip-hop lyrics. Magnify this by songs that routinely gain weekly spins nationwide in the 6 to 10,000 range and its potential impact on audiences becomes clear. Winfrey's reference to "sneakers" being so

desired by Black youth—to the extent that any of her claims are true—
would be of no surprise given that Nike, number two on the list, had
63 separate mentions that year. Rounding out that top-ten list, AK-47
assault rifles, which had 37 mentions that year. It bears repeating that
this result comes at the end of a process of musical selection and promotion that has nothing to do with artist or audience choice. Artists who
routinely produce more humane or community-supportive music are all
but banned since they are not seen as marketable. Therefore, they are not
signed or promoted, as it is quite correctly understood to be antithetical
to the needs of business and colonization to promote artists protesting
corporate dominance, conspicuous consumption, or self-directed anti-
revolutionary violence.

Further, it stands to reason that no properly functioning society or
community would blame societal flaws on children. It might behoove
those in agreement with Winfrey to question a media system that imposes
this kind of repetition on its audience, particularly its children, who have
enough products officially licensed for them—not counting the Mercedes
and AK-47s—in what has now become a $132 billion global market. The
goal here, as has long been well understood, is to attach young people to
products "before their brand decisions have been made, and before their
defenses to advertising are well developed."[526] In 2008, Nike outlasted
2007's leading brand Patron and Glock-brand handguns tied for ninth
place with Coca-Cola.[527] If this, again, is reinterpreted for a domestic colonialism and through centering the experience of young, mostly Black,
colonized residents of Washington, D.C., (or elsewhere) dangerous trends
emerge. The brands to which these young people are forcibly attached,
including the unseen and unwitting support for the harmful global labor
practices (sweatshops, etc.) involved in their production, also contribute
to negative self-images, lowered aspirations, and self or community-di-
rected criminal behavior. A wider range of images and ideas is necessary to
encourage more community-sustaining behavior among youth. Yet these
are precisely the kinds of images and ideas that are seen as antithetical to
the maintenance of colonies and, therefore, are not to be offered. They
must be generated and disseminated within colonies by the colonized and
against that which is imposed as the norm.

Theodor Adorno once described the imposition of "like." He said,
"If one seeks to find out who 'likes' a commercial piece, one cannot avoid
the suspicion that liking and disliking are inappropriate to the situation....
The familiarity of the piece is a surrogate for the quality ascribed to it. To

like it is almost the same thing as to recognize it."[528] DMX more recently
summarized the same point saying that "if you feed people dog shit long
enough they will learn to put barbeque sauce on it." In either case, both
spoke exactly to the current situation. If people are forced, through tens
of thousands of spins, to "like" certain forms of music, then they too
could be "made" to "like" other kinds. And this is precisely the issue and
the reason why so much effort is devoted to maintaining control over
which forms of expression from among the colonized will be sanctioned
for popularity. If people are routinely hearing music that is culturally up-
lifting, proud, politically radical, and so on, then their tastes, or worse,
their behavior, is also likely to change.

During a recent class, the author played for students in an all-Black
HBCU classroom a remix of Lil' Wayne's "A Milli" by Uno the Prophet
aka Nat Turner, The Devil Burner. In Turner's version "a milli" or "a million" was translated from a song about personal riches into a reference
to the tens of millions of enslaved Africans and slaughtered indigenous
people throughout the Americas and the Caribbean. After the song ended
and after some prolonged silence, the students were asked to respond.
Few had anything to say and when asked why so many were so silent one
student, who routinely did not speak in class, explained: "We are just
not used to hearing stuff like that. We don't know what to say. It was uncomfortable." Same beat, same flow, different content and political frame.
Songs about conspicuous consumption that are played tens of thousands
of times a week are seen as normal and acceptable, and though few who
listen can relate to the experiences described in these fairy tales, they are
not at all confusing or discomforting. The same basic song reworked into
one in opposition to genocide and contemporary suffering, with which
many more who hear it could identify, is met with confusion and dis-
comfort. This is the inappropriateness of "like" or "dislike" described by
Adorno and DMX, and one that must be understood in order to be intentionally developed.

CHAPTER TEN

NATIONAL PUBLIC RADIO AS FANON'S RADIO-ALGER

For NPR, Violence Is Calm if It's Violence Against Palestinians
—Fairness and Accuracy in Reporting (FAIR)

I was driving home from work the other day and torturing myself by listening to NPR...
—Noam Chomsky

In regular responses to questions of reactionary media conduct, the "liberalness" of National Public Radio (NPR), headquartered in Washington, D.C., is mentioned as part of the balance against the kinds of media practices described herein. While not mentioned above in the constellation of D.C. media, NPR certainly can be challenged in terms of its claims of serving the public. More specifically, given the current context, it can be seen as analogous in function to Fanon's description of Radio-Alger, the French National Broadcasting equivalent in the French colony of Algeria. [529] Such a claim is perhaps alarming to some. However, a closer look reveals what could be attributed to Fanon as foresight into a twenty-first century version of the same thing located at the very seat of empire. [530] *Fanon's Warning*, [531] applied to the United States, shows the brilliance of that foresight, the result of a continuing colonialism and the incompleteness of previous revolutionary movements.

In his chapter on the subject, entitled "This is the Voice of Algeria," [532] Fanon focuses on the role radio plays in maintaining both the identity of the colonized and, perhaps more importantly, the attendant identity of the colonizer. Playing its established role as a national voice, NPR does precisely what Fanon said of Radio-Alger by reminding "the settler [colonizer] of the reality of colonial power and, by its very existence, dispens[ing] safety, serenity." [533] Thus NPR's overall soft tone and careful balancing of any challenging content with lighter, and Whiter, middle-class content (cooking, movies, music, etc.). Its existence (particularly its often-publicly criticized, and sometimes self-avowed, "liberalness") provides further cover for its primary function: reassuring the settler with what Fanon calls a "daily invitation not to 'go native,' not to forget the rightfulness of his culture."[534] For example, NPR does not produce or air one single show dedicated to labor, but has the weekday business program *Marketplace*—a listener-friendly business newsmagazine designed to reassure American investors of the calm and order of the nation's economic hegemony—prominently placed on weekday evenings.[535]

The NPR-oriented struggles of African-American liberal activist-broadcaster Tavis Smiley showcase this dilemma. He described the inherently contradictory position held by his now-discontinued nationally syndicated NPR show and its existence on a network whose "demographic is overwhelmingly White. So, every day, we have to do a show that is authentically black, but at the same time not too black."[536] Smiley's public concerns are reminiscent of the claim made by cultural critic bell hooks: that once image and identity become part and parcel of the "machinery" of capitalist production, notions of authenticity are "meaningless."[537] So, too, is such a concept made irrelevant within a colonized/colonizer dialectic. The image of the colonized, in this case, becomes the product of the colonizer and, therefore, is authentic to that relationship. Smiley's acknowledged struggle, therefore, is that of combating the *function* of NPR.

Fanon understood radio's role, indeed. Radio, he said, is "a system of information, as a bearer of language, hence of message."[538] It is listened to, he argues, "solely by the representatives of power... solely by the members of the dominant authority and [who] seem magically to be avoided by the members of the 'native' society."[539] So the "authentic blackness" expected of the liberal Smiley (or any other host or producer from the non-dominant population) is that which appeases the larger need of the colonizing media: to put at ease its audience of authority.

There can be little doubt that NPR caters to America's elite. Twenty-six percent of its listeners fall within the top 10 percent of national household income, and NPR listeners are "139% more likely to live in a household that falls within the Upper Deck definition but does not derive most of its income from employment," which, of course, further indicates that they are part of society's ownership class. However, even when measuring NPR's listener income (as opposed to unearned income) 70 percent of

NPR listeners earn more than $70,000 and 73 percent are "more likely than the average U.S. adult to have household incomes of more than $100,000."[540] The median age of an NPR listener is 50, with 65 percent having at least a bachelor's degree and where they are three times as likely as the national average to have a graduate degree. 86 percent are White with a median household income of $86,000.[541]

Similarly, in a subsection titled "The Elite Majority," a report from Fairness and Accuracy in Reporting (FAIR), demonstrates the same.[542] "Elite sources dominated NPR's guest-list," the report states, noting that the list of invited guests includes "government officials, professional experts and corporate representatives—[which] accounted for 64 percent of all sources." Women were said to be represented at 1–5 ratio and republicans 61 percent versus democrats 38 percent. Similarly, think-tank representatives of NPR's programming were said to be more "right of center" at a 4–1 ratio, and for its commentators overall, 60 percent "are still White men."[543] Even by standards that (falsely) assume republicans and democrats to sufficiently cover the political spectrum, there can be said to be no "liberal bias" or clear attempt to upset the norm of mass media broadcasting of any kind at NPR.

The intentional nature can be found again in the way those actively struggling for progressive change in Washington, D.C. are dealt with via major media. This evidence, while not definitive, is suggestive of a lack of desire in or a lack of marketability of the promotion of anti-oppressive organization. In interviews conducted with representatives of Empower DC and the Youth Education Alliance respondents Parisa Norouzi[544] and Jonathan Stith,[545] each noted their organization's inability to have local Black-targeted radio in particular and D.C. media in general play a supportive role in bringing wider attention to or support for their work or the issues. Stith in particular noted the outright antagonistic relationship YEA has with the most popular commercial radio in the city (WPGC) due both to their refusal to promote issues of concern to the organization but also to the antithetical fare offered day in and day out. With few exceptions,[546] Black-targeted radio, "the people's station[s]," offer little support to organizations working to improve the material lives of D.C. residents, particularly youth. And in terms of NPR, when D.C.-based activist and organizer of the annual *National Black Luv Festival* Kymone Freeman questioned why his event would receive no coverage, he was told "because we don't see this as national news."[547] It mattered not that internationally known artists, activists, and politicians—including

Cynthia McKinney running that year for president of the United States on the Green Party ticket—would be on hand or that thousands would gather that day. News is what agenda-setting editors in a hegemonic system say it is. Therefore, natives need not expect any other response from national colonial radio.

CHAPTER ELEVEN

MANAGED OUTCOMES

[Popular culture] is not just an art form; it's a form of propaganda.
And propaganda gets Black activists killed.... if you put out the wrong
propaganda you are setting me up to be killed by my enemy.
—Dhoruba bin-Wahad

Ya'll stuck on 'Laffy-Taffy' [I'm] wonderin'
how did ya'll niggas get past me?
—Ghostface Killah

Omission is worse than lying.
—Howard Zinn

During a 2005 panel arranged by then-Congresswoman Cynthia McK-
inney (D-GA) on the history, legacy, and continued impact of the FBI's
Counter Intelligence Program (COINTELPRO), the idea of the management of information and popularity was addressed in the current
context. That is, there is an intended process, the result of which is
entertainment, "news," and academic representation—or omission—of
radicalism or varying points of view, which carries with it very real material damage suffered by those whose images or ideas are so readily
distorted. Among the panelists that day, Professor Ward Churchill offered an extended view of COINTELPRO—the FBI's secret attempts
to destroy Leftist movements in the 1960s and 1970s—as being more
than the particular moment of that effort to destroy threatening political movements and people. It was a natural offshoot of the process of
"predation" whereby the conquered must be monitored and managed.
In this case the management takes the form of the convergence of a
state-sponsored private business apparatus employing the technology of
the day to ensure the maintenance of power. What would eventually

become the FBI, and in particular its COINTELPRO operations, originated in the alignment of private policing and federal funding for the protection of the state.[548]

As expressed in their own documents, one of the core tenets of COINTELPRO was to "expose, disrupt, misdirect, discredit, or otherwise neutralize the activities of black nationalist... organizations, their leadership, [and] spokesmen... to counter their propensity for violence and civil disorder."[549] In addition, there was the primary need of preventing the "rise of a 'messiah' who could unify and electrify Black nationalist organizations."[550] However, less often discussed is the fifth element or goal, which was to "prevent the long-range growth of militant Black nationalist organizations *especially among youth*. Specific tactics to prevent these groups from *converting young people* must be developed."[551] Forty years ago, during a period of heightened rebellion among the colonized, this goal could be carried out in a manner described by an imprisoned George Jackson who wrote,

> Black capitalism, black against itself. The silliest contradiction in a long train of spineless, mindless contradictions. Another painless, ultimate remedy: be a better fascist than the fascist. *Bill Cosby, acting out the establishment agent*—what message was this soul brother conveying to our children? *I Spy* was certainly programmed to a child's mentality. This running dog in the company of a fascist with a cause, a flunky's flunky, was transmitting the credo of the slave to our youth, the mod version of the old house nigger. We can never learn to trust as long as we have them. They are as much a part of the repression, more even than the real live, rat-informer-pig. Aren't they telling our kids that it is romantic to be a running dog? The kids are so hungry to see the black male do some shooting and throw some hands that they can't help themselves from identifying with the quislings. So first they turn us against ourselves, precluding all possibility of trust, then fascism takes any latent divisible forces and develops them into divisions in fact: racism, nationalism, religions.[552]

Today, amidst a lower level of overt rebelliousness and higher levels of commercialization of youth, Cosby can return in a new role.[553] Having previously abdicated any responsibility to join or support existing political movements, he now can re-emerge as a spokesperson for neoliberal depictions of social, political, and economic inequality as the result of the behavior of the unequal. He becomes part of the "inertia" described by Fanon which, as part of the expression of the colonized, actually testifies against them.[554]

It is to this point that DaveyD spoke during the aforementioned panel in order to direct the discussion toward an investigation of the history of hip-hop—our immediate concern here as well—and particularly its origins in radical politics, as well as the ways in which access to certain forms of political hip-hop was prevented and with what impact. Speaking of the rise of numerous politically-inspired hip-hop songs, some addressing the late '80s run of Jesse Jackson for the presidential nomination of the Democratic Party, DaveyD noted how industry blockages, a lack of radio play, and an overall downplaying in popular media of these songs led to even Jackson himself being unaware of songs produced for his campaign by the hip-hop community. Ideologically speaking, the sought-after goal was met: Jackson was cut off from the youth and vice-versa. This is not to suggest, of course, that Jackson represented then or represents now the kinds of radicalism feared by the state. But it does demonstrate to some degree the need to nip in the bud any potential for the politicization and subsequent radicalization of Black youth.

This idea has also played out within the broader popular culture to include state-sponsored assaults on the image of any musician or journalist involved in anti-war activism. Speaking directly to the current concerns that the mixtape radio project described herein attempts to address, both artists and journalists who exhibited "threatening" tendencies were targeted by the "warfare state" for image or even physical assassination. Marriages were sabotaged, targets arrested for the most minor offenses, newspaper articles planted in an attempt to "[u]se misinformation to confuse or disrupt" their efforts or to even "[p]rovoke target groups into rivalries that may result in death."[555] There was a similar assault on the lives of journalists and those who operated an underground press, which "empowered many of the social movements of the 1960s."[556] Just as artists must be suppressed for fear of their influence over colonized populations, so too must journalism contend with the same repression. Just as artists were and still are targeted, journalists seeking to lay bare the horrific social arrangement that determines the order of the world around us often find themselves targeted by the colonizers. In what has been described as "The Secret War," the United States government has routinely sought to destroy underground journalists whose unconventional style and ideological position was or is now threatening to power.[557]

It is here again that it is important to reiterate the concerns raised by Glen Ford and Bruce Dixon and their calls for a News for the People Coalition.[558] In a media environment that intentionally designs an outcome devoid of news or thought-inspiring cultural expression, there must be efforts to organize challenges against this and to, as is the focus here, develop alternative forms of news and information dissemination that support those organizational efforts. The ability to determine a popular "script"[559] has the intended effect of limiting the potential for radical political organization. This has been discussed, again, in terms of a need to create "necessary illusions,"[560] which result in people who are "mindless consumers" as opposed to politically engaged critical thinkers—what bell hooks calls "enlightened witnesses"[561]—and, also, in terms of the "political necessity" required to have an internal colony accept such a position by being held collectively "out of our minds."[562]

In fact, the very field of communications study is based on the need to study the power of communication in establishing Western imperial rule over colonial subjects, or the management of outcomes and popularity.[563] In the United States, to support mass manipulation,[564] or "imperial policies," a government-sponsored series of academic studies into psychological warfare was conducted so as to maximize the ability to "suppress or distort *unauthorized communication* among subject peoples, *including domestic dissenters*."[565] Again, it has been noted that what will separate the United States as an empire is its control over mass communications and entertainment on a global scale precisely because it is understood that media, in short, produce consciousness that ultimately determines behavior.[566] So contrary to dismissive notions, media (particularly as understood by those who fund their study and who have the most ability to control and disseminate them) are tantamount and paramount to conventional forms of warfare and are employed as such to ensure their desired cognitive and behavioral outcomes. These managed outcomes are that which keep, for the most part, popular thought in line, and in support of discussions that obfuscate the underlying colonial relationships and ultimately assure that power remains unchecked.

CHAPTER TWELVE

THE MIXTAPE AND EMANCIPATORY JOURNALISM

Peace to Ron G, Brucie B, Kid Capri, Funkmaster Flex, Lovebug Starski...
—The Notorious B.I.G.

Mixtapes is the way I speak, mixtapes is the way I
communicate, mixtapes is like my radio, my TV show...
—DJ Lazy K

We're takin' over radio and wack media... nothin' can save ya!
—Cut Chemist and Al Dente

The mixtape is hip-hop's original mass medium. In fact, "there wouldn't be a rap music industry if it weren't for mixtapes... the development of hip-hop revolves around [them as] a singularly crucial but often over-looked medium."[567] The emergence of mixtapes in the 1970s initially challenged, still challenges, and must increasingly challenge convention-al means of mass communication. Emancipatory Journalism (EJ), coined by Hemant Shah, is an anti-colonial philosophy of journalism: the result of more conventional forms of journalistic practice and philosophy being insufficient for reporting and disseminating the politics of those most oppressed or marginalized.[568] EJ is, of course, part of a wider tradition of revolutionary media work that also challenged, challenges, and must continue to challenge conventional notions of journalistic practice.[569] It is intended to address contemporary and intentionally myopic views of the relationship of the press and society, as Shah explains, a "bottom up" form where journalists, encouraged to be part of social justice move-ments, apply standards of honesty, "comprehensiveness," and a willing-ness to openly dismiss notions of objectivity.[570]

This "comprehensiveness" includes the process of re-centering the experience of those communities engaged in struggle so as to re-center representatives of that community as the experts, pundits, and leaders whose views would be included if not made the basis of reporting. It is a long-played scheme in mainstream media to have hosts or programs purport to be some kind of critical challenge to power all the while having representatives of power as regular commentators or sources for that outlet's work. No matter how "radical" or challenging a journalist or media outlet claims to be, the trick of consistently returning to elite sources,[571] even if an attempt is made to criticize them, allows for those sources to shift the agenda, range of topics, or discussion away from anything of value to those without power.

Both the mixtape and EJ have origins in the irreverence of anticolonial struggle. That is, the mixtape, initially created by DJs searching for a way to disseminate their art without sanction from a mainstream corporate industry, allowed for the kinds of communication ultimately threatening to power. When Brucie B, Jazzy Joyce, DJ Hollywood, then later Ron G and Kid Capri took their artfulness to their communities by recording sessions and parties and making special custom mixes, all without institutions of state power backing them, the act itself spoke to the very tradition of unsanctioned communication that is so often seen as dangerous. It was—and is—an anti-authoritarian act, one that recalls the act of newly "freed" nations developing their own presses and traditions of journalism more suited to their national development. This would, in turn, inspire or prefigure the overtly named "Emancipatory Journalism."

The origins of each, the mixtape and EJ, are in what is initially recognized as a state of unfreedom. The act of creating a mixture of music and sounds (again, without sanction or permission) not necessarily intended by the initial artist, or—as is the case with Ron G—creating an entirely new genre of music, is ultimately (and potentially) no different from consciously deciding that new forms of media and journalism are required to popularize the movements seeking immediate material uplift and widespread social change. Hence, the tenet of EJ that challenges the very notion of Western journalism's core values of objectivity and balance: the very idea that any individual or any institution is or can be objective is seen as worse than foolish and as little more than an intentional construct meant to legitimize Western values, dominance, and the Western ability to define the world's social and economic norms. The mixtape and EJ (and their combination) are media practices meant to address Richard B. Moore's classic statement that "slaves and dogs are named by their masters. Free [women and] men name themselves."

Shah's argument exposes as fraudulent the constant underlying theme in Western discourse that, despite potential problems of capitalist monopoly or tendencies toward White supremacy, the systems of media are quite free, especially when compared with the "strictly controlled and manipulated" media of the Third World. Shah writes, "I contend that press freedom per se is not the issue that deserves close scrutiny. Rather, it is the politicization of the notion of press freedom that needs to be examined carefully."[572] He explains the debate surrounding emancipatory journalism's ideological origins in, and difference from, development journalism, which he says

> needs to be reconceptualized because deliberations about its validity and usefulness have been bogged down in arguments structured by Western notions of press freedom. The debate has diverted attention from important questions about how journalism can contribute to participatory democracy, security, peace, and other humanistic values.[573]

Ideally, we could also develop an equally "reconceptualized" notion of society, the press, copyright, the music industry, and so on, all of which also currently "divert attention from important questions" about how the mixtape can and must become part of journalism and media work produced by and in support of political organization within localized communities. When those involved in the culture make reference to something bold, unabashed, or unapologetic as "that's hip-hop!" what they speak to is the very tendency among the colonized toward anti-colonial behavior. It is precisely what Kwame Ture meant when he made clear that "the job of the conscious is to make the unconscious conscious of their unconscious behavior." When mixtape DJs noted the lack of objective balance in their colonized media environment, they re-established the rules of technology and art, making turntables into that which would allow ancient expression to be reformulated—"the turntables mimicked the tradition of looping repetition, trance-inducing sounds," and as a result threw up immediate challenges to and dents in the constructed colonized media environment.[574]

And it is just this kind of potential threat that has caused the kinds of responses to the mixtape from institutions of the colonial state. Mixtapes, like illicit drugs, are used both to pacify resistance and justify the destabilization of a colonized people. Both are supplied or contributed to by established state institutions and then used to form the basis from which arrests, harassment, imprisonment, and a generally popularized view of a community-wide tendency toward crime can be fashioned.[575] Impoverished communities may be flooded with illicit drugs by the state and then punished at will and whim for the crime of supply-and-demand (not to mention the attendant viciousness of violence, police brutality, and imprisonment associated with such enterprises), all while having their colonized condition justified to the larger population by media reports of their behavior. Similarly, intentionally impoverished communities who produce, in degrees of isolation, art forms that are not recognized by the state (as is the case initially with most colonized expression) can develop forms of communication that are also outside the very sanctioned forms that exclude them (as early Black and White radio and television excluded hip-hop) only to later be condemned and punished for those "crimes" by the very entities that had previously enlisted their support.

Indeed, the commercial exchange or sale of mixtapes, which often contain unlicensed, copyrighted material of others, is illegal. However, it is also true that many of the top DJs (Clue, Envy, Enuf, etc.) have been given exclusive tracks by major record labels, who hope to use mixtapes as a means of generating grassroots audience excitement (or "street buzz") and gaining credibility in advance of sanctioned releases of their artists' work. And yet if the young street vendors selling them are caught doing so, they are charged, incarcerated, and given permanent arrest records.[576] The more popular cases of industry crackdowns against DJ Drama or Danger Mouse speak to the somewhat randomness of the state's need to repress potentially dissident forms of communication, both in terms of content and delivery method. What is at issue here is not simply the threat to profit, as explained earlier, but the threat to unsanctioned communication taking place among those who are either already colonized, or those who are engaged in the performance, production, or distribution of culture of the colonized. A lack of attention to the methods of distribution may lead to a lack of control over message, content, and information, and therefore, the ultimate threat of behavior based on illicit forms of thought.

Three recent documentaries on the mixtape phenomenon speak to these concerns and to issues of co-optation of anti-colonial behavior. On the one hand, we must remember that this is to be expected as long as the fundamentality of colonialism remains unaddressed. There will always be a siphoning off—or an attempt to do so—of the more threatening aspects of what the colonized produce, à la Fanon, and the culture of the colonized will always become "fixed" and formed to testify against its creators. In Justo Faison's[577] *The Official Mixtape Documentary* (2005), Walter Bell's *Mixtape, Inc.* (2006), and Peter Spirer's *Black and Blue Legends of the Hip-Hop Cop* (2006), these issues are all laid bare.[578] Justo's documentary offers indispensable interviews with the legends of the mixtape, like DJs Hollywood, Brucie B, and Jazzy Joyce, who extol the virtues of the mixtape, and discuss the tradition as being original both in music selection and form of mix, all the while expressing concern over the more modern approach of simply getting record industry exclusives and throwing them on a CD with no mixing, blending, or that indefinable "umph." What once (1980s through the early 1990s) was a mixtape popularity based on DJ name, skill, or ability to craft a certain blend would eventually give way to mixtape popularity based on the tracklist and the ability of the DJ to get that exclusive first. As Brucie B explains, "I never put no track list on a tape. You got my tape because you knew it was mine and that meant it would be hot!" What he suggests, however, is the ultimate threat of the mixtape, that the DJ would be able to determine what would become popular as opposed to the industry, which itself must maintain its colonizing function of establishing the norm. The imposed system of payola, national program playlisting, and corporate ownership have removed this as an issue with radio just as exclusives are serving that same function against the mixtape.

In Bell's *Mixtape, Inc.*, this issue become clearer. Here, there is more focus on the response to mixtapes by the music industry's lobbying arm, the Recording Industry Association of America (RIAA).[579] Much like the Drug Enforcement Agency or the local police who hunt down drug dealers that they themselves helped to create and protect, so too does the RIAA seek to police those their industry supports, while petitioning Congress for more funds to expand their ability to do so. As discussed earlier, the ownership of the art in question is not in the hands of the artists. Instead, the ownership rests in the hands of the small web of elite who now must ensure that they both create a demand for their product and maintain control over the dissemination of that content. Mixtapes, as community-based, localized mechanisms of distribution, pose a threat to the process of managing the flow of ideas, which, from time to time, must be reconsolidated through punishment and example. Mixtape DJs are no different in this regard from the dope dealers who are supplied, protected, and encouraged by the very forces (especially if they consciously or not upset this relationship) who will later punish, imprison, or make examples of them.[580] As one of Bell's interviewees summarizes, "some cats sell dope and some cats sell CDs."

In an important exchange in *Mixtape, Inc.*, RIAA spokesman Erwin Chemerinsky attempts to parrot popular (and false) notions that protection of copyright ultimately serves society by offering enough fiduciary reward to artists who are then encouraged to reward the rest of us with their art. If they do not get paid, as the argument goes, they won't create and we all suffer. While he is there to promote this form of disingenuous propaganda, we must remember that such indefensible ideas are promoted to: (a) disguise the fact that few artists own their own copyright and even fewer engage in the production of art for money, which has *never* been a primary impetus for creative individuals; (b) disguise the fact that ownership of copyrights are mostly held by those the RIAA was formed to protect, namely the major labels and *not* the artists themselves; (c) disguise the fact that copyright laws or the larger body of intellectual property laws remain essential to managing who becomes popular and to whom the bulk of the financial benefits go; and to (d) disguise that this is essential to the maintenance of power, and that limiting the ability of oppressed communities to engage in unsanctioned communication is a paramount concern of those in power. Mixtapes represent one of the various mechanisms that might be well-suited to unsanctioned communication. Those punished for being engaged in such processes, like those arrested or fined for Internet downloading, are made examples of less for their "crimes" than for the kind of ungoverned exchange that can threaten empires.

For his part, Spirer, through his inclusion of a little-known story of Rudy Giuliani v. Screwball, shows how any form of unsanctioned expression can be threatening. On a mixtape released by the Queens-based rap group Screwball, a track titled "Who Shot Rudy?" caught the ear of the then-Mayor of New York City. The fictitious rhyme describing the assassination of Giuliani was seen as unacceptable. The song's author was arrested, and the question was raised as to whether this was due to the song or the fact that he has a standing bench warrant, and other members of the group were harassed by the city's finest. Screwball's track record of gangster-themed music whose focus had, before this, never crossed the racial or hierarchical order was at no time an issue. It was only when the underground communicative network of the mixtape contained media not designed to maintain appropriate authority over the colonized that it and its content became an issue further demonstrating the true nature of censorship that is always political and never linguistic.

This also speaks to the potentially appropriate use of underground media. It can and should encourage alternative methods of challenging dominating ideas and political structures. The repression incurred from those structures, both the institutions and their individual conservative and liberal defenders, must then be seen as further proof of the correctness of the initial use around which further organization would occur. In that respect we can consider just a few comments made by artists, activists, and journalists regarding the use, role, and importance of mixtapes.[581] To Head-Roc, they represent "a means for artists who don't have the financial backing of a [major] label to display his or her skills." For Badia Albanna, speaking to the emancipatory journalistic potential, mixtapes "can be incorporated into our community activism and used as a medium for getting messages out, having speakers over music, try[ing] to connect people more with the message through music." Ralph Cooper understands that mixtapes are important because "you could mix hot music with current events and news and shit so that kids aren't as stupid as they are." Unlike NPR, which, according to Cooper, "is boring as fuck and I can't convince anybody to listen to it, so you do [mixtapes] in a way that people would listen to it and that would be hot... so listen to political events with [DJ] Premier beats... but since news is a business and i'ts sold to the 40-year-old White man everybody else who ain't 40-years-old, White and educated they miss a lot of shit. And that's a lot of people."

Mixtapes represent that which was described by George Jackson when he said that "the job of the revolutionary in reactionary times is to make space for revolution to occur." In a media sense, what that means, as summarized by Toni Blackman in her response to a question about what mixtapes mean to her, is the "next shit. Newness. Authentic freestyles... sharing of love. Biggin' up the people who don't get bigged up in the mainstream... it's an opportunity for them to get some shine." And it's Rosa Clemente, whose response to a question about the viability of a mixtape radio concept truly encapsulates the immediate concern. "Our mentor," Clemente said, "Dr. [James] Turner[582] really honed in... he felt that the problem of the 21st century would be mass communication and how our people would be portrayed..." This also led her to discuss raids led by the RIAA in New York City on mixtape vendors. "So they're raiding now 'Mom and Pop' stores... and it can't be because 50 [Cent] and them ain't making money. There's something else going on here." Though

Clemente correctly noted that further use of the mixtape, regardless of politics, would likely lead to further repression, this must be used and interpreted as further justification of the concept of mixtape radio and all politically organized subversive media.

Emancipatory journalism, in its assumption of a need for journalism to serve those developing social movements, works to reject the politically-inspired myth of objectivity, which leads to "false balance"[583] or the assumption that opposing views deserve equal time. EJ is the journalistic response to the questions once raised by Amiri Baraka of Jesse Jackson's 1988 democratic primary campaign: can it ever really be that "both the slave and slave master are right? Both slavery and freedom are right?"[584] The functional need of mainstream journalism to construct fictional opposites allows for discussion to always remain safely hidden away from that which might genuinely lead audiences to new conclusions and, therefore, new (unsanctioned) behavior. Therefore, if as has been shown, most mainstream sources come from the true minority—military and government officials—and so on.[585] Even when there is debate among them, it rarely extends beyond acceptable notions of difference. Returning to Shah, Emancipatory Journalism requires a "much broader pattern of sourcing" which would be inclusive of, even centering, "…the people on the ground. The people who are experiencing issues and problems in neighborhoods and communities." These, he says, "are often the poor, people of color, people with disabilities, etc. and those are the people who aren't getting their voices heard."[586]

Shah has simplified EJ and provided a base model from which journalists seeking to employ such a form could proceed:[587]

	Prevailing model	**Emancipatory Model**
Focus of story	Events	Process
Primary Sources	Officials	Ordinary people
Writing Style	Factual	Interpretative
Legitimacy	Science	Grounded Knowledge
Purpose	Description	Explanation/orientation

In this case, mixtapes produced by the colonized populations already engaged in hip-hop (study, production, performance, journalism, etc.), which allow for their realities to be more widely disseminated within their own communities, from their own perspectives, and in their own manner or style, would be a perfect implementation of EJ.[588] That is, mixtapes can be fashioned so as to include views not just of particular events but of the underlying realities that cause those events. By interviewing people from the community who would serve as "official sources" while being fact-checked from an intellectual grounding derived from those very same communities, mixtapes could provide the space required for the sorts of interpretive change necessary to political activity.

As is shown in the documentary film *A Letter to the President* (2005), discussions of police brutality and mass incarceration are attached to systemic processes bound to White supremacy and capitalism, and we must encourage both an understanding and an awareness that activity is needed. A version of this in the form of an emancipatory mixtape would do the same thing. Rather than focus on the particular act of an individual occurrence of police brutality in a given community, the emancipatory mixtape might, in mix, tell that story as part of a cycle of police brutality. The story might be told from the perspective of community members in ways that are not possible in the context of the mainstream media that targets their communities. As an expression of locally based organizing, this mixtape radio concept might be a way to both tell the story and also encourage community participation in heightening awareness of police brutality, exposing those involved, resisting such abuses, and disseminating "Know Your Rights" flyers that arm the community with some legal basics designed to offer relative protection against a hostile police force.

Again, EJ presupposes the lack of freedom and the need for social movements and political organizations that can produce their own media and journalism. This concept of journalism is as old as political struggle.[589] Breaking with traditional notions of "development journalism," which "carries with it an aura of inferiority," the goal of EJ and its combination with the mixtape is to harmonize ideas of journalistic practice that "have [been] acquired from" colonizers "with the traditional patterns of information."[590] In other words, rather than relying on customs of journalistic practice handed down from hostile powers, EJ encourages a form of journalism that resonates with, is produced by, and is in support of those in need of some power.[591]

This is a concern facing the entire African and colonized world. As described above, it continues to be said, and as EJ demands recognition of, "there is NOTHING like a 'free press' anywhere in the world!"[592] Such false notions continue to obfuscate the reality described by Ankomah of the whole of "Western media" which has a "five-point unwritten code" of: "National interest; Government lead; Ideological leaning; historical baggage; Advertiser/Reader power."[593] This, in further agreement with An-komah, ends in a need for the colonized to practice a form of journalism that rejects this pattern of reporting in favor of something that promotes their own "national interests." Journalists must eschew the faulty tenden-cies toward mythological objectivity and embrace a form of honest, stud-ied, and informed liberating media that is joined to social movements and political organization. African America and those similarly colonized can use the mixtape as part of that project, which will also allow for reinser-tion into the larger global struggle that is ultimately needed for all to be emancipated. As Kwame Nkrumah made clear,

> [t]he press does not exist merely for the purpose of en-
> riching its proprietors or entertaining its readers. It is
> an integral part of the society, with which its purpose
> must be in consonance. It must help establish a pro-
> gressive political and economic system that will free
> [women and] men from want and poverty.... It must
> reach out to the masses, educate and inspire them,
> work for quality and the universality of [women and]
> men's rights everywhere.[594]

The combined concepts of mixtape radio and emancipatory journal-ism find renewed importance at a time when traditional news media are shifting, with newspapers going out of business (at least in their print for-mats) and especially with the continued disappearance of "ethnic media." At a moment when "42 percent of print newsrooms across the country employ no black, Asian American, Latino, or American Indian journalists at all," the cold caught by mainstream press cutbacks and consolidation is causing yet another major illness among the colonized. As a result of lost advertising revenue, "ethnic media" outlets are shutting down, cutting back on print editions and distribution, which further limits their ability to "give voice to the community, strengthen cohesion, and chronicle com-munity life." Their ability to offset the repeated misrepresentation of their communities or to offer depth in stories that the mainstream either glosses over, distorts, or omits altogether is similarly weakened.[595]

As early mixtape DJs (perhaps unwittingly) helped establish the communicative component of the development of a "hip-hop nation," contemporary emancipatory mixtape DJs and producers might revolu-tionize that now-established "nation within a nation." The need is clear, the potential boundless. Talented people must now apply their creativity and organizational capacities to alternative means of mass media-making and journalistic practice. This talent and ingenuity will be further challenged by the ever-increasing colonial pattern of forced relocation, sometimes referred to as "gentrification." This is making an obvious impact on methods of communication, as the removal of communities also means the erasure of essential public spheres. Smaller music stores and cafes, for example, which would be prime distribution points for mixtapes, are often targeted as the first to go. In recent years Washington, D.C. has witnessed its most beloved music stores such DJ Hut and Capital City Records along with favored (particularly among the politically active) coffee shops like Café Mawonaj all suffer forced removal. And this is having the predictable impact on small projects like mixtape radio, as well as on far more traditional and powerful subcultures such as D.C.'s go-go music.

Try to imagine there being no jazz in New Orleans. Or how about no blues in Mississippi? And no salsa in Panama? Or no hip-hop anywhere? It is hard to imagine and certainly makes no sense. But when noted go-go soundman Greg McNeils told us that "go-go as a culture is going to die," his words carried an uncomfortable accuracy that accompanies bad news from someone who is, unfortunately, qualified to bring it.[596] We had initially gone to interview him as part of a project for Words. Beats. Life, Inc.—a non-profit organization that educates and empowers young people using the elements of hip-hop culture. We had begun to discuss with him the impact of mixtapes and go-go P.A. tapes (named for the source of their recording being the show's sound or "public announcing" system, and often now in CD or even in mp3 formats), but what started there ended up being more about the impact on a cultural expression of colonial land-grabs (read: gentrification).

Go-go—polyrhythmic, funk, and soul music with conga drums as centerpiece—is perhaps D.C.'s most identifiable cultural export, if you don't count the half-smoke sausage. It's best enjoyed live where, as is often said, "the party don't stop," literally. Songs are merely tolerated moments between extended conga and drum solos. It's Black and spiritually powerful, like the city that birthed it. But now, McNeils says, U Street—D.C.'s "Black Broadway" during segregation and longtime home to the conga-heavy, African-inspired music since it organically developed here in the 1970s—has become Not-For-Us Street in the new District of Columbia.

Not only that, McNeils continued, those bands who are still playing in the city are allegedly banned from "hitting the pocket"—go-go's version of the hip-hop "break beat," the transitional polyrhythmic conga-driven extended drum solo. Instead, he said, bands better smooth-jazz it up and are being told straight up to *not* bring their congas. In one case, McNeils recalled, a major D.C. club venue recently told the band for which he was running sound that if they "hit the pocket," the show would be stopped. They did, and it was. No mas, no go. The pocket, like that break beat, is often considered the best part, where the percussionists take over and crowds enter those trance-like spaces where there is only the body's reaction to the groove that matters. It's where the conga players shine and take center stage. Like in hip-hop when the DJs outshined the emcee, or before that, when James Brown called for the drummer to be "given some."

No pocket for go-go artists and fans? It's like jazz with no improvisation or rap with no freestyle, beats with no samples or graffiti with no trains or walls. To go-go-lovers, D.C. with no pocket would be like the Bronx with no hip-hop. It's staggeringly symbolic. For those who have lived in the D.C. Metro area all their lives, it's painful to see the Chocolate City and vanilla suburbs of their childhood switch places, destroying the cultural continuum that made the District of Columbia a great city for Black people. No pocket for go-go. No pocket for Black people to continue to develop the Earth's most imitated culture. But plenty of new pockets—for Starbucks; Gold's Gyms; two-story, 24-hour CVS pharmacies; and all-natural grocery stores for the District of Columbia's new White and affluent residents. Those working-class Black people who are forced out of the new D.C. may hear a go-go echo sometimes—a show here, an isolated go-go mix on the radio there. They are hearing the echoes of the drums—the drums that the enslavers banned the enslaved from playing. The new D.C. has now told its colonial captives, "no more drums." Chocolate City has been dumped into the milk and is culturally drowning.[597]

There can be no denying the damage resulting from further dislocation and fragmentation caused by forced relocation. McNeils made direct connections between forced relocation and the decreasing sales of go-go P.A. tapes. He acknowledged the impact of the Internet but paid most of his attention to the smaller numbers of tapes being distributed, which he says has been the lifeline of the art for decades. With fewer tapes going around, there are fewer listeners, fewer practitioners, and ultimately, he argues, a slow decline of the cultural expression as a whole. All of the necessary space for the cultivation of the art is being choked off. Unlike hip-hop, which is now an international phenomenon, go-go, like many other

THE MIXTAPE AND EMANCIPATORY JOURNALISM

smaller, more regionally-specific genres of music, has no real international base from which it can survive these assaults and continue to flourish. Its primary communicative mechanism, the P.A. tape, is now threatened in ways never before seen that may indeed lead to a further devolution of the legendary music.

However, to the extent that mixtapes once helped bring together a hip-hop nation (and a go-go community) there is potential for them to do so again, particularly when in the hands of political organizations consciously seeking to do this work.

CHAPTER THIRTEEN

FREEMIX RADIO: THE ORIGINAL MIXTAPE RADIO SHOW

Practice without thought is blind: thought without practice is empty.
—Kwame Nkrumah

Ima hold you down, I got you. One more repetition Ima spot you. This is for my blue collar working, beer guzzlin', bootleg DVD hustlin', PUSH! Never let them place the muzzle and PUSH!
—Pharoahe Monch

A railroad too underground like Harriet Tubman. While ya'll stay strugglin' we smuggle MCs through the streets till we bubblin' on mix CDs, hustlin'. Clans see me on the block n' say freeze, I say Fuck You! I'm a man, I'm Free!
—Pharoahe Monch

FreeMix Radio: The Original Mixtape Radio Show, as mixtape radio, was conceived originally to be the violent reclamation of media as an extension of a now-defunct community-based political organization. Its goal, now as then, is to demonstrate a model of the mixtape as underground press, anti-colonial media, and support mechanism and extension of political organization. This includes the utilization of the mixtape as a space where forms of cultural expression, news, politics, and musical/sonic blends can be developed and disseminated. An understated function is also to demonstrate the fallacy of any "end" to hip-hop or political rap music. Each edition proves as false the notion that artists today are not as talented as their predecessor or capable of expressing radical politics in the twenty-first century. Each edition demonstrates the intentional process of eliminating popular expression of these ideas, as opposed to any lack of such expression. Those who routinely lament the absence of political or radical rap music without acknowledging the suppressed mass of other forms—or who themselves do little to highlight or make room for those "alternatives"—do so foolishly or ignorantly and to tremendous political detriment to hip-hop in general and, in particular, those (mostly) Black progenitors. This is evidenced in each edition of FreeMix Radio.

No one familiar with the artists featured on FreeMix Radio over the years can claim a death of hip-hop or an end of political rap music. Instead, they would be forced to confront levels of talent that cannot be dismissed as undeserving or lacking the necessary quality that popular exposure is said to demand. Quite the opposite. Were we to do a FreeMix Radio "roll call" à la Senior Love Daddy[598] we would have to thank and appreciate Head-Roc, Godisheus, KRS-One, Hueman Prophets, Face, Rakim, Immortal Technique, Dead Prez, Mos Def, Talib Kweli, Murs, Rebel Diaz, Wise Intelligent, NY Oil, Son of Nun, Precise Science, Self-Scientific, The Cornel West Theory, Asheru and The Els, Ben Sharpa, Diamond District, DJ Eurok, DJ Underdog, Lone Catalysts, Lauryn Hill, Myka9, Carolyn Malachi, Brothas Keepa, Emoni Fela, Dilated Peoples, Blitz the Ambassador, Hasan Salaam, De la Soul… These and the countless others whose erasure from popular media—who receive no radio or video airplay, who are consigned to the margins (despite having significant national and international following)—is the intended result of a system of mass media and popular culture designed to protect the colonialism still in process. These artists' exclusion is *necessary* to the function of the popular form to in perpetuity "testify against" the communities from which they come.

To the extent that it has continued largely as the work of one person—namely myself—speaks loudly to this author's failure in helping the development of that organization and in convincing others of this project's viability for their own goals. However, such criticism, far from some attempt at individual humility or pessimism, is meant to be instructive. Whether as the single form of organizational outreach or a component within a larger media plan mixtape radio remains a viable, cost-effective, and mostly legal method of producing the kinds of media that are more necessary than ever.[599] So just as Kwame Ture said in response to a critic of socialism, "you cannot judge Socialism by Socialists" just as you would not "judge Christianity by Christians," we can add that "you cannot judge mixtape radio by The Funkinest Journalist."

The idea is a good one. It began to crystallize while I was working in pizza delivery where long hours spent in the car for the first time truly drove home just how homogenized and painful commercial music and news radio are. Tips meant that everyday cash was in-hand and available, which began lending itself to routine trips to Baltimore, Md.'s Everyone's Place bookstore and African cultural shop, or Washington, D.C.'s House of Kemit or the now defunct Pyramid Books. I purchased lecture tapes, which exposed me to the worldviews of African-centered, pan-Africanist, nationalist, Marxist, and atheist educators, most notable among them scholars with and without portfolio such as Malcolm X, John Henrik Clarke, James Turner, Marimba Ani, Kwame Ture, Cheikh Anta Diop, Charles Finch, Ivan Van Sertima, Steve Cokely, Yosef ben-Jochannan, Ayele Bekerie, Runnoko Rashidi, Jacob Carruthers, Greg Carr, Angela Davis, Amiri Baraka, Ward Churchill, Dhoruba bin-Wahad, Elombe Brath, John G. Jackson, and many others.

Similarly, regular visits to Baltimore, D.C., New York, and elsewhere to purchase mixtapes developed a kind of radical new media environment in the car where music, news, and worldviews that few others were exposed to became the norm and then foundational. Already prone to the emotions described once by Malcolm X that "all Negroes are angry and I am the angriest of them all," the combination of lecture and underground mixes, exclusive blends, unreleased tracks, and so on, and the immediacy of the difference between them and the mainstream deepened these tendencies. And, when coupled with long hours and poor tips from customers, this new environment developed an individualized sense of what has been described as "intriguing… the extent to which African Americans have fantasized about political violence—specifically, violent revolt."[600]

Years later, the idea emerged to combine the two traditions of the lecture and the mixtape into a kind of regularly produced underground press. It was an idea born also of the work done within a grassroots organization, itself an offshoot of the late Damu Smith's Black Voices for Peace, Organized Community of United People (Organized COUP[601]), which began in 2001, selling copies of mixtapes (non-journalistic ones) to raise funds. The concept of emancipatory journalism, even before being officially known as such, seemed perfectly suited to that organization's goals of localized community-based organization whose resources would come only from the community to ensure as much liberty in action as could be hoped. The idea was, and remains, that groups such as Organized COUP need forms of mass press that can help to increase their ranks, encourage wider support for their programs, and remain free enough to be relevant to their audience. The concept of an organizationally-funded and freely-distributed mixtape that contained (mostly) politically progressive or radical music and journalism made—and still makes—great sense.

So far the "why" of it all has been laid out. The "how" is much simpler. With the help and guidance of locally-based D.C. artists and others, the idea arose to purchase bulk lots of plain CDs that could be burned and duplicated on anywhere from seven to fifteen CD-stack burners.[602] The original audio was and is compiled from a variety of sources, any source. Artists, many of whom know full well their lack of access to commercial media and who respect the potential personal value of having their work distributed on thousands of mixtapes, often offer their music. Interviews, sound clippings (from television, radio, or film), and speeches are added using basic audio-editing software, and finally, there is an attempt to mix, blend, or arrange it all into a flowing, interesting, and hype final product.

From there, similar bulk label procurement or even the scrounging of used labels, CD jackets, and covers, etc. allows for the production cost to be kept to around $20 for a burned stack of 100. The goal is 3000 per run and the initial goal was to double the number and make a new edition each month. From there, the use of cafes, bookstores, barbershops and beauty salons, trains, street vendors, and hand-to-hand distribution remains the greatest challenge and the brightest reward. Handing people a mixtape (and usually having to explain that this is *not* me asking, "please listen to my demo…") often requires follow-up discussion of why such a project is being conducted. It expands the range of the organization involved but also the topics related to colonialism and mass media that recipients are not likely to ever encounter. The free distribution offers legal cover for use of unlicensed copyrighted material and helps to undermine a philosophy of capitalist exchange.[603] The communal nature of the funding, the organizational "subsidy" of its own media, is also a powerful exercise for future struggles and access of internal strength resulting in greater degrees of media practice and freedom.

However, the failure to maintain organization and develop the required talent to produce FreeMix Radio regularly and with great skill have combined to weaken this individual project. Its disconnect from any organization and its lack of communal production and distribution are examples of its own inability to realize the fundamental tenet of Emancipatory Journalism and has rendered it an individual exercise in practicing theory by the author. It cannot be said enough: this is an absolute failure. However, this does not speak to or at all change what is the correctness of the idea or the politics or theory attached. What it means is that those more solidly involved in organization might consider the project and, in the best traditions of hip-hop, do it better.

This issue of "do it better" also helps to provide some legal cover to the project and its intended goals. By keeping a particular mixtape radio project local, with limited and free distribution, and under its own individual name and logo greater protection under copyright law is afforded.[604] It also ensures that there is a decentralized mechanism that is most relevant to the organizations operating in any given location. Perhaps one day there will be Mixtape Summits, à la Bandung,[605] where mixtape radio producers will gather to unify the efforts of the organizations they have helped to grow and thrive by their journalistic mixtape work. In any event, mixtape radio projects in their versatility are meant to be supportive of underserved grassroots communities and, as such, are perfectly suited to support those engaged in a variety of other politically similar media efforts. Mixtapes are perfect for low-power, community, and college radio stations to take and set in rotation (perhaps with some slight editing). In an interview with low-power or pirate radio activist Mbanna Kantako, he noted having run his besieged low-power radio broadcasts using multi-disc CD players from which he could set in motion up to 24-hours worth of programming to be aired without anyone physically being present.[606] What this might mean for similar guerrilla radio projects were they to have at their disposal numerous mixtape radio programs is unpredictable but exciting to consider.

Mixtape radio is not designed for fame or national or international exposure. It is meant to demonstrate freedom of thought and action and to encourage the people to organize for more. George Jackson once cited three elements to a successful revolution: the first he said was a "secret army"; the second, a political party; and the third, an "underground press with a mass appeal" that could help popularize the concept of revolution. Let it be hoped that the mixtape can serve as the latter, which will encourage the former so as to make the first unnecessary. That part, unfortunately, is not up to the colonized. Toward the third, an underground press, however, the service and support of DJs working in tandem with journalists so as to combine the expertise of each into a viable mixtape radio program would be of great benefit to existing and future political organizations in local communities. DJs could, at a minimum, seek out or allow for journalists who find them, so that there could be infused in mixes some manner of organizational promotion, news, interview—some for thought-provoking, action-inspiring media—that would be produced by, and for those in, a given community. The popularity of the DJ, the mix, and the mixtape itself would support the organizational work and would give them a much needed outlet.

Those who dabble in both DJ-ing and journalism could seek to expand the role of the mixtape in their work. Those in organizations could seek out members or allies to perform the same functions. Again, the cost is roughly $20 for 100 copies burned and out the door, and 3000 copies for $600. These are not costs that are beyond the reach of community organizations whose membership is viable and supportive. It is local, freely distributed, and a means to reach community members in a way that is culturally relevant and that circumvents existing media structures that are designed to prevent just such media work and reach. Hand them out and engage the community in not only the work of the organization but in the media environment itself, which necessitates this kind of hand-to-hand, community-based, free exchange. Mixtape radio is necessary simply because, as mixtape enthusiasts already know, what you can put on a mixtape you cannot put on the radio. The key and core difference is that censorship, though often described in terms strictly linguistic, is, in fact, political. Young Buck's song was not omitted from his album release because he said "Fuck." It was because he said "Fuck the police!"[607]

CHAPTER FOURTEEN

WHITE LIBERALISM AND "PROGRESSIVE" JOURNALISM

*For the vast majority of White Americans, the past decade—the
first phase—had been a struggle to treat the Negro with a degree of
decency, not of equality. White America was ready to demand that the
Negro should be spared the lash of brutality and coarse degradation,
but it had never been truly committed to helping him out of poverty,
exploitation, or all forms of discrimination. The outraged White
citizen had been sincere when he snatched the whips from the Southern
sheriffs and forbade them more cruelties. But when this was to a
degree accomplished, the emotions that had momentarily inflamed him
melted away. White Americans left the Negro on the ground and in
devastating numbers walked off with the aggressor. It appeared that
the White segregationist and the ordinary White citizen had more
in common with one another than either had with the Negro.*
—Dr. Martin Luther King, Jr.

*Many people want to know why, out of the entire White segment of society,
we want to criticize the liberals. We have to criticize them because they
represent the liaison between both groups, between the oppressed and the
oppressor. The liberal tries to become an arbitrator, but he is incapable
of solving the problems. He promises the oppressor that he can keep the
oppressed under control; that he will stop them from becoming illegal (in
this case illegal means violent). At the same time, he promises the oppressed
that he will be able to alleviate their suffering—in due time. Historically,
of course, we know this is impossible, and our era will not escape history.*
—Kwame Ture

The Black liberation struggle (or any other) in this country has always
been aided by (*not started by, nor run by, nor beholden to!*) the White

Left and the media and journalism they produce. Black struggles for independence have traditionally inspired sympathetic White supporters to use their station in life, positions within the press or ability to generate new presses to give light and attention to those struggles. Even the White mainstream, pushed by events here and abroad, sought to engage that struggle by shaping which forms would be made acceptable. In doing so, it made the never-to-be-repeated mistake of giving Malcolm X a national (and international) audience in the 1959 documentary *The Hate That Hate Produced*. This had the *unintended* effect of generating tremendous notoriety and support for him, the Nation of Islam, and other African or Black nationalist groups and individuals. This will never happen again.[608] But what this also means is that not only are those interested in Black liberation or genuine freedom for all humankind going to need to be more involved in political organization and media production, but so too will the White Left media reformers. And here, there is too little evidence today to suggest that this will occur.

The kinds of inattention to African America in White mainstream or "radical" media criticism is mirrored by a similar inattention in White liberal journalism. Few stories focused on the colonized here (or abroad) appear in the leading White left liberal media outlets or scholarship. Stories of police brutality, mass incarceration—specifically the incarceration of political prisoners—get very little run.[609] This is sadly also the case within much of the Black press, but as explained previously, that press is largely weak and incapable of breaking established mores as they are certainly more bound to corporate ties than the White Left are. The White Left has an access to funding to which few who might evolve into some kind of dissident force could likely aspire.

The long-running Project Censored series, for example, which prides itself on publishing annual accounts of the most underreported stories of the year, routinely does not include stories about Black America (or Latino or Native America for that matter). In 2006, their publication has only one story about Black America (as a subset of another issue about children being used as guinea pigs for AIDS research)—and their one story that mentions "lynching" is about the mistreatment of White journalist Dan Rather. Their 2007 edition contains only one story that would only be specifically relevant to Black people were it connected to the history of detention centers being planned should there be "radical negroes" deserving of them. The 2008 and 2009 editions contain no stories directly about Black America. The "Katrina's Hidden Race War" story in their 2010 edition is one of just two stories that deal with African America.[610]

Similar trends exist across the leading White Left media outlets, including *Democracy Now!* Host Amy Goodman cites as inspiration pan-Africanist thinkers and Black activists, but rarely devotes her daily national broadcast to the issues facing Black (Latino or Indigenous) people. In prior research conducted on this subject it was noted that of the 176 possible shows (weekdays) for the calendar year of 2005 prior to the levee flooding following Hurricane Katrina, only 21 (or 12 percent) had a focus on Black America. Of that small number, ten were historical references to the Civil Rights era with two about Emmitt Till. Four of the 21 had Damu Smith as guest and only four shows were about some contemporary issue.[611] Post-levees, like all media, there was a boost in coverage, but then, like all media, trends and tendencies return. This study was updated more recently only to show that while some were focused on news that 74 percent of episodes of NBC's flagship news and interview program *Meet the Press* contained no Black guests, 88 percent of the episodes of the White Left's flagship news/interview program *Democracy Now!* had no Black guests.[612] In many ways it was surreal to hear Noam Chomsky speak to this on *Democracy Now!*, saying:

> The drug war is used as a pretext to drive the superfluous population, mostly black, back to the prisons, also providing a new supply of prison labor in state and private prisons, much of it in violation of international labor conventions. In fact, for many African Americans, since they were exported to the colonies, life has scarcely escaped the bonds of slavery, or sometimes worse.... If you look at the history of Afro-America... *if that's not headline news I don't know what is.*[613]

Of course, the "drug war" or African America having "scarcely escaped the bonds of slavery" is rarely headline news on *Democracy Now!* or any other in the White Left media constellation.

Media Matters with Bob McChesney, during that same initial 2005 calendar year, did two shows on race where in each case White men were the invited guests. Twice they mentioned Glen Ford and his work but Ford never appeared on the show himself.[614] This has since changed to some degree, but it is still sad that the Blackest element of McChesney's show is his use of Thelonious Monk's "Straight No Chaser" as his introductory music (which is, of course, not all that different than *Democracy Now!*'s use of Incognito's "Need to Know"). It may well be the media equivalent to Washington, D.C.'s gentrified U Street having a new Ellington House apartments with no (or few?) Dukes.

Others, like Fairness and Accuracy in Reporting (FAIR), deal very little with Black America in part because their task is to critique the mainstream press (who too often ignore African America), which—though not necessarily forming a permanent barrier—largely prevents them from making sweeping change in agenda and limits even their scope of what then should be given more attention. Janine Jackson, program director with FAIR and an African American, when asked about these concerns said little more than, "Well, help us out, send us stories." When asked about what appears as a preference for stories about Palestinians or the so-called Middle East in general, the response was, "Well, we are at war."[615] All well and good. But this, of course, presupposes that wars on poverty, drugs, racial inequality, homelessness, or police brutality and mass incarceration are over.

Of course, this is the point. In a manner slightly better than that described with respect to NPR, the White Left media reformers reify their own settler status by critiquing the myopia of corporate media and calling for policy reform rather than, for instance, performing the kinds of journalism that might encourage societal, as opposed to media, reform. Rather than focus on the uncomfortable inequality at home, their gaze is placed more comfortably elsewhere as if to say, "We have already done Civil Rights and anti-racism, anti-poverty work. The '60s are over. You are now equal, have your opportunity, and even have your own president! We simply find your concerns passé."

Even when one of the White Left's most impressive scholars writes on the subject, as did Robert Jensen in his book *The Heart of Whiteness* (2005), there remains a scramble for solutions that prevent recognition of their own field's potential contribution. Jensen's work, like much coming from the liberal White Left, is reminiscent of Hanno Hardt's claim of some years ago that

> the dilemma of American communication stud-
> ies continues to lie in its *failure to comprehend and
> overcome limitations of its own intellectual history,*
> not only by failing to address the theoretical and

methodological problems of an established academic
discipline, but also by failing to recognize the potential of radical thought.[616]

After writing eloquently about White privilege and the need to center Whiteness as the problem, Jensen struggles to "attempt any statement
about solutions" and then cannot move beyond the popular but empty
rhetoric of going "toward that which most frightens us" or to realize that
"we [Whites] are the problem," and so on. It is interesting that one solution that did not come from this journalist and journalism professor is the
use of their platforms to report, uncover, make known (whether through
regular coverage of or discussion with) those colonized right here in their
own country. One way to attack that White privilege would be to use it to
confront, via their media work (at least), the ravages of White supremacy
at home. It is far easier, as they demonstrate, to talk about Iraqis, Palestinians, and even people in the African diaspora—and it is certainly not to
say here that these people do not deserve or need it—than it is for them
to focus on the people for whose suffering they are most responsible and,
most importantly, most able to address. Audiences of their programs may
identify and sympathize with all the folks around the world who appear in
these media but there can be no similar sense of "I can fix this" as would
arise if the stories dealt with people literally right down the street.

But, perhaps, this is the point. Settlers, even the "nice ones," are
not likely to want to address that which might really upset their status
or that from which they, in the end, benefit. White liberals have always
made money and fame by "supporting" those that their societies destroy.
It becomes a safe cottage industry, one that does not challenge them to
confront their own complicity. An industry supported by the larger body
of White liberals now satiated (and, of course, with the necessary disposable income) who are the audience. In a media sense, it becomes what
Dr. King described as a tendency to "walk off with the aggressors" of the
mainstream. By centering the mainstream, even for the purposes of per-
sistent critique, there is a dangerous validation still conferred upon that
mainstream that sets definitive limits on that criticism's ultimate impact.

In a media sense, the White Left have realized their political equivalent by inhabiting the role once defined by Kwame Ture, "the least powerful element of White America." Politically, their role is to stem the potential for Black (or other) violent rebellion. In terms of media, their role is
to limit violent reclamation of media space, practice, and focus. That is,

their function is to limit ranges of debate, ranges that might include the unsanctioned practice of media, forms that are more culturally and practically relevant, or which might contain points of reference that differ from their own. The White Left, in both media studies and practice, often—even after levying powerful and informed critiques—still prefer that we remain shackled to notions of government petition, inclusive ownership, more diverse staffs, etc. This, again, returns to the fundamental gaps that remain between liberal criticism and the genuinely threatening rebellious behavior that existed in more popular political movements and continues unchecked. This nation's press has never existed outside its "original sins" of race and class bias, and has always been used as part of the "machinery of control"[617] or as a weapon against the majority, women, the poor, and the Indigenous or African-descended populations.[618]

So while it remains important to incorporate the work produced by the White Left, it is equally important to recognize that their existence as institutionalized critics makes that work the result of loyal opposition or more supportive of existing media and their function than threatening. Their studies of race, class, gender, corporate consolidation, assaults on public broadcasting, etc. are ultimately limited to the safe confines of liberal reform and, therefore, ultimately support the continuance of that which they claim to challenge. In this sense, whereas previously Kwame Ture spoke of illegal as meaning "violent," illegal here means "mixtapes" or any other form of unsanctioned media production whose purpose is in support of political organization and mass movement as opposed to FCC and government changes in regulation and corporate diversity.

Bootlegging, in this sense, is a revolutionary activity, as opposed to petitioning the FCC or local government for media policy reform or for more inclusion of women or non-white faces in positions of leadership or practice. The "violence" represented here is the suggestion that oppressed people take to producing their own journalism and media based on their own experiences, with low-tech, locally-based apparatuses that are absent of permission from above and divorced from the hopeful, eventual shift in media policy. It is "violence" in service of political organizations and social movements and with no illusions of White liberal or non-profit money. It is the "divinely [journalistically and intellectually] violent... refusal to normalize the crime" or to "make it part of the ordinary/explicable/accountable flow of things, to integrate it into a consistent and meaningful life-narrative." In this case it is the crime of a White liberal colonial reification of patterns established by those considered "experts" or the perspectives from which all grand interpretations must emerge. In another similar sense, continuing Žižek's theme: "When a subject is hurt in such a devastating way that the very idea of revenge according to *ius talionis* is no less ridiculous than the premise of the reconciliation with the perpetrator after the perpetrator's atonement, the only thing that remains is to persist in the 'unremitting denunciation of injustice.'"[619]

"Revenge" here, to remain true to Žižek's larger point, is against a colonialism that creates even a White liberal media that itself, by definition, cannot raise consistent and fundamental challenges to state function and purpose. They serve to set the acceptable parameters of resistance, as had always been their function, and do little to raise up new voices—new majority "non-White" voices—who might reorganize bodies and movements into more threatening positions. The White Left is less likely to cover the concerns of Black women than the White mainstream is to cover the concerns of Black women before the White Left makes it a story. This was on full display when coverage of post-Katrina, post-levees New Orleans only occurred in response to Eve Ensler "politicizing" her *Vagina Monologues* during a "V Day" benefit for women.[620] And since this is also true of the Black press, not taking up a story before the White Left, it makes the role of the White liberal that much more important and their impotence that much more heavily felt. It also makes important the need for communities left out of these discussions to return to traditions of a different kind of journalism for inspiration in the modern era. A tradition of, in this case, Black radical journalism or anti-colonial journalism and the naturally anti-colonial origins of the mixtape itself is one worthy of new attention.

For these and other reasons, the "media reform movement," as it is called, suffers. An emphasis on FCC regulations and petitioning elected officials while downplaying or ignoring peoples' struggles weakens the potential development of the social movements necessary to determine media (or any other public) policy. As one critic concludes, if a media reform movement "is to last beyond the next round of FCC hearings—and if it is to have a progressive impact on media systems under a Democratic administration—it seems vital that media reformers articulate their concerns and fashion their demands in relation to the structures of dominance, the routines and ideologies, which comprise the building blocks that enabled the frightening phenomenon of consolidated media ownership to emerge."[621] Extending from this point, another asks, "how different would the media reform movement look if it were focused on issues of social justice, centering racial justice, feminism, queer liberation, workers' rights, and others as core tenants in a global fight against corporate ownership of the media?... [T]he media reform movement [needs] to move from, in the words of Martin Luther King, Jr., 'thing-oriented'—i.e., who should control the technology movement to a 'person'-oriented'—that is, who and *how can we use technology for broad social change*, because a 'civilization can flounder as readily in the face of moral... bankruptcy as it can through financial bankruptcy.'"[622]

This present critique is, again, not meant to discount the important contributions made by the White Left to understanding and organizing around issues of media content and policy. Nor is this critique meant to discount White *progressives* and *radicals* who overtly and covertly engage in other less liberal activities, which include, for example, the establishment of unsanctioned low-power radio stations.[623] However, covert acts of unsanctioned rebelliousness cannot be seen as an appropriate counterbalance to overt acts of soft liberalism. This confuses, weakens, and limits, rather than inspires, more threatening activity.

And for the colonized, no one is coming. Renewed energy is needed in terms of media and journalism production and methods of distribution. Updated theory or perspective must be applied to political organizing because where attention is being paid to these issues, rarely are the concerns of the most oppressed truly a concern. Mixtape radio is conceptually grounded in the need for the colonized to assume leadership within a broader social movement that uses media effectively, as opposed to being marginalized within a media reform movement that assumes incorrectly (and if at all) that the conditions of the most oppressed will improve with a moderately reshaped media policy.

CONCLUSION

This concept of changing people's minds in a context of a reactionary scheme is very difficult. We are bombarded by incredible amounts of propaganda, that's what it is. That includes some of the hip-hop movement... not the movement, because it's not a movement.... I'm not talking about "bitches" and "hoes." I'm talking about these totally reactionary things. I'm not talking about the language.... I'm not talking about the Don Imus piece.... I'm talking about the fact that you have Russell Simmons out here totally involved in some very reactionary activity and at the height of the game. And we know that it's Sony and all these others. So the people who do have something to say within this certain cultural paradigm of hip-hop are obviously not going to get in to the mass mind because they are not in control of the mass media... so the problem is that we're not in control of any of this.... [W]e've got to create the conditions to get to people's minds. We have no means by which to pound the population of this country with information. Whether its through music, or whether its through rhetoric... the concrete conditions are not there for us to do that. We've got to find ways to get enough resources... and have bigger voices to get out to the people so that people can have some new ideas about what they might want to do.
—Elaine Brown

When one says "terrorism" in a democratic society, one also says "media." For terrorism by its very nature is a psychological weapon which depends upon communicating a threat to a wider society. This, in essence, is why terrorism and the media enjoy a symbiotic relationship.
—Paul Wilkinson

When James Cone described the very existence of ghettoes and a prison industrial complex as contemporary "mass crucifixions and lynchings" of African and Latin Americans, which are meant to control, via terror," the entire community, he was describing the still existent, and permanent, moment of danger out of which hip-hop and the rap music mixtape emerge.[624] Or, as John Henrik Clarke would say, "history is never old. Everything that has ever happened continues to happen."[625] The adoption of a colonial model of analysis to be applied to African America was done so as to shatter myths of "citizen," "freedom," and "democracy" in order that these fraudulent concepts be replaced with more liberating ideas surrounding an end to colonialism here and abroad. Continued reference to these dead concepts returns us back to predictable responses and to equally predictable, and unfortunate, material realities. The forces that maintain colonialism continue largely unchecked, even unnoticed, and the colonized continue to suffer in an equally unchecked and un-noticed manner. For them, help is not on the way and hence the mixtape radio concept is offered as a potentially affordable, low-tech (therefore, accessible) source for the support of their own organizational and pro-motional work.

The colonial model approach, or that of internal colonialism theory, is also essential in supporting the idea of mixtape radio (or any form of revolutionary media) in a U.S. media and legal environment that stands in direct and powerful opposition to the use of more traditional or sanc-tioned means of communication. Recognizing the colonial relationship can only assist in developing more appropriate media practices and re-sponses that allow individuals to engage in the practice of revolutionary media—that which is "illegal and subversive mass communication utiliz-ing the press and broadcasting to overthrow government or wrest control from alien rulers."[626] As a form of what Streitmatter calls a "dissident" press, this mixtape radio concept contains "a differing view of society [and also seeks] to change society in some discernible way." Similarly, a mix-tape radio project can function as a hip-hop nation "zine" in that it is also "non-commercial, non-professional, small [in] circulation... [where] creators produce, publish and distribute by themselves."[627]

Given the conditions of the African American colony, it stands to reason that more media be produced with at least the goal of wresting "control from alien rulers," these being the unjust forces that strip Black people of their ability to own land or homes, making it impossible to ex-ist without police and legal terror, or to not have their labor and wealth extracted to enrich those whose concerns for them do not exist. And such a model of analysis and a call for this kind of media response is meant to highlight and address the sort of twisted logic in the quote above from Wilkinson.[628] Despite his having properly noted the symbiotic relation-ship between terrorism and mass media, he promulgates a dangerous inversion of the fact that it is not terrorists who use media to carry out their goals against a powerful enemy. It is instead the powerful enemy who terrorizes the colonized via their media. In terms of U.S. mass media, and hip-hop specifically, colonized African America is targeted and then assaulted by intentionally-selected damaging forms of its own cultural expression buttressed by an entire lack of news.[629] As the Colonialism and Mass Media model attempts to show, popularity is determined not by the consumers but by the entities in control of dissemination. These corporate, private equity, and internationally-connected entities have the larger political needs of managing populations and, therefore, have no interest—which has been demonstrated and detailed for centuries—in willfully altering that relationship or use of mass media.

Borrowing from, and making relevant via a colonialism model of analysis, the work of Naomi Klein and her discussion of *The Shock Doctrine* (2007), a summary of her discussion and the notion of genocide borrowed from Ward Churchill help further the current argument.[630] That is, once contextualized in the colonialism that continues to grip African America, the Shock Doctrine is more clearly seen as Frantz Fanon's description, from some forty years earlier, of the "psychic violence" that is waged against the colonized, whose colonial status marks them as the targets of genocide. Even more directly, the concept of mixtape radio takes on a deeper meaning given the history of media's role in service of conquerors who understand that, "before we enter into warfare or genocide we first dehumanize those we mean to eliminate."[631]

In light of the above-cited conditions of African America and the larger imperial design of the U.S. as an empire holding colonies and within which are held subjects as opposed to citizens, all of this taking place on the territory conquered from a preserved Indigenous "Fourth World," it stands to reason that issues of genocide and terrorism be brought to bear on discussions of mass media. Churchill describes a definition of genocide arrived at by the United Nations in 1947 which is applied to "'national' or 'oppressed' groups" and includes "'*racial*, national linguistic, religious [and] *political* groups' as falling under the law's rubric." "Genocide," Churchill continues, "itself is defined in a two-fold way, encompassing all policies intended to precipitate '1) the destruction of [such] a group' and 2) *preventing its preservation and development*.'"[632]

Churchill goes on to describe three categories under which genocide is definable. They are, "Physical Genocide" or that which is both the "direct/immediate extermination," or what are considered "slow death measures"

152 I MIX WHAT I LIKE!

"or "subjection to conditions of life which, owing to lack of proper housing, clothing, food, hygiene and medical care or excessive work or physical exertion are likely to result in the debilitation [and] death of individuals ..." Secondly, there is "Biological Genocide" which includes "sterilization" or "any other policies intended to prevent births within a target group." But lastly, "Cultural Genocide" speaks more to the immediate topic. This involves, "the imposition of [an] alien national pattern," which "includes all policies aimed at destroying the specific characteristics by which a target group is defined, or defines itself, thereby forcing them to become something else." This includes assaults on the target population's "books... language... religious works... destruction or dispersion of objects of... artistic... value."633 This is the "cultural chaos" of Marable and the cultural "mummification" of Fanon previously described.

or "subjection to conditions of life which, owing to lack of proper housing, clothing, food, hygiene and medical care or excessive work or physical exertion are likely to result in the debilitation [and] death of individuals ..." Secondly, there is "Biological Genocide" which includes "sterilization" or "any other policies intended to prevent births within a target group." But lastly, "Cultural Genocide" speaks more to the immediate topic. This involves, "the imposition of [an] alien national pattern," which "includes all policies aimed at destroying the specific characteristics by which a target group is defined, or defines itself, thereby forcing them to become something else." This includes assaults on the target population's "books... language... religious works... destruction or dispersion of objects of... artistic... value."633 This is the "cultural chaos" of Marable and the cultural "mummification" of Fanon previously described.

These points are important when considering, for example, Chuck D's description of the forced/imposed change in hip-hop resulting from copyright laws and their impact on sampling, or his other statements regarding the "three year shift" resulting from "a marketing scheme" that replaced popular hip-hop discussions of "Fight the Power" in 1989 with "Gin and Juice" in 1992.634 Within a colonial framework, this has to be interpreted as part of a genocidal targeting of Black people as part of the imposition of an "alien national pattern... forcing them to become something else." Musically speaking, and in addition to the qualitative analysis previously offered, a recent study argues that it has shown quantitatively that "[m]usic represents an important form of communication of shared social reality for teenagers. This meta-analysis supports the conclusion that music does correlate with anti-social outcomes..."635 In the present context, and in accordance with the previously developed media model, these conclusions must, like Klein's description of torture and terror, be so vetted as to see them as predetermined and necessary to the function of a continued colonialism.

In making her macro-economic analysis of imposed suffering on oppressed communities, Klein's definitions of terror and torture taken from CIA documents become instructive when applied within the U.S. colonies. She notes how the "economic shock doctrine" is employed after terrifying events (natural disasters, war, etc.), when an unwitting population is too weak to realize or to respond. Given some of the history of African America described herein, it can be argued that Black America has been in a collective permanent state of shock as a result of enslavement, Reconstruction, and re-enslavement. DuBois described this as a process meant to take African America "back toward slavery," sharecropping, lynching, debt-peonage, Jim/Jane Crow—and Yolanda Denise King's "James Crow, Jr. Esquire"—police brutality, mass incarceration, segregated and inferior housing and education, insufficient healthcare (or Harriet Washington's "medical apartheid"), the levees in New Orleans, and the recent imposition of a brand-marketed, propaganda-driven neo-colonial president.[636] Given even this brief and ultimately polite overview of that history, it must then be concluded that African America has never fully escaped the terror that precedes the implementation of shock doctrine policies.

Klein notes that shock leads to compliance where subjects are "far more open to suggestion" (including the imposition of "leaders"), and that this "trauma" is "collective" or felt throughout whole societies. This shock reduces subjects to "a childlike status" which, again, makes people more compliant. This is eerily similar to the discussion of popular, mainstream commercial hip-hop as encouraging a "perpetual childhood,"[637] or the "auto-colonialism" wherein, through sheer imposition, victims "consciously or unconsciously, participate in their own oppression."[638] Klein goes on to describe CIA-manual descriptions of torture, including isolation, which helps assist in the ultimate goal of reducing the victim's capacity for awareness of her or his surroundings, of what precisely is happening, and limiting her or his ability to communicate with those who might be in a similar circumstance or able to explain. Here, again, issues of a fragmented media take new meaning. As put by a panelist at the youth speak-out in Oakland, Calif. during the 2006 FCC hearings, "as a society we have distorted and fragmented understanding of what is going on in our country.... Sometimes [there is] no public understanding at all of what is happening in the communities that are treated as disposable."[639] This is the domestic application of the techniques of colonization.

During a 1991 panel concerning the then soon-to-be released film *Malcolm X* by Spike Lee, participants John Henrik Clarke, Amiri Baraka, and Dhoruba bin-Wahad all took aim at the film as part of what distorts—for political purposes—the image of Black people and their struggles for liberation. Their concerns that early versions of the film's script pointed to (what would eventually be validated by the film's final released version) a bastardization, a Hollywood-ization of Malcolm X's life, which would both damage his legacy and also prohibit that legacy from pushing contemporary Black politics toward a more genuine threat to power. Wahad, a former Black Panther and political prisoner of nineteen years, focused on the direct correlation between popular image and treatment of those engaged in such activity. His statement on popular culture deserves a second quoting. "It is not just an art form," said Wahad,

> it's a form of propaganda. And propaganda gets Black activists killed… if you put out the wrong propaganda you are setting me up to be killed by my enemy. Because you see, it was propaganda and the definitions of the Black Panther Party that the enemy put out (and that many of these negroes went along with) that got us killed. Those [political prisoners] wouldn't be sitting in jail if they weren't branded criminals and half of us believed it.[640]

This, much like Klein's suggestion, is the political equivalent to a Shock Doctrine. People are shocked into an image of others that conditions the message recipient's perspective to accept the image, and ultimately, the treatment of the subject.

In terms of mass communication, this has long been recognized as the very function of that field's study. Mass Communication Studies was developed in the U.S. and institutionalized to understand and develop just these kinds of techniques. CIA experiments conducted during the civil/human rights struggles of the Vietnam era "in the social psychology of controlling unrest in U.S. client states" through the use of propaganda directed at positioning target groups as "the real terrorists" were "based in large part on the sociological methods and theories on communication and society," which themselves were the foundation of the academic field of mass communication studies. The field was developed by the higher circles described above at the nexus of the military, political, and social elite to develop the journalist, public relations, and advertising class who would be the nation's "ideological workers." This class, including the CIA's predecessor, the Office of Strategic Services (OSS), provided 96 percent of the field's funding to develop the notion of "communication-as-domination," or psychological or "worldview" warfare into "a full fourth arm of the U.S. military." This explicit goal was the "scientific application of propaganda, *terror*, and state pressure as a means of securing an ideological victory over one's enemies." [641]

Again, given the previously discussed goals of COINTELPRO and their concerns over the influence of racial politics on Black youth, we gain a new clarity of vision into the workings of a U.S. media system that predetermines which forms of Black politics and art become popular. This predetermination is a political necessity, one essential to the "proper" function of the state. It is not an accidental public or commercial policy nor can it be changed by simple appeals via electoral politics. It cannot be changed as one might change a single defective component of a larger mechanism. The entire mechanism demands that this component—mass media and the study thereof—function in just such a manner. Mass communication research was developed in part to *"prolong the agony of colonized* peoples and they continued to be used for that purpose today."[642] Hence, the aforementioned importance of returning African America— for purposes of analyses and strategy—back to its rightful placement among the world's colonized populations. This remains the most useful and relevant analytic tool for the study of African America in general, and specifically for examining the role and function of hip-hop as mass media, even in the twenty-first century.

And, though some will most certainly seek to dismiss this as regurgitating dead rhetoric, they do so themselves to dismiss the questionable foundation upon which they build their own analyses. Changing the description, finding new euphemisms or methods of evasion does not change the reality. It defies them. Unfortunately, those who would challenge the theoretical basis of this work can offer no substantive replacement that can explain the material condition of the world's majority in such a way that does not include it being the result of their own innate cultural or character flaws. As said, those notions are simply rejected from the start. Instead, once recognized as the result of a continuing predetermined, intentional system—colonialism—those conditions are better interpreted and, therefore, the response must, and will, naturally look and sound unorthodox. This too is understandable. The current orthodoxy and its popular representation via media, journalism, popular culture, academia, and so on would by its nature offer little support to those seeking a genuine and fundamental change. So it stands to reason that an attempt among the colonized to express themselves, organize around that expression, and develop a sustained challenge to the colonialism that binds them would also be met with resistance, confusion, or dismissal. No matter. As an expression of the colonized, the mixtape remains a kind of unsanctioned or dissident communication exercised by oppressed populations seeking to disrupt imposed media environments, which of necessity narrowly limit the roles and function of communication.[643] The mixtape, evolving out of colonial antagonisms, asks for no permission, is bound by no laws of the state, and disseminates a national mythology essential to all national groupings. Mixtapes are freedom incarnate and can and must be used to support efforts whose goals are the same—more freedom.

To again paraphrase DuBois' initial concern with the treatment of African America, this much smaller effort is a response to those who, "[a]ssuming, therefore, the endless inferiority of [Black people]," continue to fill the shelves, airwaves, and web pages with "misinterpreted, distorted" descriptions and solutions of an ongoing inequity that has "ignored any fact that has challenged or contradicted this assumption." These are the analyses that may even pay lip-service to the statistics demonstrating the intent of a system, but do so in such a way as to return the onus onto the oppressed by suggesting that an alternative reality is possible would they only conform better to the established rules or norms of this society. How else could one conclude that appeals to the legal or governing structure are their only or primary source of response? How else could one conclude that currently acceptable uses of media technology are the pathway to genuine change? "But," as DuBois reminds us, this wave of propaganda— that which Bernays summarized as "the establishing of reciprocal understanding between an individual and a group"—is only truly understood when viewed in terms of its "fidelity against the Negro since emancipation in this land, [where] we face one of the most stupendous efforts the world ever saw to discredit human beings, an effort involving universities, history, science, social life, and religion."[644] And to this enormity of production and function we have only added mass media.

The problems facing the colonized can only be addressed at the point when *they determine*, through organization, that their conditions must change and in ways that *they define*. The peace that is the promise of such organized struggle is, as Fred Hampton said, the reward of those who fight for it. This fight can be buttressed by turning off the radio and sticking a fucking mixtape (radio!) in instead.

SELECTED BIBLIOGRAPHY

"UN Report: At 45%, Gaza unemployment is highest in the world." July 28, 2008. *Haaretz Service*. Retrieved July 19, 2009 from http://www.haaretz.com/hasen/spages/1006282.html.

Achbar, M. (Director). (1992). *Manufacturing Consent: Noam Chomsky and the Media*. [Film]. Canada: Necessary Illusions Productions.

Adorno, T. and Horkheimer, M. (1944). *Dialectic of Enlightenment*. New York: Continuum.

Allen, R. L. (1969/1990). *Black Awakening in Capitalist America*. Trenton: Africa World Press.

Allen, R. L. (2006). "Reassessing the Internal (Neo) Colonialism Theory." *The Black Scholar*, Vol. 35, no. 1.

Allen, R. L. (Winter 2008). "Barack Obama and the Children of Globalization." *The Black Scholar*, Vol. 38, no. 4.

Alterman, E. (2002). *What Liberal Media? The Truth About Bias and the News*. New York: Basic Books.

Altschull, H. J. (1984). *Agents of Power*. New York: Longman.

Ani, M. (1994). *Yurugu: An African-Centered Critique of European Cultural Thought and Behavior*. Trenton: Africa World Press.

Ards, A. (2004). "Organizing the Hip-Hop Generation." In *That's the Joint! The Hip-Hop Studies Reader*. New York: Routledge, pp. 311–323.

Armstrong, D. (1981). *A Trumpet to Arms*. Boston: South End Press.

Atkinson, P. (1993). *Brown vs. Topeka: Desegregation and Miseducation: An African American's View*. New York: African American Images.

Atton, C. (2002). *Alternative Media*. London: Sage Publications.

Asante, M. K. (2008). *It's Bigger than Hip-Hop: The Rise of the Post-Hip-Hop Generation*. New York: St. Martin's Press.

Bagdikian, B. (2004). *The New Media Monopoly*. Boston: Beacon Press.

Ball, J. A. (Winter 2008). "Barack Obama, 'Connected Distance': Race and Twenty-first Century Neo-colonialism." *The Black Scholar*, Vol. 38 Issue 4.

Ball, J. A. (Fall 2008). "*Mixtape Inc.* and the Definitive Incorporation of Dissident Culture." [Film Review]. *The Global Journal of Hip-Hop Culture from Words, Beats and Life*, Vol. 3, no. 2.

Ball, J. A. (March 2009). "FreeMix Radio: The Original Mixtape Radio Show: A Case Study in Mixtape 'Radio' and Emancipatory Journalism." *The Journal of Black Studies*, Vol. 39, no. 4.

Ball, J. A. (2009). "A Bronx Mix: Mixtapes Then and Now." [Audio]. *Voxunion. com.* Retrieved from: http://www.voxunion.com/?p=1562.

Ball, J. A. (2010). "Communicating Liberation in Washington, D.C." In *Democratic Destiny and the District of Columbia: Federal Politics and Public Policy.* Lanham, MD: Lexington Books.

Ball, J. A. (February 23, 2010). "The Titans of Technology: The Internet, Radio and *Our* Newton's Laws." *BlackAgendaReport.com.* Retrieved from http://tns1.blackagendareport.com/?q=content/titans-technology-internet-radio-and-our-newton%E2%80%99s-laws.

Ball, Jared A. (April 14, 2010). "Save the Internet But Start a Social Movement." *BlackAgendaReport.com.* Retrieved from http://www.blackagendareport.com/?q=node/11709.

Baran, P. A. and Sweezy, P. M. (1966). *Monopoly Capital: An Essay on the American Economic and Social Order.* New York: Monthly Review Press.

Barker, L. J.; Jones, M. H.; and Tate, K. (1999). *African Americans and the American Political System.* Upper Saddle River: Prentice Press.

Barlow, W. (1995). "Black Music on Radio During the Jazz Age." *African American Review*, 29(2), pp. 325–328.

Barlow, W. (1999). *Voice Over: The Making of Black Radio.* Philadelphia: Temple University Press.

Barsamian, D. (2001). *The Decline and Fall of Public Broadcasting.* Cambridge: South End Press.

Bell, D. (2004). *Silent Covenants: Brown v. Board of Education and the Unfulfilled Hopes for Racial Reform.* Oxford: Oxford University Press.

Bernays, E. (1928/2005). *Propaganda.* Brooklyn: IG Publishing.

Berry, D. and Theobald, J. (eds.). (2006). *Radical Mass Media Criticism: A Cultural Genealogy.* Montreal: Black Rose Books.

Blauner, R. (1972). *Racial Oppression in America.* New York: Harper & Row.

Boehlert, E. (May 14, 2001). "Pay For Play: Why Does Radio Suck?" Salon.com. Retreived from http://www.salon.com/ent/feature/2001/03/14/payola/.

Boehlert, E. (January 5, 2005). "Payola is Dead! Now What Will We Listen To?" Salon.com. Retrieved from http://www.salon.com/news/feature/2005/01/05/payola/.

Breed, W. (1955). "Social control in the newsroom: A functional analysis." *Social Forces*, 33(4), pp. 326–335.

Brewster, B. and Broughton, F. (2000). *Last Night a DJ Saved My Life: The History of the Disc Jockey*. New York: Grove Press.

Brzezinski, Z. (1997). *The Grand Chessboard: American Primacy and Its Geostrategic Imperatives*. New York: Basic Books.

Cabral, A. (1973). *Return to the Source*. New York: Monthly Review Press.

Carmichael, S. and Hamilton, C.V. (1967). *Black Power: The Politics of Liberation*. New York: Dimensions Books.

Carr, G. (2008). *A Conversation About Race*. [Television]. MSNBC. Retrieved July 19, 2009 from http://www.msnbc.msn.com/id/21134540/vp/24076911#24076911.

Churchill, W. and Vander Wall, J. (1990). *The COINTELPRO Papers: Documents from the FBI's Secret Wars Against Dissent in the United States*. Boston: South End Press.

Churchill, W. (2004). *Kill the Indian and Save the Man: The Genocidal Impact of American Indian Residential Schools*. San Francisco: City Lights Books.

Clemens, R. (2005). *State of Black America Report*. National Urban League. Washington, D.C.

Cosby, B. and Poussaint, A. (2009). [Television]. *Meet The Press*. Transcript retrieved July 19, 2009 from http://www.msnbc.msn.com/id/28605356/.

Creamer, M. (Oct. 17, 2008). "Obama Wins!... Ad Age's Marketer of the Year." *Advertising Age*. Retrieved July 19, 2009 from http://adage.com/moy2008/article?article_id=131810.

Cruse, H. (1967/1984). *The Crisis of the Negro Intellectual*. New York: Quill.

Dannen, F. (1991). *Hit Men*. New York: Vintage Books.

Davis, A. (2003). *Are Prisons Obsolete?* Boston: Seven Stories Press.

Delaney, M. (1852/2004). *The Condition, Elevation, Emigration, and Destiny of the Colored People of the United States and Official Report of the Niger Valley Exploring Party*. New York: Humanity Books.

Downing, J. and Husband, C. (2005). *Representing "Race": Racisms, Ethnicities and Media*. London: Sage Publications.

DuBois, W.E.B. (1935). *Black Reconstruction in America 1860–1880*. New York: Simon and Schuster.

Entman, R. M. and Rajecki, A. (2000). *The Black Image in the White Mind: Media and Race in America*. Chicago: The University of Chicago Press.

Fanon, F. (1963). *The Wretched of the Earth*. New York: Grove Press.

Fanon, F. (1964). *Toward the African Revolution*. New York: Grove Press.

Fanon, F. (1965). *A Dying Colonialism*. New York: Grove Press.

Ford, G. (2009). "The Shrinking American Empire." *Black Agenda Report*. Retrieved July 17, 2009 from http://www.blackagendareport.

com/?q=content/shrinking-american-empire.

Gaiter, C. (June 8, 2005). "Visualizing a Revolution: Emory Douglas and The Black Panther Newspaper." *AIGA*. Retrieved from http://www.aiga.org/content.cfm/visualizing-a-revolution-emory-douglas-and-the-black-panther-new.

Galbraith, J. (2008). *The Predator State: How Conservatives Abandoned the Free Market and Why Liberals Should Too*. New York: Free Press.

George, N. (1988). *The Death of Rhythm and Blues*. New York: Pantheon Books.

George. N. (1998). *HipHop America*. New York: Penguin Books.

Golding, P. and Murdock, G. (1991). "Culture, communications, and political economy." In *Mass media and society*. London: Edward Arnold, pp. 15–32.

Goodman, A. and Goodman, D. (2004). *The Exception to the Rulers*. New York: Hyperion.

Hall, S. et al. (1980). *Encoding/Decoding. Culture, Media, Language*. London: Hutchinson.

Harris, W.J. (Ed.) (1991). *The Leroi Jones/Amiri Baraka Reader*. New York: Thunder's Mouth Press.

Heider, D. (2000). *White News: Why Local News Programs Don't Cover People of Color*. Mahwah, NJ: Lawrence Erlbaum.

Heider, D. (ed.). (2004). *Class and News*. Lanham, Md: Rowman & Littlefield.

Hilliard, D. and Weise, D. (2002). *The Huey P. Newton Reader*. New York: Seven Stories Press.

INCITE! Women of Color Against Violence. (2007). *The Revolution Will Not Be Funded: Beyond the Non-Profit Industrial Complex*. Boston: South End Press.

Innis, H. (1951). *The Bias of Communication*. Toronto: The University of Toronto Press.

Jackson, G. (1971/1990). *Blood in My Eye*. Baltimore: Black Classic Press.

Joseph, P. E. (Feb. 2008). "From Black Power to Barack Obama." *The Brooklyn Rail*.

Kamenka, E. (1983). *The Portable Karl Marx*. New York: Penguin Books.

Kirk, M. (writer, producer, director). (2004). *The Way the Music Died*. [Television]. Boston: WGBH Educational Foundation.

Kofsky, F. (1970, 1988). *Black Nationalism and the Revolution in Music*. New York: Pathfinder Press.

Kozol, J. (2005). *Shame of the Nation*. New York: HarperCollins Publishers.

Kouddous, S. A. (December 19, 2008). "Katrina's Hidden Race War." *Democracy Now!* Podcast transcript retrieved from http://www.democracynow.org/2008/12/19/katrinas_hidden_race_war_in_aftermath.

Krasilovsky, M. W. and Shemel, S. (2000). *This Business of Music*. New York: Billboard Books.

Kunjufu, J. (2002). *Black Economics: Solutions for Economic and Community Empowerment*. Chicago: African American Images.

Lewis, D. L. (1995). *W.E.B. DuBois: A Reader*. New York: Henry Holt and Company, Inc.

Lippmann, W. (1921/1997). *Public Opinion*. New York: Free Press.

Lipsitz, G. (1998). *The Possessive Investment in Whiteness: How White People Profit from Identity Politics*. Philadelphia: Temple University Press.

Lugard, F .S. (1906/1997). *A Tropical Dependency: An Outline of the Ancient History of Western Sudan with an Account of the Modern Settlement of Northern Nigeria*. Baltimore: Black Classic Press.

Marx, K. (1976). *Capital*. New York: Penguin.

McChesney, R. (2004). *The Problem of the Media: U.S. Communication Politics in the 21st Century*. New York: Monthly Review Press.

McChesney, R. Newman, R. and Scott, B. (2005). *The Future of Media: Resistance and Reform in the 21st Century*. New York: Seven Stories Press.

McChesney, R. (2008). *The Political Economy of Media: Enduring Issues, Emerging Dilemmas*. New York: Monthly Review Press.

McLeod, K. (2005). *Freedom of expression: Overzealous copyright bozos and other enemies of creativity*. London: Doubldeday.

Memmi, A. (1965). *The Colonizer and the Colonized*. Boston: Beacon Press.

Moreno, S. (October 24, 2007). "Poverty Rate Grows Amid an Economic Boom D.C.'s Poorest Left Behind By Renewal, Report Finds." *The Washington Post*.

Moyers, B. (November 23, 2007). Interview with James H. Cone. *Bill Moyers Journal*. Transcript retrieved from http://www.pbs.org/moyers/journal/11232007/profile.html.

Muhammad, D., Davis A., Leondor-Wright, B., and Lui, M. (2004). *The State of the Dream 2004: Enduring Disparities in Black and White*. Boston: United for a Fair Economy.

Neal, M. A. (1999). *What the Music Said*. New York: Routledge.

Nelson, J. (2001). *Police Brutality: An Anthology*. New York: W.W. Norton.

Osayande, E. (2004). "Art at War: Revolutionary Art Against Cultural Imperialism. *Black Commentator*. Retrieved from http://www.blackcommentator.com/108/108_guest_osayande_pf.html.

Palast, G. (2002). *The Best Democracy Money Can Buy*. London: Pluto Press.

Patel, R. (July 31, 2008). *Democracy Now!* Interview. Retrieved July 17, 2009 from http://www.democracynow.org/2008/7/31/raj_patel_on_the_collapse_of.

Peck, J. (2008). *The Age of Oprah: Cultural Icon for the Neoliberal Era*. New York: Paradigm Publishers.

Perkins, J. (2004). *Confessions of an Economic Hit Man*. San Francisco: Berrett-Koehler.

Pinderhughes, C. (April 10, 2009). *Robert Allen Celebrated: A 40th Anniversary Tribute to Black Awakening in Capitalist America*. Berkeley, CA. Podcast retrieved from http://www.voxunion.com/?p=1089.

Rivera, A.; Cotto-Escalera, B.; Desai, A.; Huezo, J.; Muhammad, D. (2008). *Foreclosed: State of the Dream 2008*. Boston: United for a Fair Economy.

Rose, T. (1994). *Black Noise*. Middletown: Wesleyan University Press.

Rose, T. (2004). "Contracting rap: An interview with Carmen Ashhurst-Watson." In M. Forman & M. A. Neal (Eds.), *That's the Joint! The Hip-Hop Studies Reader*. New York: Routledge: pp. 311–323.

Ross, T. (1992). "Copyright and the Invention of Tradition." *Eighteenth-Century Studies*, 26, 1–27.

Shah, H. (May 1996). "Modernization, Marginalization, and Emancipation: Toward a Normative Model of Journalism and National Development." *Communication Theory*, vol. 6, no. 2: 143–166.

Shah, H. (June 2007). "Journalism in an Age of Mass Media Globalization." Retrieved from http://www.idsnet.org/Papers/Communications/HEMANT_SHAH.HTM.

Simpson, C. (1993). "U.S. Mass Communication Research, Counterinsurgency, and Scientific 'Reality.'" *Ruthless Criticism: New Perspectives in U.S. Communication History*. Minneapolis: University of Minnesota Press.

Simpson, C. (1994). *Science of Coercion: Communication Research and Psychological Warfare 1945–1960*. New York: Oxford University Press.

Simpson, C. (ed.) (1999). *Universities and Empire: Money and Politics in the Social Sciences During the Cold War*. New York: New Press.

Smith, A. (1776/1991). *Wealth of Nations*. Amherst: Prometheus Books.

Spady, J., Alim, H.S., and Meghelli, S. (2006). *The Global Cipha: Hip-Hop Culture and Consciousness*. Philadelphia: Black History Museum Press.

Spivey, D. (1978). *Schooling for the New Slavery: Black Industrial Education, 1868– 1915*. Westport: Greenwood Press.

Street, P. (2008). *Barack Obama and the Future of American Politics*. New York: Paradigm Publishers.

Streitmatter, R. (2001). *Voices of Revolution: The Dissident Press in America*. New York: Columbia University Press.

Tabb, W. K. (1970). *The Political Economy of the Black Ghetto*. New York: Norton.

Tate, Greg (ed.) (2003). *Everything but the Burden*. New York: Broadway Books.

Thall, P. M. (2002). *What They'll Never Tell You About the Music Business: The Myths, the Secrets, the Lies (and a Few Truths)*. New York: Watson-Guptill.

Turner, J. (March/April 1977). "Black America: Colonial Economy Under Siege." *FirstWorld: An International Journal of Black Thought*. vol. 1, no. 2: pp. 7–11.

Williams, E. (1935). *Capitalism and Slavery*. Chapel Hill: University of North Carolina Press.

Wilson, A. (1993). *The Falsification of Afrikan Consciousness*. New York: Afrikan World Infosystems.

Wilson, A. (1998). *Blueprint for Black Power: A Moral, Political, and Economic Imperative for the Twenty-First Century*. New York: Afrikan World Infosystems.

Van Dijk, T. A. (1991). *Racism and the Press: Critical Studies in Racism and Migration*. London: Routledge.

Zinn, H. (1999). *A People's History of the United States*. New York: Harpers-Collins Press.

Žižek, S. (2008). *In Defense of Lost Causes*. London: Verso Books.

Žižek, S. (2008). *Violence*. New York: Picador.

1 Steve Biko, *I Write What I Like: Selected Writings*, ed. Aelred Stubbs C.R., (Chicago: University of Chicago, 2002).

2 "Hip-hop" and "hip-hop mixtape" are terms used to clarify that (a) we are talking about aspects of an African expression that include various "elements," such as the emcee, DJ, graffiti artists, and dancers; and (b) that we are discussing the tradition of the rap music mixtape, that is, hip-hop's particular and specific use of the mixtape as a communicative tool. Our focus is the mixtape as developed within a hip-hop culture that emerged in the U.S. circa the 1970s that is itself an expression of a Diasporan African culture.

3 Frantz Fanon, *Toward the African Revolution* (New York: Grove Press, 1964), 34.

4 Frank Wilderson (author of *Incognegro: A Memoir of Apartheid and Exile* [Boston: South End Press, 2008]) in discussion with the author, April 2010.

5 Greg Thomas, *The Sexual Demon of Colonial Power: Pan-African Embodiment and Erotic Schemes of Empire* (Bloomington: Indiana University, 2007), ix.

6 Jacob Carruthers, *MDU NTR: Divine Speech: A Historiographical Reflection of African Deep Thought from the Time of Pharaohs to the Present* (London: Karnak House, 1995), 82. For more on how rap music lyrics form part of a "Black rhetorical tradition" and a "guerrilla rhetoric" that continues to subvert attempts to destroy its transformational capacity see Baruti N. Kopano, "Rap Music as an Extension of the Black Rhetorical Tradition: 'Keepin' It Real'," *The Western Journal of Black Studies*, vol. 26, no. 4, 2002.

7 Predator as a concept is borrowed initially from the works of John Trudell and Ward Churchill in, for example, *Struggle for the Land: Native North American Resistance to Genocide, Ecocide, and Colonization* (San Francisco: City Lights, 2002.) And let's not put it all on these brothers. Consider, for example, *Predator's Ball: The Inside Story of Drexel Burnham and the Rise of the Junk Bond Raiders* (1989); and more recently, J. Galbraith, *The Predator State: How Conservatives Abandoned the Free Market and Why Liberals Should Too* (New York: Free Press, 2008), in which the author describes the lack of levee preparation that prefigured the suffering during and after Hurricane Katrina as the "erosion of capability," which itself is the result of a "rot in the system." This "rot" is for Galbraith the result of "predation: the systematic abuse

of public institutions for private profit or, equivalently, the systematic undermining of public protection for the benefit of private clients" (xii–xiii). It must also be added that the continuing suffering of the victims of this New Orleans-based predation has not improved even under the Obama administration. This was detailed recently during the event "Nobel Prize for Peace, But 'D+' for New Orleans: Obama, Mass Media and 'Katrina'," a panel discussion held at Howard University on October 13, 2009. Available online at: http://www.voxunion.com/?p=1873.

8 C. F. Volney, *The Ruins of Empires* (Baltimore: Black Classic Press, 1991), 150, original emphasis.

9 Sigmund Freud, *Moses and Monotheism* (New York: Vintage Books, 1939), 16.

10 Gerald Massey, *The Historical Jesus and the Mythical Christ* (New York: A&B Publishers, 1828), 134.

11 Volney, *The Ruins of Empires*, 17, original emphasis.

12 Mark Crispin Miller in his introduction to *Propaganda* by Edward Bernays (Brooklyn: IG Publishing, 2005), 12.

13 Marshall McLuhan quoted in Kevin McMahon, dir., *McLuhan's Wake* [Film] (National Film Board of Canada, 2008). "It's like fish in the water. We don't know who discovered water but we know it wasn't a fish. A pervasive medium, a pervasive environment is always beyond perception."

14 For more on how this system of non-profits works to siphon off radical struggle where they can be safely corralled within the confines of capitalism see Incite! Women of Color Against Violence, *The Revolution Will Not Be Funded: Beyond the Non-Profit Industrial Complex* (Boston: South End Press, 2007).

15 Though focused on Black or African America, the intent here to is follow the trajectory of classification as established in, for instance, Michele Stephenson's *Faces of Change* [Film] (Rada Films, 2005), in which an international White supremacy defines and reduces darker-skinned people around the world to "Black," which, of course, lowers their relative position on the colonial pyramid. The film traces this phenomenon in the U.S., India, "Arabicized" Africa, and Bulgaria.

16 W.E.B. DuBois, *Black Reconstruction in America 1860–1880* (New York: Touchstone, 1935), xviiii, emphasis added.

17 Slavoj Žižek, *In Defense of Lost Causes* (London: Verso Books, 2008), 1.

18 As has long-been noted, the use of "Amen" is part of the imperial project of Western religion and is co-opted, as is Judaism, Christianity, and Islam, from African philosophy and spirituality. "Amen," despite false claims to it meaning "so be it," is the truncated form of "Amen-Ra" the unified deity of a unified Kemet (Egypt) during the eighteenth dynasty.

19 Stephen Wrage, "Pirates and Parasites," *The Washington Post*, October 20, 2001, A27.

20 Cornelius Mays, personal communication with the author, December 16, 2002.

21 Michael Arrington, "'360' Music Deals Become Mandatory as Labels Prepare for Free Music," *TechCrunch,* November 8, 2008. Available online at: http://techcrunch. com/2008/11/08/360-music-deals-become-mandatory-as-labels-prepare-for-free-music/.

22 Herbert Schiller in the foreword to Dennis W. Mazzocco, *Networks of Power: Corporate TV's Threat to Democracy* (Boston: South End Press, 1994), ix.

23 Marshall McLuhan quoted in Kevin McMahon, dir., *McLuhan's Wake* [Film], (National Film Board of Canada, 2002).

24 Mazzocco, *Networks of Power,* xiii–xiv.

25 "Emancipatory Journalism," to be more fully explained below, is a phrase coined by Hemant Shah in "Modernization, Marginalization, and Emancipation: Toward a Normative Model of Journalism and National Development," *Communication Theory,* vol. 6, no. 2, May 1996, 143–166. "Lost causes" is taken from Žižek, *In Defense of Lost Causes.* For Žižek such a "'defense of lost causes' is not to defend Stalinist terror, and so on, but to render problematic the all-too-easy liberal-democratic alternative" (6). Here too, the goal is not to defend as perfect the theoretical approach of a colonialism model, and so on, but to "render problematic" notions of Black progress, equality, and meritorious rises to fame, wealth, and political power.

26 Stokely Carmichael and Charles V. Hamilton, *Black Power: The Politics of Liberation* (New York: Dimensions Books, 1967).

27 Jared A. Ball, "Barack Obama, 'Connected Distance,' Race and 21st Century Neo-Colonialism," *Black Scholar,* vol. 38, no. 4, 2008.

28 Robin Kelley, *Freedom Dreams: The Black Radical Imagination* (Boston: Beacon, 2002).

29 Ibid.

30 *"On Pan-Africanism."* A Speech given to the Patrice Lumumba Coalition in New York City, June 1996.

31 December 12, 2005. Available online from North Bay Indymedia at: http://www. indybay.org/newsitems/2005/12/12/17897041.php.

32 Fanon, *Toward the African Revolution.*

33 Naomi Klein, *The Shock Doctrine: The Rise of Disaster Capitalism* (New York: Picador, 2007). The definition of terror/torture as summarized by Klein in her companion video introduction to the book: (http://www.youtube.com/watch?v=aSF0e6oO_tw). This also speaks loudly to the concern raised by Harold Cruse in *The Crisis of the Negro Intellectual* (New York: Quill, 1984). He said that "White intellectuals should be more in touch with Black intellectuals."

34 For more, see J. K. Lee, "The Effect of the Internet on Homogeneity of the Media Agenda: A Test of the Fragmentation Thesis," *Journalism and Mass Communication Quarterly,* vol. 84, no. 4, Winter 2007, 745–760. Despite varying media outlets,

and the Internet replete with a wide array of content and blogs, "people are likely exposed to a fairly stable agenda across mainstream media and internet news outlets, despite the diversification of information channels." For more on the devastating impact of media fragmentation on oppressed communities see also *Yo TV!* California State Conference: 19th Annual NAACP State Convention FCC Forum in Oakland, Ca. (October 26–29, 2006). Available online at: http://www.youtube.com/watch?v=mR8CHfxgQ-I.

35 For more, see T. A. Van Dijk, *Racism and the Press: Critical Studies in Racism and Migration* (London: Routledge, 1991) and R. M. Entman and A. Rajecki, *The Black Image in the White Mind: Media and Race in America* (Chicago: University of Chicago, 2000). See also John Downing and Charles Husband, *Representing 'Race': Racisms, Ethnicities and Media* (London: Sage Publications, 2005).

36 Glen Ford, "Who Killed Black Radio News?" *BlackCommentator.com*, May 23, 2003.

37 Jared A. Ball, "FreeMix Radio: The Original Mixtape Radio Show: A Case Study in Mixtape Radio and Emancipatory Journalism," *Journal of Black Studies*, vol. 39, no. 4, March 2009, 614–634.

38 C. Wright Mills, *The Power Elite* (New York: Oxford University, 1959).

39 Fanon, *Toward the African Revolution*, 34.

40 Meant as "conceptual anchor" as described by Kwasi Konadu in his *Truth Crushed to the Earth Will Rise Again: The East Organization and the Principles and Practice of Black Nationalist Development* (Trenton, N.J.: Africa World Press, 2005). Konadu, quoting a statement from The East organization writes that "[t]he African-American cultural identity has been and continues to be influenced by the U.S. social context, but it is essential to note that the African-American cultural orientation also represents an experiential context. Thus, while African-Americans exist within the U.S. social context, they also exist within an African historical-cultural continuum that predates that social context and would continue to exist even if the nation-state and its social arrangements were to transform or demise" (xiv). However, unless specified, here the term "Black American" will at times be used for clarity and recognition of its contemporary popularity interchangeably with "Africans in America" or simply African people.

41 An amendment made to Albert Memmi's colonial "pyramid of petty tyrants" (*The Colonizer and the Colonized* [Boston: Beacon Press, 1965], 17) to be explained more fully below. Simply, it means that most of us lead relatively freer lives than others but only in relation to their condition and *as a result* of their condition.

42 See, for example, Charles Pinderhuges' work, "African Americans and Internal Colonial Theory," American Sociological Association, Boston: July 31, 2008. Available online at: http://www.allacademic.com/meta/p_mla_apa_research_citation/2/4/3/0/8/p243088_index.html. Pinderhuges' presentation on the subject during the event

"Robert Allen Celebrated: A 40th Anniversary Tribute to Black Awakening in Capitalist America" is available online at: http://www.voxunion.com/?p=1089.

43 Chela Sandoval, *Methodology of the Oppressed* (Minneapolis: University of Minnesota, 2000).

44 Jack O'Dell quoted in Robert Allen's *Black Awakening in Capitalist America* (Trenton, N.J.: Africa World Press, 1969/1990), 8, original emphasis.

45 Tim Lake, "Postcolonial Theory and the African American Experience," *The Journal of Pan African Studies*, vol. 1, no. 10, November 2007.

46 Adam Haupt defines empire in his own *Stealing Empire: P2P, Intellectual Property and Hip-Hop Subversion* (South Africa: Human Sciences Research Council, 2008) as "a form of supranational cooperation between the U.S. and the former imperial powers of Western Europe that allows them to act in ways that benefit them economically, militarily, culturally and politically." Just as Haupt uses an unconventional definition of empire so too does *I Mix What I Like!* suggest an unconventional definition of colonialism. Noam Chomsky, discussing the presence of the U.S. military abroad, has said, "The United States cannot commit aggression, by definition, we do not commit aggression… our forces are not foreign; they are indigenous. We are indigenous everywhere." As empire, founded as such from the beginning, "expansion is the path to security," and if the world is yours then everywhere is home and everyone else is to one degree or another foreign. Available online at: http://www.youtube.com/watch?v=rnLWSC5p1XE.

47 This is not to deny distinctions or shifts in colonialism from one moment to the next but rather to suggest that "neo-colonialism" is just that, neo or new but not ended. Nkrumah's discussion, in *Neo-Colonialism: The Last Stage of Imperialism* (London: Thomas Nelson and Sons, 1965), of this shift is still powerfully relevant as it describes a modern shift in "independence" and "corporate" dominance as part of this continuance and advancement of colonialism.

48 "Hip-hop" is recognized *not* as a distinct culture but an *extension* of a more pan-African diasporic cultural tradition. Its African world origins are herein taken for granted whereas it is recognized that all may (and should) participate but on this basis and with this particular historical and cultural understanding. Hip-hop is also understood to include rap, graffiti, dance, DJ-ing, and various other expressions as well.

49 Both the phrase "hip-hop" and the word "mixtape" carry many definitions. "Hip-hop," which I've given some definition of in the previous note, is used here specifically because I think of the mixtape as part of the collective elements of what is characterized as "hip-hop culture." In this sense I mean to suggest it as an "eleventh element," that of the underground mass medium. As for the mixtape and its many definitions, a few of which I will describe below, the form that is to be the

subject here is that of the rap music variety.

50 For a more broad discussion of the tradition, history, and impact of the Black
community's street corner orator, see Jared A. Ball, *Still Speaking: An Intellectual
History of John Henrik Clarke*, Masters thesis, The Africana Studies and Research
Center at Cornell University (Ithaca, N.Y.: 2001). For more on the history of Black
Talk Radio and for a better understanding of the relationship of that medium to
Black America, including radio as a "public sphere" essential to open discussions
of political problems and solutions that was once a powerful force in assisting
progressive change but today "no longer exists," see Catherine Squires, "Black Talk
Radio: Defining Community Needs and Identity," in *The Black Studies Reader*, eds.
Jacqueline Bobo, Cynthia Hudley, and Claudine Michel (New York: Routledge,
2004), 193–210. See also William Barlow's *Voice Over: The Making of Black Radio*
(Philadelphia: Temple University, 1999).

51 "Well over 90% of Black consumers aged 12 years and over listen to the radio each
week—a higher penetration than television, magazines, newspapers or the internet.
Radio reaches Black audiences everywhere they are: at home, at work, and in the
car; in stores and restaurants; online; and, more recently, via cell phones. Regardless
of age, time of day, or geography, radio is the true media companion of Black
consumers." *Black Radio Today*, Arbitron: 2008. Available online at: http://www.
arbitron.com/study/blackrt.asp.

52 Radical in this sense, to quote David Berry means "to move beyond the boundaries
of *mere critique*, not necessarily by stepping outside, but rather by *stepping beyond!*"
(5, original emphasis). We also mean, since Berry and Theobald refer little to
any African tradition of media criticism, to step beyond them in a definition of
radicalism, analysis, and activity.

53 Kevin Phillips, *Wealth and Democracy: A Political History of the American Rich*,
(New York: Broadway Books, 2002). See also Huey P. Newton, "The Technology
Question," in *The Huey P. Newton Reader*, ed. David Hilliard (New York: Seven
Stories Press, 2002), 257. Also James K. Galbraith, in *The Predator State: How
Conservatives Abandoned the Free Market and Why Liberals Should Too*, describes
how a *growing income inequality* is often explained away by those in power as the
result of technological advances in society that reward an educational "skill bias"
that only a select few attain (89).

54 Angela Ards, "Organizing the Hip-Hop Generation," in *That's the Joint! The Hip-
Hop Studies Reader*, *eds.* Murray Forman and Mark Anthony Neal, (New York:
Routledge, 2004), 311–323.

55 Justo Faison, dir., *The Mixtape Documentary* [Film] (2005), and William Bell, dir.,
Mixtape, Inc. [Film] (Pixel Propaganda: 2006).

56 Recently introduced legislation may have a positive impact on the status of low-

power radio. The "Local Community Radio Act of 2009" would, in part, respond to findings of the Federal Communications Commission (FCC) that describe the negative impact on local communities of media consolidation. Reponses would include opening more broadcast licenses to low-power radio operators in urban areas. Follow this bill online at: http://thomas.loc.gov/cgi-bin/query/z?c111:H.R.1147.

57 According to a recent "Home Broadband Adoption 2009" report from the Pew Research Center, "Data released earlier this year by the Pew Internet and American Life Project found that broadband adoption was at 35 percent among Americans living in households with annual incomes under $20,000. The survey also found that 46 percent of blacks had broadband at home, while the home adoption rate among the adult population in general was 63 percent." Available online at: http://www.pewinternet.org/Reports/2009/10-Home-Broadband-Adoption-2009.aspx?r=1. For more details, see Shireen Mitchell discussing the issue of the digital divide, or lack of Internet access for impoverished communities. Available online at: http://www.freepress.net/node/38188.

58 Joe Torres, "Will Obama Abandon the Open Internet?" *HuffingtonPost.com*, June 23, 2010. Available online at: http://www.huffingtonpost.com/joe-torres/will-president-obamaaban_b_623148.html.

59 Peter Whoriskey, "Giant of Internet Radio Nears Its 'Last Stand': Pandora, Other Webcasters Struggle Under High Song Fees," *The Washington Post*, August 16, 2008.

60 Jared A. Ball, "Save the Internet, But Start a Social Movement," *BlackAgendaReport.com*, April 14, 2010.

61 Jared A. Ball, "The Titans of Technology: The Internet, Radio and *Our* Newton's Laws," *BlackAgendaReport.com*, February 24, 2010. Available online at: http://www.blackagendareport.com/?q=content/titans-technology-internet-radio-and-our-newton%E2%80%99s-laws.

62 Newton, "The Technology Question," 257.

63 Compare and contrast how *FreeMix Radio* is situated legally to the discussion and repression of mixtape vendors and the legal arguments surrounding low-power FM. This is also not to say that there need be any particular or healthy respect for such unjust laws that in the end are established to maintain this process of colonization.

64 For a broader overview of this concept's history and use, see R. Scott Heath, "True Heads: Historicizing the Hip-Hop 'Nation' in Context," *Callaloo*, vol. 29, no. 3, Summer 2006, 846–866, 849.

65 Edward Said, *Culture and Imperialism* (New York: Vintage Books, 1994), 9.

66 Jack O'Dell quoted in Allen, *Black Awakening in Capitalist America*, 8, original emphasis.

67 Sandoval, *Methodology of the Oppressed*, 164, emphasis added.

68 Marshall McLuhan quoted in Kevin McMahon, dir., *McLuhan's Wake* [Film]

(National Film Board of Canada, 2002).

69 R. Scott Heath, "True Heads: Historicizing the Hip-Hop 'Nation' in Context," 849.

70 Derrick Bell, "Great Expectations: Defining the Divide Between Blacks and Jews," in *Strangers and Neighbors: Relations Between Blacks and Jews in the United States*, eds. Maurianne Adams and John H. Bracey (Amherst: University of Massachusetts, 1999), 806.

71 Ronald Walters, *White Nationalism, Black Interests: Conservative Public Policy and the Black Community* (Detroit: Wayne State University, 2003), 23, emphasis added.

72 Memmi, *The Colonizer and the Colonized*.

73 Robert McChesney, Interview with Economist Michael Perelman on *Media Matters with Bob McChesney*, WILL 580 AM Radio, Urbana-Champaign, July 20, 2008. Available online at: http://will.illinois.edu/mediamatters/show/july-20-2008/.

74 Bill Moyers, Interview with James Cone on *Bill Moyers Journal*, Public Broadcasting System, November 23, 2007. Available online at: http://www.pbs.org/moyers/journal/11232007/profile.html.

75 Angela Davis, *Are Prisons Obsolete?* (Boston: Seven Stories Press, 2003) and Nancy A. Heitzeg, "Visiting a Modern-Day Slave Plantation," *Truthout.org*, February 22, 2010. Available online at: http://www.truthout.org/visiting-a-modern-day-slave-plantation57098.

76 William K. Tabb, *The Political Economy of the Black Ghetto* (New York: W.W. Norton, 1970).

77 Aaron Levine, "Ogletree Highlights King Weekend Celebration," *The Chronicle*, June 20, 2004. Available online at: http://dukechronicle.com/article/ogletree-highlights-king-weekend-celebrations.

78 Algernon Austin, "What Recession Means for Black America," *Economic Policy Institute*, January 2008. Available online at: http://www.epi.org/publications/entry/ib241/.

79 Said, *Culture and Imperialism*, 282, emphasis added.

80 Gilbert G. Gonzalez, "A Critique of the Internal Colony Model," *Latin American Perspectives*, vol. 1, no. 1, 1974, 154–160.

81 Ernest Gellner, *Nations and Nationalism* (Ithaca, N.Y.: Cornell University, 1983), 6–7.

82 Katherin Verdery, "Whither 'Nation' and 'Nationalism'?" *Daedalus*, vol. 122, no. 3, 1993, 37–46.

83 Phillip L. Kohl, "Nationalism and Archaeology: On the Constructions of Nations and the Reconstruction of the Remote Past," *Annual Review of Anthropology* 27, 1998, 223–246.

84 A new book from KRS-One discussed in Jared A. Ball, "May Day and Hip-Hop Nationalism," *BlackAgendaReport.com*, May 5, 2010. Available online at: http://www.blackagendareport.com/?q=content/may-day-and-hip-hop-nationalism.

85 Marimba Ani, *Yurugu: An African-Centered Critique of European Cultural Thought and Behavior* (Trenton, N.J.: Africa World Press, 1994), 22–23.

86 See, for example, "On the Streets of Algeria, Palestine, and Egypt: Pan-African and Pan-Islamic Hip-Hop Cultural Movement," in James Spady, Charles G. Lee, and H. S. Alim, *Street Conscious Rap* (Philadelphia: Black History Museum Umum/ Loh Publishers, 1999), 17. The authors detail how colonized people around the globe routinely use hip-hop to express their anti-colonial hatred and are with equal consistency condemned for it.

87 Charise Cheney, *Brothers Gonna Work It Out: Sexual Politics in the Golden Age of Rap Nationalism* (New York: NYU Press, 2005), 14–15.

88 Cheney, *Brothers Gonna Work It Out...*, 18.

89 George Lipsitz, *Dangerous Crossroads: Popular Music, Postmodernism and the Poetics of Place* (London: Verso, 1994).

90 Joseph D. Eure and James G. Spady, *Nation Conscious Rap* (New York: PC International Press, 1991), 159.

91 Eure and Spady, *Nation Conscious Rap*, 162.

92 Memmi, *The Colonizer and the Colonized*.

93 Frantz Fanon, *A Dying Colonialism* (New York: Grove Press, 1959), 71.

94 Greg Tate quoted in Jeff Chang, *Total Chaos: The Art and Aesthetics of Hip-Hop*, 36.

95 James Spady, Charles G. Lee, and H.S. Alim, *Street Conscious Rap* (Philadelphia: Black History Museum Umum/Loh Publishers, 1999), xvii, original emphasis.

96 M. K. Asante, *It's Bigger Than Hip-Hop: The Rise of the Post-Hip-Hop Generation* (New York: St. Martin's Press, 2008), 249–251, 259, original emphasis.

97 Chris Simpson, "U.S. Mass Communication Research, Counterinsurgency, and Scientific 'Reality,'" in *Ruthless Criticism: New Perspectives in U.S. Communication History*, eds. William S. Solomon and Robert W. McChesney (Minneapolis: University of Minnesota, 1993). Simpson also expressed agreement in the application of an internal colonial model to African America and the similar application of mass media against them as such. This was expressed via personal communication with the author in July 2009.

98 Sandoval, *Methodology of the Oppressed*, 3.

99 John Brenkman quoted in John O. Calmore, "Critical Race Theory, Archie Schepp, and Fire Music: Securing An Authentic Intellectual Life in a Multicultural World," in *Critical Race Theory: The Key Writings That Formed the Movement*, eds. Kimberle Crenshaw, Neil Gotanda, Gary Peller, Kendall Thomas (New York: New Press, 1995), 319.

100 Walter Lippmann, *Public Opinion* (New York: Free Press, 1997), 63, emphasis added as the "our" is meant by Lippmann to represent the White male power elite.

101 James Baldwin, *Notes of Native Son* (Boston: Beacon Press, 1955), 146.

102 Norman Kelley, *R&B, Rhythm and Business: The Political Economy of Black Music* (New York: Akashic Books, 2005), xv.

103 Hear a variety of scholars and activists discuss the continued relevance of internal colonialism theory during a tribute to the fortieth anniversary of Robert Allen's *Black Awakening in Capitalist America*, which remains seminal in its application of a model of internal neo-colonialism (April 10, 2009 at UC Berkeley). Available online at: http://www.voxunion.com/?p=1089.

104 Peter Calvert, "Internal Colonisation, Development and Environment," *Third World Quarterly*, vol. 22, no. 1, February 2001, 51–63.

105 Martin R. Delany, *Condition, Elevation, Emigration and Destiny of the Colored People of the United States* (1852), 12–13, emphasis added.

106 For example, George Soros has said that "the United States cannot do whatever it wants but nothing can happen unless it says so," in George Soros, *George Soros on Globalization* (New York: Perseus Books, 2002), 150. See also Noam Chomsky's discussion of empire in his "Authors @ Google" lecture, April 25, 2008. Available online at: http://blogoscoped.com/archive/2008-05-12-n55.html.

107 For more on this concept and its broader context and meaning, see also Besenia Rodriguez, "Long Live Third World Unity! Long Live Internationalism: Huey P. Newton's Revolutionary Intercommunalism," *Souls*, vol. 8, no. 3, 2006, 119–141.

108 See also *The Nation* forum on an evolving, malleable capitalism where this is discussed by, for example, Tariq Ali in his "Capitalism's Deadly Logic," March 4, 2009. Available online at: http://www.thenation.com/doc/20090323/ali.

109 "In order to be classified as a (neo)colony, he contended, a territory must have the capacity to return to its former state. 'What happens when the raw materials are extracted and labor is exploited within a territory dispersed over the entire globe?' Newton asked rhetorically. 'When the riches of the whole earth are depleted and used to feed a gigantic industrial machine in the imperialist's home?' 'The people and the economy are so integrated into the imperialist empire that it's impossible to 'decolonize,' to return to the former conditions of existence,' he explained. If colonies cannot 'return to their original existence as nations,' Newton contended, 'then nations no longer exist.... And since there must be nations for revolutionary nationalism or internationalism to make sense... we say that the world today is a dispersed collection of communities.' Newton defined a community as a small entity with a collection of institutions that exist in order to serve a small group of people. The global struggle, according to Newton's analysis, is between the small clique of individuals—and its ruling police force—that 'administers and profits from the empire of the United States, and the peoples of the world who want to determine their own destinies.' He termed the current age, in which a ruling circle uses technology to controls all other people, is reactionary intercommunalism."

Rodriguez, "Long Live Third World Unity! Long Live Internationalism," 119–141.

110 However, by "decline," I by no means intend to suggest that this speaks to some improved condition. The decline of the U.S. as empire does not promise that a new and improved system is on the rise.

111 Jared A. Ball, "The Titans of Technology."

112 Newton, "The Technology Question," 256.

113 For those interested in more of the social-science heavy-lifting that explains how the Internet is *not* giving "voice to the voiceless," the work of Matthew Hindman should suffice, *The Myth of Digital Democracy* (Princeton, N.J.: Princeton University, 2008. People can also use the Internet to see him, and others, speaking at Stanford University during a panel session titled "New Media and Political Communication." Available online at: http://www.youtube.com/watch?v=y6l5QGuHqOY&feature=related.

114 Besenia Rodriguez, "Long Live Third World Unity! Long Live Internationalism," 119–141, 132, emphasis added.

115 Ibid, 133.

116 The conference proceedings and presentations can all be heard online at: http://www.voxunion.com/?p=1089.

117 Stokely Carmichael and Charles V. Hamilton, *Black Power: The Politics of Liberation* (New York: Dimensions Books, 1967). Charles Pinderhughes, while arguing that there are multiple colonies held in various parts throughout the United States, as opposed to one Black nation, he continues to note the fundamentality of these communities being distinct spatially, ethnically, racially, and so on, and ruled from the outside. Available online at: http://www.voxunion.com/?p=1089.

118 Ahmad A. Rahman, *The Regime Change of Kwame Nkrumah* (New York: Palgrave Macmillan, 2007), 12.

119 This does not mean to dismiss the ways in which hip-hop has become a vehicle for educational or pedagogical improvement as exemplified in the work of Words. Beats. Life., Inc.'s Saturday Academy, or *Journal of Hip-Hop and Global Culture*, or *The Hip-Hop Education Guidebook* from Marcella Runnell and Martha Diaz or the Hip-Hop Educational Literacy Program (H.E.L.P.) from Gabriel "Asheru" Benn. The point here, however, is that neither the institution of education nor its function have been altered. These efforts struggle against a system described below that continues to function successfully.

120 Not even the election of a Black president changes this. For more, see Jared A. Ball, "Barack Obama, 'Connected Distance,' Race and 21st Century Neo-Colonialism."

121 Of course, Walter Rodney's discussion of this remains essential. *How Europe Underdeveloped Africa* (Washington, D.C.: Howard University, 1972).

122 Ollie A. Johnson, III, "Locating Blacks in Brazilian Politics: Afro-Brazilian Activism,

New Political Parties, and Pro-Black Public Policies," *International Journal of Africana Studies*, vol. 12, no. 2, 2006, 170–193, 172, original emphasis. Johnson argues that this view "obscure[s]" Afro-Brazilian activism and I do not mean to argue that particular point. I am only seeking to emphasize what are seen as strategies of blunting activism by colonial powers and noting a similarity in strategies deployed by the Brazilian and U.S. power elite.

123 Frantz Fanon, *Toward the African Revolution*, 34.

124 Ward Churchill, "The Fourth World: Struggles for Traditional Lands and Ways of Life," *Left Turn*, June 16, 2007. "The Third Worldist formulation was afflicted from the outset by many deficiencies. Insufficient weight was placed upon the prospect that the extent of colonialism's often protracted underdevelopment of the Third World might have created structural conditions within the newly independent countries that would leave them virtually defenseless against 'neocolonialist' exploitation by their former colonizers. Nor—despite the warnings implicit to pioneering studies undertaken by Fanon, Memmi, and others—was the virulence and intractability of the psychological maiming inflicted upon those subjugated under colonialism's genocidal yoke ever truly taken into account." And further: "Thus, while 'liberation' was seen by Third Worldists as the transformation of Europe's overseas colonies into states independently governed by their former subjects, the subjects themselves often envisioned it in dramatically different terms, i.e.: the restoration of control over their traditional territory to each of the peoples encompassed within colonial boundaries and, on that basis, resumption of their self-determining modes of governance, social organization, and economy. In substance, these indigenous peoples—nations, actually—comprised a 'Fourth World,' unmentioned by Mao, upon the expropriation of whose lands and resources all states depend for their very existence."

125 Dr. Alex Pietersie, personal communication with the author, July 6, 2008.

126 Hence the centuries-old discussions of "Manifest Destiny," "White man's burden," "assimilation," "integration," and "being American."

127 Fanon, *Toward the African Revolution*.

128 Naomi Klein, *The Shock Doctrine*.

129 Donald Spivey, *Schooling for the New Slavery: Black Industrial Education, 1868–1915* (Wesport: Greenwood Press, 1978), ix.

130 Ward Churchill, *Kill the Indian and Save the Man: The Genocidal Impact of American Indian Residential Schools* (San Francisco: City Lights, 2004).

131 David Levering Lewis, *W.E.B. DuBois: A Reader* (New York: Henry Holt and Company, 1995), 677. Note also that he was *not* talking about Black America though he would eventually, and though the description is indeed fully analogous.

132 From "Colonies, Democracy and Peace After the War," in *Against Racism: Unpublished*

Essays, Papers, Addresses 1887–1961, ed. Herbert Aptheker (Boston: University of Massachusetts, 1985), 229–252. For a much more in-depth look at DuBois, colonialism, and Black radical theory, see the work of Dr. Reiland Rabaka, who can be heard discussing his work on the subject in our "Jazz and Justice" interview conducted on November 2, 2009. Available online at: http://www.voxunion. com/?p=1902.

133 Michelle Alexander, *The New Jim Crow: Mass Incarceration in the Age of Colorblindness* (New York: New Press, 2009). Alexander details conditions of mass incarceration that lead there to being more Black people in prison in the United States now than in pre-Mandela-release apartheid South Africa. See also United for a Fair Economy reports from 2004 to 2008 and National Urban League (Clemens, 2005).

134 Dedrick Muhammad, Attieno Davis, Meizhu Lui, Betsy Leondar-Wright, *The State of the Dream 2004: Enduring Disparities in Black and White* (Boston: United for a Fair Economy, 2004). See also the nearly annual reports subsequent to this one that continue to show similar disparities in these and many other indicators including health care and housing.

135 Austin, "What Recession Means for Black America." See also Chris McGreal, "A $95,000 Question: Why Are Whites Five Times Richer than Blacks in the U.S.?" *The Guardian,* May 17, 2010. Available online at: http://www.guardian.co.uk/ world/2010/may/17/white-people-95000-richer-black. The article describes the recent report from Brandeis University whose conclusion is that the gap in wealth between Black and White Americans has worsened over the last twenty-five years.

136 The more than $200 billion loss for Black America has been called the "greatest loss of wealth for people of color" by United For a Fair Economy, January 2008. Available online at: http://www.faireconomy.org/news/subprime_lending_causes_greatest_ loss_of_wealth_for_people_of_color_in_modern_history.

137 See, for instance, Jill Nelson's *Police Brutality: An Anthology* (New York: W.W. Norton, 2000).

138 Jared A. Ball, "Et Tu, Michael Eric Dyson? Fraternizing with the Devil," *BlackCommentator.com,* March 26, 2006. Available online at: http://www. blackcommentator.com/175/175_dyson_ball_guest. This critique of the then-newly developing Radio One syndicated talk show featuring Michael Eric Dyson and his routine friendly discussions with John McWhorter focuses on the role of think tanks, specially placed "pundits" and their societal function related to poisoning and limiting debate. This also should be put in the context of national use of propaganda as a means of creating and spreading a national will or "public opinion." See, for example, the work of George Creel, Walter Lippmann, and Edward Bernays. Propaganda has always been used and is, in fact, a (the) primary component or foundation of the field of mass communications itself. For more,

see Chris Simpson's *Science of Coercion* (New York: Oxford University, 1994) and Everett Rogers, *A History of Communication Study* (New York: Free Press, 1994).

139 Greg Carr on MSNBC's "Conversation About Race," July 2, 2008. Available online at: http://www.voxunion.com/?p=73.

140 The John McWhorter-styled argument in which too often "the overall [historical] message is a grim saga of victimization. This kind of history is deeply damaging to Blacks." Oppression doesn't cause as much damage as the telling of it seems to. Quoted from "Toward a Usable Black History," *City Journal,* Summer 2001. Available online at: http://www.city-journal.org/html/11_3_toward_a_usable. html.

141 See, for example, Steven Pimpare, author of *A People's History of Poverty in America* (New York: New Press, 2008), discuss this particular point on his website. Available at: http://web.me.com/stephenpimpare/webpage/Interviews.html.

142 First president of "independent" Ghana (1957), one-time member of the Harlem History Club and underappreciated by many as a result of what Kevin Gaines has well argued were "concerted diplomatic, economic, and political U.S. government strategies for 'containment' of Ghana's influence in world affairs" (139). Kevin Gaines, "The Cold War and the African American Expatriate Community in Nkrumah's Ghana," in *Universities and Empires: Money and Politics in the Social Sciences During the Cold War,* ed. Chris Simpson (New York: New Press, 1998). This was part of what Gaines describes as the fear inspired within empire that Ghana's freedom and pan-Africanist tendencies were a threat not only on the continent of Africa but also within the diaspora and the African American population in the United States. Their goal was to prevent the application of such theoretical approaches in those communities.

143 "Letter from Engels to J. Bloch, London, 21–22 September 1890," quoted in Kwame Nkrumah, *Consciencism: Philosophy and Ideology for De-Colonization* (London: Thomas Nelson and Sons, 1964), 1.

144 Nkrumah, *Consciencism,* 72.

145 Robert L. Allen, "Reassessing the Internal (Neo) Colonialism Theory" in *The Black Scholar,* vol. 35, no. 1, 2006. Allen here, in part building on his earlier work, *Black Awakenings in Capitalist America* (Trenton, N.J.: Africa World Press, 1969), reasserts the value of a colonialism model of analysis. Two points most related to this current work are that the American South-applied "direct rule" and the North "indirect neocolonialism," defined in part by the encouraged growth of a Black "middle-class… buffer" group who would be the face of rule over the domestic colony. This neo-colonial class division among the colonized plays out to this day within African and Latin American communities where, according to the Pew Research Center, "the wealthiest 25 percent of households own over 90 percent of the total wealth in

the Hispanic and Black communities" (Rakesh Kochhar, "The Wealth of Hispanic Household: 1996–2002," *The Pew Hispanic Center*. October, 18, 2004. Available online at: http://pewhispanic.org/reports/report.php?ReportID=34). Allen goes on, "Significantly, in the era of globalization, a group of Latin American scholars and activists has developed a concept that links what is happening in many 'third world' countries to what is happening to 'third world' peoples in the U.S. Anibal Quijano, Walter Mignolo, and most recently Ramon Grosfoguel have elaborated the concept of 'coloniality' of power, by which is meant the continuation of the colonial relationship without the formal colonial administration (Grosfoguel). They argue that the granting of independence by a colonial power does not mean decolonization; rather, the colonial relationship continues through economic and cultural domination and the dependence on imperialism of the native bourgeoisie. As Grosfoguel has remarked, there is no 'post' in colonialism" (10).

146 See also Norm Stamper, *Breaking Rank: A Top Cop's Expose of the Dark Side of American Policing* (New York: Nation Books, 2006) for his discussion of White "fear" of Black men (in particular) and the militarized police force that sees these African communities as just that—African communities—and as such a threat from a foreign sub-human colony.

147 It is important to note that slavery in the United States remains perfectly legal. The 13th Amendment reads clearly: "Section 1. Neither slavery nor involuntary servitude, *except as a punishment for crime* whereof the party shall have been duly convicted, shall exist within the United States, or any place subject to their jurisdiction. Section 2. Congress shall have power to enforce this article by appropriate legislation" (emphasis added). For more on this history and the continuities of slavery in modern-day imprisonment, see the works of Adrienne Davis, Angela Davis, Derrick Bell and Kimberle Crenshaw, Ruth Wilson Gilmore, Larry Bobo, Glen Loury, and Malik Russell. In fact, Larry Bobo has described mass incarceration as a part of a historic "strategy of removal," where "free Blacks" who threatened the social order of Black inferiority had to be removed from that society. He goes on to describe the prison industry as creating a series of "internal colonies" throughout the United States. See the 2007 Tanner Lecture Series "Racial Stigma, Mass Incarceration, and American Values" by Stanford University.

148 Jawanza Kunjufu, *Black Economics: Solutions for Economic and Community Empowerment* (Chicago: African American Images, 2002). Kunjufu does connect these statistics to the conditions of internal colonization.

149 See Derrick Bell, *Silent Covenants: Brown v. Board of Education and the Unfulfilled Hopes for Racial Reform* (New York: Oxford University, 2004). See also more recently *Democracy Now!* (January 16, 2009) for a report on continued school segregation rates that rival those of the 1950s.

150 "The psychological occupation of Black America by White America is an ongoing phenomenon resulting, in large measure, from the mechanism of cultural repression which permeates the institution of education in the American system of internal colonialism, whereby Black America exists as a domestic colony of White America." Pansye Atkinson, *Brown vs. Topeka: Desegregation and Miseducation: An African American's View* (New York: African American Images, 1993), 3. See also Jonathan Kozol, who calls it "the cognitive decapitation of inner-city children. We're locking them out of the competition for empowerment from the very beginning." Retrieved April 5, 2010 from: http://www.campusprogress.org/features/552/five-minutes-with-jonathan-kozol.

151 "The United States boasts of being one of the most culturally diverse nations in the modern world yet it is also one of the most socially segmented. In fact, in a recent report by the Milton S. Eisenhower Foundation (1998), *it was discovered that our nation is parallel to the state of the nation in 1968*. At that time, the National Advisory Council on Civil Disorders (otherwise known as the Kerner Commission) released its report stating, "Our nation is moving toward two societies, one Black, one White, separate, hostile and unequal"Quoted in "White Student Confessions About a Black Male Professor: A Cultural Contracts Theory Approach to Intimate Conversations About Race and Worldview," *Journal of Men's Studies*, vol. 12, no. 1, September 2003, 25, emphasis added.

152 Jonathan Kozol, *Shame of the Nation* (New York: HarperCollins, 2005), 153. Mark Achbar, dir., *Manufacturing Consent: Noam Chomsky and the Media* [Film], (Necessary Illusions Productions, 1992).

154 See again, for example, Pimpare's discussion at at: http://web.me.com/stephenpimpare/webpage/Interviews.html.

155 Stacy Peralta, dir., *Crips and Bloods: Made in America* [Film] (Gang Documentary, 2008).

156 Edward Bernays, *Propaganda* (Brooklyn: IG Publishing, 1928/2005).

157 C. Wright Mills, *The Power Elite.*

158 Jamie Johnson, dir., *The One Percent*, [Film] (HBO Documentary Films, 2006).

159 Kevin Phillips, *Wealth and Democracy*, xiii.

160 Raj Patel, interviewed by *Democracy Now!* July 31, 2008. Available online at: http://www.democracynow.org/2008/7/31/raj_patel_on_the_collapse_of.

161 Jamie Johnson, dir., *Born Rich*, [Film] (HBO Documentary Films, 2003).

162 Michael Parenti, *Democracy for the Few* (Boston: Bedford/St. Martin's Press, 2002), 9.

163 Interview with economist Michael Perelman *on Media Matters with Bob McChesney*, WILL AM 580 Radio, Urbana-Champaign, Ill. July 20, 2008. Retrieved from: http://will.illinois.edu/mediamatters/show/july-20–2008/.

164 Maude Barlow, "The World Has Divided into Rich and Poor as at No Time in

History," *DemocracyNow.org*. A speech made at the G–20 summit in Toronto, Canada, July 2, 2010, emphasis added. Available online at: http://www. democracynow.org/2010/7/2/maude. We would only argue that this is no "new wave of colonialism," but part of a process never ended.

165 Parenti, *Democracy for the Few*, 11.

166 Noam Chomsky, *Rogue States: The Rule of Force in World Affairs* (Boston: South End Press, 2000). Available online at: http://www.thirdworldtraveler.com/Chomsky/ SocioSovereign_RSChom.html. By this, Chomsky means an elite whose daily, hourly, and by-the-minute investment decisions act like referenda on national policies, even those determined by democratic vote. That is, should this elite not like the direction taken by any given nation, it can simply withhold investment or place it elsewhere, thereby putting strangleholds on states deemed out of line.

167 Kevin Phillips, *Wealth and Democracy*, xv.

168 Ibid., xvii.

169 Ibid., xix.

170 Joseph Salerno in Murray N. Rothbard, *A History of Money and Banking in the United States: The Colonial Era to World War II* (Auburn: Ludwig von Mises Institute, 2005), xxx, emphasis added. This not to say that we agree with all that Salerno or the Austrian School of economic theory has to offer. However, we mean only to demonstrate the ways in which varying perspectives can acknowledge some fundamental aspects of state power and economic order. The point here is also to raise a critical view of the state.

171 Walters, *White Nationalism and Black Interests*. Walters describes a history of this nation that has been about the consolidation of power among a White elite whose expressed goals dating as far back as the mid-nineteenth century included the effectuation of a "racial purification" by carefully limiting (if not removing altogether) Black populations geographically in a fashion that concludes today with the aforementioned spatial separateness, gentrification. Elliot Jaspin, *Buried in the Bitter Waters: The Hidden History of Racial Cleansing in America* (New York: Basic Books, 2007). Walters also details how "gains" accrued during the Civil Rights struggles have benefited White Americans more than African or others.

172 Derrick Bell, "Great Expectations: Defining the Divide between Blacks and Jews," 806.

173 Where of course then we must ignore the highly anti-colonial question of George Jackson: "What is an honest election after the fact of monopoly capital?" *Blood In My Eye* (Baltimore: Black Classic Press, 1990), 28.

174 Žižek, *In Defense of Lost Causes*, 5–7. Whereas Žižek sees this as a struggle between those "public intellectuals" who would choose safer arguments careful to avoid those around the "dictatorship of the proletariat" or "revolutionary state terror," here the

limits of his Eurocentrism are extended to include colonialism or anti-colonial struggle as primary "lost causes," those which "public sphere" scholars avoid.

175 Sandoval, *Methodology of the Oppressed*, 2000.

176 Tabb, *The Political Economy of the Black Ghetto*, 3.

177 Fanon, *Toward the African Revolution*, 40, emphasis added. And hence, for example, the conclusions reached by the United Nations Special Rapportuer, which included the continued prevalence and pervasiveness of racism in the U.S. "U.N. Expert Calls on U.S. to Address Ongoing Issues of Racism: Special Rapporteur Presents Findings Before U.N. Human Rights Council," *American Civil Liberties Union* report, June 17, 2009. Available online at: http://yubanet.com/usa/U-N-Expert-Calls-On-U-S-To-Address-Ongoing-Issues-Of-Racism2.php. And hear the Special Rapporteur deliver his findings (June 6, 2008) online at: http://www.voxunion.com/?p=65.

178 Fanon, *Toward the African Revolution*, 37, emphasis added.

179 United Nations General Assembly Resolution, 1987. Quoted in Noam Chomsky, *Letters from Lexington: Reflections on Propaganda* (Monroe, Maine: Common Courage, 1993), 44.

180 Including the tendency in hip-hop and media studies to refer to one or another aspect of people's lives as being "colonized" without this or the *primacy of colonialism* itself ever being the foundation of that particular intellectual enterprise.

181 Examples include Fanon, *Toward the African Revolution*; Memmi, *The Colonizer and the Colonized*; Carmichael and Hamilton, *Black Power*; Allen, *Black Awakening in Capitalist America*; Kofsky, *Black Nationalism and the Revolution in Music*; Tabb, *The Political Economy of the Black Ghetto*; Blauner, *Racial Oppression in America*; Cabral, *Return to the Source*; Turner; Atkinson, *Brown vs. Topeka*; Barker, et al.; Kunjufu, *Black Economics*.

182 Tim Lake, "Postcolonial Theory and the African American Experience," *The Journal of Pan African Studies*, vol. 1, no. 10, November 2007, 2/80.

183 Bob Blauner, *Racial Oppression in America* (New York: HarperCollins, 1972), 12, emphasis added.

184 Tom Engelhardt, "The Cartography of Death," *The Nation,* October 5, 2000. The main point of this article is that much of the violence that appears in the so-called "Third World" is actually the result of Western imperialism as it spreads throughout the world. I simply would extend this thesis back into the U.S. and place much of the blame for the violence and crime of the internal "Third World" on their colonized status: lack of jobs, resources, space, privacy, etc.

185 The majority of the people in this nation and world are women, poor, and so-called "people of color," reminding us that *the only true minority* are elite White men.

186 Marshall McLuhan, *Understanding the Media: The Extensions of Man* (New York: McGraw-Hill, 1964), 29. See also the first several chapters of Zinn's *A People's History*

of the United States (New York: Harper Perennial, 1999). And, of course, Michael Moore depicts this concept in Bush's statements of preferring a "dictatorship" in *Fahrenheit 911* (Lion's Gate, 2004).

187 Parenti, *Democracy for the Few,* 43. Similarly, Baran and Sweezy explain that "the Civil War was not fought by the Northern ruling class to free the slaves, as many mistakenly believe. It was fought to check the ambitions of the Southern *slave-owning oligarchy,* which wanted to escape from what was essentially a *colonial relation* to Northern capital. The abolition of slavery was a by-product not its purpose, and Northern capitalism had no intention... of liberating the Negro in any meaningful sense." Paul Baran and Paul Sweezy, *Monopoly Capital: An Essay on the American Economic and Social Order* (New York: Monthly Review, 1966), 252, emphasis added.

188 Zinn *A People's History of the United States,* 98.

189 Cedric Robinson, *Black Marxism: The Making of the Black Radical Tradition* (Chapel Hill, N.C.: University of North Carolina, 1983), 186. The development of "nation-states and political reigns precipitate the development of founding myths—myths of origins in the language of anthropologists." That is, they are essential and common to all with the impact varying dependent upon the particular positioning within the colonial pyramid.

190 Who, as John Jay wrote in his *Federalist Paper #2,* had the divine "providence" bestowed upon "one united people—a people descended from the same ancestors." Clinton Rossiter, *The Federalist Papers* (New York: Penguin Books, 1961), 38. His intent clearly was to forever associate this with and as a nation for a White elite.

191 Words of James Madison in his *Federalist Paper #10,* also in Rossiter (84). Madison also preferred republicanism due to its imperial openness and extension of elite influence over a greater distance or territory.

192 Noam Chomsky, *Failed States* (New York: Metropolitan Books, 2000), 215–216, where the Trilateral Commission saw and sees this "crisis of democracy" as "even more dangerous by the components of the elite spectrum to the right of the commission and by the business world in general."

193 Parenti, *Democracy for the Few.*

194 Glen Ford, "Study Shows Blacks Will NEVER Gain Wealth Parity With Whites Under the Current System," *BlackAgendaReport.com,* May 19, 2010.

195 Bernays, *Propaganda.*

196 Laurence Shoup, quoted in Paul Street, *Barack Obama and the Future of American Politics* (Boulder, Co.: Paradigm Publishers, 2008), ix.

197 Noam Chomsky, "What Next? The Elections, the Economy, and the World," *Democracy Now!,* November 24, 2008. Available online at: http://www.democracynow.org/2008/11/24/noam_chomsky_what_next_the_elections.

198 Thomas Ferguson, *The Golden Rule: The Investment Theory of Politics* (Chicago: University of Chicago, 1995).

199 Greg Palast, *The Best Democracy Money Can Buy* (London: Pluto Press, 2002).

200 Blauner, *Racial Oppression in America*, 12, emphasis added.

201 Carmichael and Hamilton, *Black Power*.

202 Eric Williams explains in *Capitalism and Slavery* (Chapel Hill, N.C.: University of North Carolina, 1994) the use of colonies as either places for resettlement, as in the North American colonies, or as suppliers of raw materials and natural resources, as in the islands of the Caribbean (4). He also further explains Rhodes' concerns by showing how "two-thirds of the immigrants to Pennsylvania during the eighteenth century were White servants" and how "convicts provided another steady source of White labor" (10–11). The need to secure colonies and rid homelands of excess population led to the establishment of severe "transportation" laws. Initially feudal England had over 300 crimes punishable by hanging and by 1745 shipment to the colonies was sentence for crimes as low as "the theft of a silver spoon and a gold watch" (11–12). Massive importation of these "convicted criminals" from England led Benjamin Franklin to lament the reception of "outcasts from the Old [World]," suggesting that the colonies in the "New" return the favor by shipping "rattlesnakes" back to England (12). But as Williams reminds us, the "great increase of indentured servants and free emigrants would have tended to render the convict influence innocuous, as increasing quantities of water poured in a glass containing poison" (12). And few saw the negative as did Franklin. The vast majority of the elite recognized the need for the cheap labor and the wealth (i.e. power) that would be incurred as a result (12). It is this recognition that would lead Lenin to note the fact that by the end of the nineteenth century, "all the free territory of the globe, with the exception of China, [had] been occupied by the powers of Europe and North America" (86). Among the reasons for this vast spread of European and North American capital investment (or economic control) was that "in the colonial market it is easier to eliminate competition" because, there, opportunities for "monopoly" control over labor-pools and natural resources were possible (84). There was no greater way to gain so much. The trade of enslaved Africans was the initial builder of Western European power. Their way of maintaining such power and remaining in the intra-European competition was and is through colonies. According to John Henrik Clarke and Flora S. Lugard, "Lady Lugard" was, before becoming wife to the man responsible for establishing colonial rule over Britain's territories, "one of the first female journalists" and "a supporter of empire [who] went out to the British-governed protectorate that would later become Nigeria to write a series of articles in defense of the British takeover of this territory" (Lugard, 1906/1997, i). She later wrote in her book *A Tropical Dependency* (1906/1997) of the "diverse" nature of

empire. Explaining, again, the need of colonies for the accumulation of wealth and power beyond the scope of one's immediate society, she begins, "It has become the habit of the British mind to think of the British Empire as a White empire. But, as a matter of fact, we all know that ours is not a White empire." This is not to say that White supremacy was any less important at the time of her writing in 1906. She was simply explaining the need for a White elite to project its interests onto others in order to attain and maintain inordinate wealth and power. She continues, "Out of an estimated population of 413,000,000, only 52,000,000 or one in eight are White" (1). In other words, once one accounted for all the people in British-held Africa and India—seven out of eight people—whose exploitation was essential to British wealth and dominance, the empire was awfully "diverse."

203 Adam Smith, *Wealth of Nations* (Amherst: Prometheus Books, 1776/1991); Karl Marx, *Capital* (New York: Penguin, 1976); Williams, *Capitalism and Slavery*; Tabb, *The Political Economy of the Black Ghetto*; Blauner, *Racial Oppression in America*; Kunjufu, *Black Economics*.

204 See, for instance, Eileen Southern, *The Music of Black Americans: A History* (New York: W.W. Norton, 1997).

205 See, for instance, Frank Kofsky, *Black Nationalism and the Revolution in Music* (New York: Pathfinder Press, 1970/1988).

206 See, for example, Jeff Chang's allusion to hip-hop as a new raw material, and even again where he describes "local hip-hop undergrounds" becoming "veins of gold to be exploited," in *Can't Stop, Won't Stop: A History of the Hip-Hop Generation* (New York: St. Martin's Press, 2005), 443.

207 Adam Smith in *Wealth of Nations* was clear about the importance of colonies to historical Europe. For Greece, Smith explained, colonies were meant to rid the country of surplus populations, "when the people in any one [territory] multiplied beyond what the territory easily maintained, a part of them was sent in quest of a new habitation" (414). Of Columbus and his voyage to St. Domingo, Smith further explains the importance of colonies, saying that the "pious purpose of converting [Indigenous People] to Christianity sanctified the injustice of the project," but the search for gold and silver for the crown was the "sole motive" (420).

208 Aimé Césaire, *Discourse on Colonialism* (New York: Monthly Review, 1955/2000), 41–42.

209 V. I. Lenin, *Imperialism: The Highest Stage of Capitalism* (New York: International Publishers, 1939/2000), 79. See Bernard Magubane in *The Making of a Racist State* (Trenton, N.J.: Africa World Press, 1996) for more on Rhodes and his connection to African colonization, the establishment of DeBeers diamond mines, and his goals for world White dominion. He greatly lamented the eighteenth-century split between the U.S. and England, the reunification of which he sought as an absolute

necessity. He planned to contribute to this in his expressed desire to conquer Africa from "the Cape to Cairo" (97–120).

210 Interestingly, Joseph Stiglitz, former chief economist of the World Bank, was forced to retire because of his continued reminders that these basic relationships continue to exist on a heightened and global scale. As he wrote in *Globalization and Its Discontents* (New York: W.W. Norton, 2002), international lending agencies are "pretending to help developing countries by forcing them to open up their markets to the goods of the advanced industrial countries [Mother Countries] while keeping their own markets protected, policies that make the rich richer and the poor more impoverished" (xv). Further, John Perkins has written recently in *Confessions of an Economic Hit Man* (New York: Plume, 2004) that his role as such meant that he was part of a group of "highly paid professionals who cheat countries around the globe out of trillions of dollars. They [Economic Hit Men or EHMs] funnel money from the World Bank, the U.S. Agency for International Development (USAID), and other foreign 'aid' organizations into the coffers of huge corporations and the pockets of a few wealthy families who control the planet's natural resources. Their tools include fraudulent financial reports, rigged elections, payoffs, extortion, sex, and murder. They play a game as old as empire, but one that has taken on new and terrifying dimensions during this time of globalization" (ix).

211 Kwame Nkrumah, *Neo-Colonialism: The Last Stage of Imperialism* (London: Thomas Nelson and Sons, 1965).

212 John Perkins, *The Secret History of the American Empire: The Truth About Economic Hit Men, Jackals, and How to Change the World* (New York: Plume, 2008) 223–224. And see Patrick Bond's *Fanon's Warning: A Civil Society Reader On The New Partnership For Africa's Development* (Trenton, N.J.: Africa World Press, 2005) for updates on this process and the use of NEPAD (New Partnership for African Development) to bring it to fruition.

213 Noam Chomsky, *Necessary Illusions: Thought Control in Democratic Societies* (Boston: South End Press, 1989).

214 Charles Mills, *The Racial Contract* (Ithaca, N.Y.: Cornell University, 1997). "*Thus, in matters of race, the Racial Contract prescribes for its signatories an inverted epistemology, an epistemology of ignorance, a particular pattern of localized and global cognitive dysfunctions (which are psychologically and socially functional), producing the ironic outcome that whites will in general be unable to understand the world they themselves have made*" (18, original emphasis).

215 Memmi, *The Colonizer and the Colonized*. "Such is the history of the pyramid of petty tyrants: each one, being socially oppressed by one more powerful than he, always finds a less powerful one on whom to lean, and becomes a tyrant in his turn" (17).

216 Martin Luther King, Jr., *Where Do We Go From Here? Chaos Or Community* (New

York: Harper and Row, 1967). "Negroes have proceeded from a premise that equality means what is says, and they have taken White Americans at their word when they talked of it as an objective. But most Whites in America in 1967, including many persons of goodwill, proceed from a premise that equality is a loose expression for improvement. White America is not even psychologically organized to close the gap—essentially it seeks only to make it less painful and less obvious but in most respects to retain it. Most of the abrasions between Negroes and White liberals arose from this fact" (9).

217 "The great beauty of capitalist production consists in this, that it not only constantly reproduces the wage-laborer as a wage-laborer, but also always produces a relative surplus population of wage-laborers in proportion to the accumulation of capital. Thus the law of supply and demand as applied to labor is kept on the right lines, the oscillation of wages is confined within limits satisfactory to capitalist exploitation, and lastly, the *social dependence* of the worker on the capitalist, which is indispensable, is secured. At home, in the mother country, the smug deceitfulness of the political economist can turn this *relation of absolute dependence* into a free contract between buyer and seller, between equally independent owners of commodities, the owner of the commodity capital on one side, the owner of the commodity labor on the other." Karl Marx, *Capital,* 935, emphasis added.

218 Ibid.

219 Eugene Kamenka, *The Portable Karl Marx* (New York: Penguin Books, 1983), 499–501.

220 Marx explains this by making clear that capital only exists "under circumstances in which they serve at the same time as a means of exploitation and subjection of the laborer" (Kamenka, 495). In other words, money is only valuable based on its ability to affect a social relationship whereby people do what they are told in order to earn it. A dollar bill will not itself build a house. However, it will allow for the purchase of tools and those who will wield them to build. Parenti (*Democracy for the Few*) explains how "wealth is created by the labor power of workers." And quoting Adam Smith, he continues, "Labor… is alone the ultimate real standard by which the value of all commodities can at all times be estimated and compared. It is their real price; money is their nominal price only" (7). More directly related to my immediate topic Marx wrote, "*Capital is not a thing, but a social relation between persons which is mediated through things....* A negro is a negro. In certain relations he becomes a slave. A mule is a machine for spinning cotton. Only in certain relations does it become capital. Outside these circumstances, it is no more capital than gold is intrinsically money, or sugar is the price of sugar.... Capital is a *social relation* of production" (Marx, *Capital*, 932, emphasis added). In fact, it is interesting to note Adam Smith's own description of the history of money altogether (29–35). The development of

coin and money was only intended to create a social relationship where none could previously exist. Prior to the advent of coin and money, people traded based on the barter of tangible items. I need your goat, you need my cow, we switch. If I needed your goat but had nothing in exchange of any value to you, a substitute had to be offered and its value (real or nominal) created in order to facilitate an exchange. As Smith says, "When the division of labor has been once thoroughly established," an individual must rely on the work of others to procure certain items or have certain work accomplished. The individual no longer is self-sufficient" (29). Therefore, coin and money are created, a value attached and a social relationship (for better or worse) ensues. You need work, I need money, I then must behave accordingly; do what I am told to earn what I need. And my power as a worker only exists to the extent that labor is organized and has needs that can be appeased absent the employer. To the extent that it is highly concentrated, and it certainly is, "wealth," as Smith accurately quotes Thomas Hobbes, "is power" (37). This continues as more recently Kevin Phillips has said, "Power and money represent one of the world's enduring covert partnerships" (xix). And in his discussion of *Public Opinion*, or the "manufacture of consent" (158), Walter Lippmann traces this to the origins of this nation. He describes the development of "fiscal measures" by Alexander Hamilton designed to "attach the provincial notables," such as "the gentry, the public creditors, manufacturers, shippers and traders... to the new government." This was necessary, for, according to Lippmann, it is an "inversion of the truth to argue that [Hamilton] made the Union to protect class privileges, instead of saying that he used class privileges to make the Union" (177). So, for instance, the installation of a central banking system was designed, in part, to regulate the wealth or value of money so as to assure that these classes of men would have their consent to a Union manufactured in the same way middle- and upper-class interests today are created out of an allegiance to a society that protects their standing and even insists that they act against those further down the colonial pyramid. It too must be noted that part of the colonizing mission of Europe was to force the colonized to accept the European form of currency. The United States used the American "greenback" to subdue Native Americans. As described by Lame Deer, "the idea of an Indian having to pay for a [license] in order to be allowed to hunt on his own land to feed his own, genuine, red man's belly seemed like a bad joke to me" (*From Outside of Western Civilization, eds.* Eira Patnaik, Gersham Nelson, and Jorn K. Bramann [Frostburg, Md.: G. Austin Nelson Books, 1991], 75). The British, who in Kenya could not afford to kill the very people needed for continued labor, used this method to help subdue that nation. Of course, this was not entirely successful as the Kenyan Land and Freedom Party (inaccurately called "Mau Mau") found this unacceptable.

221 See, for example, the film from Ana Maria Garcia, dir., *La Operación*, (Latin

American Film Project, 1982). This explains how corporations in need of land have encouraged forced sterilization to limit the damages (i.e. revolutionary fervor) caused by their land-theft-inspired overpopulation. That is, rather than provide space and jobs for those whose land and resources they stole, it was felt more profitable and safer to prevent newborns who might grow up angry enough at their poverty and overcrowding from rebelling.

222 (1969/1992), 16.

223 Though this idea of Marx is challenged by the description of his involvement in labor unions and other political organizations by Kurt Krueger, "Principles of Communism and the Communist Manifesto." Speech delivered during the Socialism 2009 Conference in San Francisco, July 2009.

224 Ayi Kwei Armah, "Masks and Marx: The Marxist Ethos Vis-à-Vis African Revolutionary Theory and Praxis," *Presence Africaine* (Dakar, Senegal), 36–64.

225 (1963), 40.

226 Jean-Paul Sartre, *Colonialism and Neocolonialism* (New York: Routledge. 2001), 31.

227 D. McQuail, *McQuail's Mass Communication Theory* (London: Sage Press, 2000), 14.

228 John Downing, "Social Movement Theories and Alternative Media: An Evaluation and Critique," *Communication, Culture & Critique,* International Communication Association, 2008, 40–50, original emphasis.

229 K. McLeish, ed., *Key Ideas in Human Thought* (Rocklin: Prima Publishing, 1995), 459, 207.

230 Walters, *White Nationalism, Black Interests: Conservative Public Policy and the Black Community*, 1.

231 McQuail, 4.

232 Kamenka, 462–463.

233 Greg Tate, ed., *Everything But the Burden* (New York: Broadway Books, 2003), 4.

234 John Downing and Charles Husband, *Representing 'Race': Racisms, Ethnicities and Media* (London: Sage Publications, 2005). They talk about this forcing of race(s) into "distinct categories defined by bi-polar extremes," which forms part of a "mental economy" generated once these core concepts are set to media (2–3).

235 Amos Wilson, *Democracy Now!*-aired speech. Again, this should be seen as a point of departure for any group's relationship to media within a colony. That is not to say that experiences or impacts are universally the same (even within a common group) but that alternate forms of consciousness among any group represent threats to power.

236 Sanchez, quoted in Greg Thomas, "To Make the Revolution Come Quicker: For Sex, Hip-Hop, and Black Radical Tradition (A Riff in Three Movements)," *The Global Journal of Hip-Hop Culture,* The Sex Issue, Words.Beats.Life., Spring 2010.

237 Clifford Geertz, *Interpretation of Cultures* (New York: Basic Books, 1973), 44–45. It

must also be noted that Geertz "worked cheek-by-jowl with men whom many people consider to be *professional terrorists* specializing in the suppression of indigenous democracy" (Simpson, xix, emphasis added). In other words, his work was used to develop U.S. national security strategies involving communication and propaganda.

238 Wade Nobles quoted in Ani, *Yurugu*, 4.

239 Ngugi Wa Thiong'o, *Decolonizing the Mind: The Politics of African Literature* (New Hampshire: Heinemann, 1986), 15.

240 Edward Said, *Culture and Imperialism* (New York: Vintage Books, 1994), xiii, xiv.

241 As described by Dr. Greg Carr during an MSNBC-broadcast discussion of race at Howard University, July 2, 2008. Available online at: http://www.voxunion.com/?p=73.

242 Frantz Fanon, *Wretched of the Earth (New York: Grove Press, 1965),* 43.

243 While this work would not likely satisfy all the requirements necessary to be considered fully Afrocentric or African-centered, it remains respectful and in full acknowledgement of the debt owed to those scholars for, at a minimum, complicating the more popular and acceptable ranges of discussion. It must be repeated that this tradition is old, varied, and powerfully deep, solidifying it as worthy of more attention and more honest critiques than it often receives. As a summary of why this may occur, readers might see Jacob Carruthers' *Intellectual Warfare* (Chicago: Third World Press, 1999), which details some of the kinds of misleading criticism of the field. But more recently, leading Black scholars have taken unfortunate and often uninformed shots at African-centered thought: the works of Norman Kelley, such as *The Head Negro in Charge Syndrome: The Dead End of Black Politics* (New York: Nation Books, 2004) and the works of Patricia Hill Collins, such as *Black Power to Hip-Hop: Racism, Nationalism, and Feminism* (Philadelphia: Temple University, 2006), for example. The effort that these and others put into their broader and often strong analyses in other areas is simply not applied to their criticism of African-centered thought. Kelley simply says that Afrocentricity had "potential" but is now simply "a window into race fantasy" (45). He cites or mentions no scholars of the field nor any of the voluminous texts or even the debates within the field. He goes almost immediately, and exclusively, to Louis Farrakhan who would not likely be included by any scholar of African-centered thought as a member, much less a representative, of that community. Collins, who has offered a more substantive critique in *Black Feminist Thought: Knowledge, Consciousness and the Politics of Empowerment* (New York: Routledge, 1991), extends none of that thought to her comments in 2006 and does not respond to the twenty or more years of critical response to her earlier work. See, for example, Clenora Hudson-Weems, *Africana Womanism* (New York: Bedford/St. Martins, 1993).

244 Amos Wilson, "The Impact of Media on the African Psyche." Speech aired on

Democracy Now!, February 5, 1999. Available online at: http://www.democracynow. org/1999/2/5/amos_wilson_the_impact_of_the.

245 Amos Wilson, *Blueprint for Black Power: A Moral, Political, and Economic Imperative for the Twenty-First Century* (New York: Afrikan World Infosystems, 1998), 61.

246 Achbar, *Manufacturing Consent: Noam Chomsky and the Media.*

247 Lippmann, *Public Opinion.*

248 "Americas" is meant to—though not done properly here—extend the focus to Africans in the hemisphere as would be properly necessary in accounting for the influence of Africa, the Caribbean, and South, Central, and North America, all of which have contributed to hip-hop.

249 Wilson, *Blueprint for Black Power,* 63.

250 According to Memmi, the "ideology of the dominant class is adopted in large measure by the governed classes...*the dominated classes practically confirm the role assigned them*" (*The Colonizer and the Colonized,* 88, emphasis added).

251 Manning Marable, *How Capitalism Underdeveloped Black America* (Cambridge: South End Press, 1983/2000), 3, emphasis added.

252 (2005), 2–3.

253 From the beginning, Thomas Jefferson noted the need to graft a developing "Whiteness" onto the "heterogeneous, incoherent, distracted mass of European immigrants" in Leon Wynter's *American Skin: Pop Culture, Big Business, the End of White America* (New York: Crown Publishers, 2002), 16. See also Grace Elizabeth Hale's *Making Whiteness* (New York: Vintage Books, 1998) for a history of the development of "Whiteness" as a consciousness to help shape a post-enslavement American South and establish the colonial pyramid. See also George Lipsitz's *Possessive Investment in Whiteness* (Philadelphia: Temple University, 1998) and Robert Jensen's *The Heart of Whiteness* (San Francisco: City Lights, 2005) for White male discussions of White male (and female) privilege and how that privilege manifests itself materially.

254 As James Baldwin said, "What white people have to do is to try to find out in their own hearts why it was necessary to have a nigger in the first place, because I'm not a nigger, I'm a man, but if you think I'm a nigger, it means you need it. Why?... If I'm not a nigger here and you, the white people, invented him, then you've got to find out why." Fred Standley and Louis H. Pratt, eds., *Conversations with James Baldwin,* (Jackson, Miss.: University Press of Mississippi, 1989), 45.

255 Aided by the fact that the World Trade Organization has classified water as a human "want" as opposed to a human "need," which would prevent it from being made into a commodity. As Maude Barlow explains, "The fact that water is *not* now an acknowledged human right has allowed decision-making over water policy to shift from the U.N. and governments toward institutions and organizations that favor the private water companies and the commodification of water." Maude Barlow,

"It's Time for the U.N. to Make Water a Human Right," *Alternet.org*, February 21, 2008, emphasis added. Available online at: http://www.alternet.org/water/77350/.

256 This is so regardless of whether we embark on an analysis of rap music, or the entire hip-hop nation, as being "located within a continuum of Black cultural movements including the Harlem Renaissance of the 1920s and the Black Arts Movement of the 1960s," or "through an evolution of African American musical production, with the blues, jazz, and R&B as its predecessors," or "mapped diasporically as a point of convergence for African polyrhythms, Brazilian capoeira, and Jamaican sound systems." R. Scott Heath, "True Heads: Historicizing the Hip-Hop 'Nation' in Context," *Callaloo,* Summer 2006, 846–866, 849. See this cycle in Nelson George's *The Death of R&B* (New York: Plume, 1988), as well as Mark Anthony Neal's *What the Music Said* (New York: Routledge, 1999).

257 See, for example, Ward Churchill, *Struggle for the Land.* Some will be surprised at the wealth still to this day derived by the United States from Indigenous lands. For a more recent study, see "Who Will Profit from Native Energy?" from *Project Censored.* "According to the Indigenous Environmental Network, 35 percent of the fossil fuel resources in the U.S. are within Indian country. The Department of the Interior estimates that Indian lands hold undiscovered reserves of almost 54 billion tons of coal, 38 trillion cubic feet of natural gas, and 5.4 billion barrels of oil. Tribal lands also contain enormous amounts of alternative energy." Available online at: http://www.projectcensored.org/top-stories/articles/25-who-will-profit-from-native-energy/.

258 See for example Gerald Massey's *The Historical Jesus and the Mythical Christ* (San Diego: Book Tree,1828) and John G. Jackson's *Christianity Before Christ* (Austin, Texas: American Atheists, 1985) for discussions of the political impact of African metaphysics being reinvented into European religions, imagery, and philosophy.

259 "As a rule, human beings do not kill other human beings, [and therefore] before we enter into warfare or genocide we first dehumanize those we mean to eliminate." Sam Keen quoted in Barbara Hawk, ed., *Africa's Media Image* (Santa Barbara: Praeger Publishers, 1993).

260 Ed. Barbara Hawk, *Africa's Media Image* (Santa Barbara: Praeger Publishers, 1993) and Milton Allimadi, *The Heart of Darkness: How White Writers Created The Racist Image of Africa* (New York: Black Star , 2003).

261 Eds. Janette Dates and William Barlow, *Split Image: African Americans in the Mass Media* (Washington, D.C.: Howard University, 1993). They describe this as a "war of images" (4).

262 Ed. Edmund Ghareeb, *Split Vision: The Portrayal of Arabs in the American Media* (Washington, D.C.: American-Arab Affairs Council, 1983). See also J. Linnéa Hussein, "Reel Bad Arabs: How Hollywood Vilifies a People" [Film Review], in

Film and History, vol. 40, no. 1, Spring 2010), 118–120: "Shaheen's film argues that the visual vilification of the Arab people has been going on for more than a century, starting with early European depictions of the Orient in art and increasing in visual media after WWII with the founding of Israel, the Arab oil embargo in the 1970s, and the Iranian Revolution" (118–119).

263 See, for example, Dana Mastro and Elizabeth Behm-Morawitz, "Latino Representation on Prime-time Television," *Journalism and Mass Communication Quarterly*, vol. 82, no. 1, 2005, 110–130. More than just an issue of television, this article chronicles a decades-long problem of both under-representation in popular media and the kinds of limited, usually derogatory, depictions of Latin Americans in U.S. popular media. And these depictions run similar to those of African America: "Content analyses have also established that, when depicted, Latinos have historically been confined to a narrow set of stereotypic, often-times negative characterizations. They include the criminal, the law enforcer, the Latin lover, the Harlot, and the comic buffoon" (111).

264 Hemant Shah, "Assimilation and 'Third World' Modernization Communication and Nation Building: Comparing U.S. Models of Ethnic Gazette," *The International Journal for Communication Studies*, vol. 65, no. 2, 2003, 165–181.

265 Mills, *The Racial Contract*, 1–3.

266 Ibid., 98.

267 Ibid., 98–99.

268 Ibid., 98–101.

269 Clovis E. Semmes, *Cultural Hegemony and African American Development* (Westport: Praeger Publishers, 1995), 1–40.

270 Fanon, *Toward the African Revolution,* 35.

271 Blauner, *Racial Oppression in America,* 67.

272 Cabral, *Return to the Source*, 40. However, Cabral never agreed with the colonial model being applied to African America. His argument is not clear beyond his claim that a colonial situation requires a "continuity of territories," which Black America does not have (78). We will simply disagree with our dear departed comrade. A lack of contiguous borders, as argued by Pinderhughes, does not change the overall spatial relations of African America vis-à-vis White America that remain distinct physically and socially, and in direct opposition to one another regarding political or colonial power versus dependence. Similarly, Cabral suggests (in an unrelated discussion) that in "classic colonialism," the dominated are "subjected to the following experiences": (a) "Total destruction" or the physical violence that precedes the establishment of a colony. This element seems satisfied here in the U.S. by the removal and replacement of Indigenous people and the enslavement of Africans who both became part of the new population and the displaced internal colony;

(b) "partial destruction"; (c) "ostensible preservation," which he says involves the "restriction of indigenous people in geographical areas or special reserves usually without means of living." This too as a tenet would seem to have been met by "Indian Reservations" and Black America "ghettoes," "'hoods," and so on (66).

273 Fanon, *Toward the African Revolution*, 34.

274 Sut Jhally, dir., *bell hooks: Cultural Criticism and Transformation* [Film] (Media Education Foundation, 1996).

275 Memmi, *The Colonizer and the Colonized*, 79.

276 Fanon, *Toward the African Revolution*, 34, emphasis added.

277 Zbigniew Brzezinski, *The Grand Chessboard: American Primacy and Its Geostrategic Imperatives* (New York: Basic Books, 1997), 24–25, emphasis added.

278 Stuart Hall makes a good point in *Encoding/Decoding* (New York: Routledge, 1980): Media promotes the dominant idea and its ability to limit the range of acceptable responses, thus blunting total agency. But here his point could be expanded to indicate that though not all messages are received as they are intended by the encoder, they still serve the primary purpose that he describes as the "dominant meaning" in support of a "dominant cultural order" (172).

279 Sandoval, *Methodology of the Oppressed*.

280 Incidentally, this is the point made by a father-son exchange in *Thank You for Smoking* (Fox Searchlight, 2005) when, in a demonstration of powerful argumentation (as a public relations rep for "Big Tobacco"), the father makes seemingly inane comments about vanilla ice cream being better than chocolate ice cream. When his son remarks about the ridiculousness of his argument, the father responds by pointing to a crowd and saying, "I'm not arguing to beat you, I'm arguing to get them."

281 Rodriguez, "Long Live Third World Unity! Long Live Internationalism," 133.

282 As Herbert J. Altschull has said in *Agents of Power* (New York: Longman, 1984): "Such an assumption was inevitable, for the leaders of the new ['post-colonial' African] nations had themselves been schooled in the lore of the capitalist states; their ideas derived from those of Britain and France, Belgium, and Holland, and the political giant that had been spawned by all of them, the United States. Belief was universal in the power of *the press and its companion in education, the schools*, to raise a citizenry dedicated to the principles of democracy and social justice" (149), emphasis added. This would be both challenged and amended and will be discussed later, but the statement is meant to describe the taken-for-granted nature (correctly) that education and journalism are equally essential in maintaining ranges of thought and are both linked intimately to maintenance of power.

283 Education in the United States for its African and Latin populations resembles in function that which is described by Walter Rodney of Africa: "The main purpose of the colonial school system was to train Africans to help man the local administration

at the lowest ranks and to staff the private capitalist firms owned by Europeans....
It was not an educational system that grew out of the African environment or one
that was designed to promote the most rational use of material and social resource.
It was not an educational system designed to give young people confidence and
pride as members of African societies, but one which sought to instill a sense of
deference towards all that was European and capitalist." Marable, *How Capitalism
Underdeveloped Black America*, xxx.

284 Herbert Marcuse quoted in James Curran, Michael Gurevitch, Janet Woollacott,
"The Study of the Media: Theoretical Approaches." In Boyd-Barrett and Newbold,
eds., *Approaches to Media: A Reader* (London: Oxford University, 1995), 105.

285 Lippmann, *Public Opinion*, 19, emphasis added. In other words, for the news to make
sense or to have the desired impact of limiting the thought of its audience or targets,
general opinions of what is covered must already have been set. The news can never
raise, discuss, or spend too much time illuminating various topics, as it only exists
to reify or amplify existing views.

286 And in the vein of Harold Cruse's question regarding popular culture and the
popularity of that cultural expression globally, the value of becoming a staple
within North America's "cultural store," it is not a positive but the result of a
cultural imperial reach needed to create misunderstandings about this nation, its
organization, or its goals.

287 Williams H. Watkins, *The White Architects of Black Education: Ideology and Power in
America, 1865–1954* (Williston, Vt.: Teacher's College Press, 2001), 11.

288 Ibid., 11.

289 Ibid., 12. It must also be noted again that these men, those who developed systems of
educating African and Indigenous people in the U.S., were also "directly involved in
developing colonial policies in Africa." Robin D. G. Kelley quoted in his foreword
to Watkins, *The White Architects of Black Education*, xii.

290 Again, this is not to deny an agency among African people or anyone else. It is meant
to highlight the structural demands of those it makes famous. There is "wiggle"
room where individual entertainers can make at times poignant and biting criticism
or deep humor (Dave Chapelle, for instance). But they do so going against a grain,
which can be exhausting and is often short-lived (again, Chapelle). These efforts are
also made against that which has been established as the norm.

291 DuBois, *Black Reconstruction in America*.

292 Lake Mohonk, N.Y., in 1893, where the "industrial schooling" and residential schools
for First Nations people were discussed, and Capon Spring, W.V., in 1898 where
Industrial Education was discussed and planned for African America.

293 Spivey, *Schooling for the New Slavery*, ix.

294 See Herbert Aptheker's *American Negro Slave Revolts* (New York: Columbia

University, 1943) and also Owen 'Alik Shahadah's *500 Years Later* [Film] (Halaqah Media, 2008) for in-depth descriptions of the fact that Black rebellion or the "Fear of Revolt" ended the *manner* in which people were to be maintained in various forms of involuntary servitude.

295 Baran and Sweezy, *Monopoly Capital.*

296 Spivey, *Schooling for the New Slavery,* 17.

297 Many of the same figures who established a system of education for Africans in America did so throughout the colonized African world. See also Kenneth King, *Pan-Africanism in Education (Oxford: Clarendon, 1971).*

298 James D. Anderson, "Northern Foundations and the Shaping of Southern Black Rural Education, 1902–1935," *History of Education Quarterly*, vol. 18, no. 4, Winter 1978, 371–396.

299 Ibid., 379.

300 Carter G. Woodson, *Education of the Negro* (Brooklyn: A&B Books, 1919/1999), 1–2.

301 Watkins, *The White Architects of Black Education,* 9. And "ideology" being that which "helps *organize* our world and explains it in relation to power and vested interests" (2, original emphasis).

302 Nkrumah, *Consciencism*, 57.

303 See note 52 for Galbraith's description of the "rot in the system," which results from "predation" or the nature of the social relationship, which predetermines the end result.

304 See Derrick Bell's *Silent Covenants*, and see also Stan Karp speak on No Child Left Behind in an interview with *CounterSpin,* May 1–May 7, 2009. Available online at: http://www.fair.org/index.php?page=3778.

305 Kozol, *Shame of the Nation..*

306 John Taylor Gatto, *The Underground History of American Education* (New York: Odysseus Group, 2003). Interestingly, though not surprisingly, though he is considered an influential thinker within the field of media and communication studies, the work of Harold Innis—*The Bias of Communication* (Toronto: University of Toronto, 1951)—is rarely considered for what it says about technology reifying power (as opposed to overthrowing it) or the author's cautioning about the ideological biases in teaching history.

307 Ibid.

308 Watkins, *The White Architects of Black Education.* "The Rockefeller family and its associated were major actors in shaping scientific, early-twentieth-century corporate philanthropy and its accompanying political philosophy.... The Rockefeller people contributed to articulating ideological strategy and tactic for the new corporate industrial order" (118, 134).

309 Simpson, *The Science of Coercion*, 8, emphasis added. "During the second half of the 1930s, the Rockefeller Foundation underwrote much of the most innovative communication research then under way in the United States.... The Rockefeller Foundation clearly favored efforts designed to find a 'democratic prophylaxis' that could immunize the United States' large immigrant population from the effects of Soviet and Axis propaganda" (22).

310 Churchill, *Kill the Indian and Save the Man*. See also the works of Jonathan Kozol who has compared modern public schools to "plantations."

311 Ahati N. N. Toure, *John Henrik Clarke and the Power of Africana History: Africalogical Quest for Decolonization and Sovereignty* (Trenton, N.J.: Africa World Press, 2008), 29.

312 The Harlem History Club would be called the "most important institution in the development of Black Nationalism" by Greg Carr. This society produced and influenced intellectual giants from around the globe, from John G. Jackson, John Henrik Clarke, and Willis N. Huggins, to Kwame Nkrumah and Ho Chi Minh. For more, see Greg Kimathi Carr, "The African-Centered Philosophy of History: An Exploratory Essay on the Genealogy of Foundationalist Historical Thought and African Nationalist Identity Construction" in *African World History Project: The Preliminary Challenge*, eds. Jacob Carruthers and Leon Harris (Los Angeles: Association of the Study of Classical African Civilization, 2002). For more on these societies and the history of the Black Studies Movement and African-centered education, see Elinor Des Verney Sinnette's *Arthur Alfonso Schomburg: Black Bibliophile and Collector* (1989), and see also Toure, *John Henrik Clarke and the Power of Africana History,* 63–65.

313 Ricky Jones, "Obama Mania and Black Political Possibilities," panel presentation at the *National Council of Black Studies*, Atlanta, Ga., March 23, 2009. Available online at: http://www.voxunion.com/?p=1004.

314 Carruthers, *Intellectual Warfare*.

315 Stuart Hall, *Encoding/Decoding*, 170.

316 Or, as was said by Antonio Gramsci, "Everything which influences or is able to influence public opinion, directly or indirectly, belongs to [the ideological structure]: libraries, schools, associations, and clubs of various kinds, even architecture and the layout and names of streets" (381).

317 See Alterman; Palast, *The Best Democracy Money Can Buy*; Ben Bagdikian, *The New Media Monopoly* (Boston: Beacon Press, 2004).

318 Van Dijk, *Racism and the Press*; Entman and Rajecki, *The Black Image in the White Mind* ; Heider.

319 Josh Stearns, "News For Sale," *FreePress.net*, July 2, 2009. Available online at: http://www.stopbigmedia.com/blog/2009/07/news-for-sale/.

320 Heider.

321 See also the works of Breed; Dates and Barlow, *Split Image*; Klein, *No Logo: Taking Aim at the Brand Bullies* (New York: Picador, 2000); Alterman; Bagdikian, *The New Media Monopoly*; Goodman and Goodman, *The Exception to the Rulers: Exposing Oily Politicians, War Profiteers, and the Media That Love Them* (New York: Hyperion, 2004); McChesney, *The Problem of the Media: U.S. Communication Politics in the 21st Century* (New York: Monthly Review, 2004); Robert McChesney, Russell Newman, and Ben Scott, eds., *The Future of Media: Resistance and Reform in the 21st Century* (New York: Seven Stories, 2005).

322 Todd Steven Burroughs, *Drums in the Global Village: Toward an Ideological History of Black Media*. Unpublished doctoral dissertation, University of Maryland, College Park, 2001.

323 Recognizing the fraudulence of Lincoln's Proclamation and his being "forced into glory" as so well argued by Leronne Bennett, Jr. in *Forced into Glory: Abraham Lincoln's White Dream* (Chicago: Johnson Publishing, 2000).

324 See, for example, Howard C. Perkins, "The Defense of Slavery in the Northern Press on the Eve of the Civil War," *The Journal of Southern History*, vol. 9, no. 4, November 1943, 501–531. See also Alexander Saxton, "Problems of Class and Race in the Origins of the Mass Circulation Press," *American Quarterly*, vol. 36, no. 2, Summer 1984, 211–234.

325 Hale, *Making Whiteness*. This is also why Ida B. Wells worked tirelessly and through great frustration and risk to get reports of lynching published. She had no alternative given the state of the dominant press. Wells, who had herself been forcibly removed from a train in 1884 for refusing to give up her seat in the White section, would use her *Memphis Free Press* to combat the local and national coverage of lynching. At the time, much of the existing coverage was tantamount to promotion of lynching where actions resulting from the calls for the attendance at and participation in White mobs would be covered in the press by "special correspondents" who would "civilize" the participants (Hale, 212–213). Postcards and photos would be widely and inexpensively distributed, often to those who could not afford or who were not fortunate enough to have access to the more highly coveted body parts of the victims. Newspapers, as well as the previously described Associated Press, would happily write invitations to join "lynch parties." One San Francisco paper referred to lynching as "an American institution." This particular paper went so far as to conclude that "the strangest delusion in connection with lynching is that it is the victim who suffers most. In reality it is the community who is lynched" (Hale, 120). Wells would eventually have to carry her work north as death threats and violence silenced her Southern voice.

326 Saxton, "Problems of Class and Race in the Origins of the Mass Circulation Press,"

211–234.

327 And as James Turner has said, "The enduring value of the Appeal is centered in its conscious African-centered perspective... that organizes itself around a social theory of reality meant to implement change in the society towards freedom. If Walker had a dictum it would have been that *freedom must be actualized by oppressed people themselves*, which requires them to assume an independent methodology to analyze their world in order to change it.... David Walker's heirs—both conscious and unconscious—have been legion." James Turner, *David Walker's Appeal: To the Coloured Citizens of the World but in Particular, and Expressly, to Those of the United States of America* (Baltimore: Black Classic Press, 1830/1993), 14.

328 Carole Boyce Davies, *To the Left of Karl Marx: The Political Life of Black Communist Claudia Jones* (Durham, N.C.: Duke University, 2007), 272.

329 John Downing, *Radical Media: The Political Experience of Alternative Communication* (Boston: South End, 1984).

330 This is somewhat similar to the not-so-suspicious assassination of his White contemporary Elijah Lovejoy who was shot to death by a "mob" in Alton, Illinois on November 7, 1837. His death, in Illinois, would later be praised in political speeches given by then-campaigning senatorial aspirant Abraham Lincoln: "I have heard you have abolitionists here. We have a few in Illinois and we shot one the other day." Bennett, *Forced Into Glory*, 57, 85.

331 Not only was there the founding of *Freedom's Journal* (1827) and later the *North Star* (1847), there would later come, among many other examples, Garvey's *Negro World*; Ida B. Wells' *The Red Record*; The Nation of Islam's *Muhammad Speaks*; Robert and Mabel Williams' *The Crusader*; The Black Panther Party's *The Black Panther*; *The Abolitionist Press*, The Left Underground Press of the 1960s; Claudia Jones' work in the Black press of her day and within the Communist Party U.S.A.; the "Hood News" concept from rap group Dead Prez, and so on.

332 Interview by the author with former editor of *Emerge* magazine, George Curry, June 7, 2008.

333 Personal communication with the author, June 3, 2008.

334 Greg Carr, during the aforementioned MSNBC 2008 discussion of race at Howard University.

335 For example, Mark Lloyd's *Prologue to a Farce: Communication and Democracy in America* (Champaign, Ill.: University of Illinois, 2006) is one example in which a Black writer, one who has written of the importance of communications as a "Civil Rights issue," still remains within the more traditional mode of discussing communications history in the U.S. Lloyd continues an acceptance of conventional approaches to this nation's history and development as a "Republic" or a "Democracy" without properly investigating or exposing either as political chicanery masking

deeper more exploitative goals (i.e. colonialism). This perspective is locked safely within the confines of the worldviews of Lincoln and Madison, and Lloyd's own appreciation for a "largely unrestricted commercial media" and focus on changing "public policy" as opposed to the development of alternative, underground media in response to a public policy that is just what is necessary or desired in a colonial setting. Were it simply a matter of public policy, the almost counterintuitive study of the history as conducted by McChesney (*The Political Economy of Media: Enduring Issues, Emerging Dilemmas* [New York: Monthly Review, 2008]) would have seen those policy struggles he describes as occurring throughout the early twentieth century have a different outcome. So, unlike both of them, the perspective described herein represents the "no one" that McChesney writes of who "thinks any longer that media reform is an issue to solve 'after the revolution'" (499).

336 Bruce Cosby raises brilliant points about this overall historical relationship of Africans to technology and demonstrates that, as mentioned above, said technology has been consistently used to exploit. He most importantly notes that technology leads to gadgets that are all those colonized are able to access. So the technology that allows for use of a cell phone or computer is held in tight control by those in power, whereas the gadgets—the computers and phones themselves—are doled out to those with no power over the technology or the wealth and power they generate.

337 According to Harold Cruse, "During the 1920s, the development in America of mass cultural communications media—radio, films, recording industry, and ultimately, television—drastically altered the classic character of capitalism as described by Karl Marx. This new feature very obviously presented new problems (as well as opportunities) for all the anti-capitalistic radicals; problems which they apparently never appreciated. The capitalist class, according to the Marxists, have the political and economic power through class ownership of all the industrial and technological means of production, to exploit the working class and control opinions through the press. If that be so, then consider the added range and persuasiveness, the augmented class power, the enhanced political control and prerogatives of decision making that result from the new mass communications industry. *What happens to the scope of popular democracy when this new technological electronic apparatus spreads throughout the lands, bombarding the collective mind with controlled images?*" (64, emphasis added).

338 Southern, *The Music of Black Americans*, 505–510.

339 Cedric J. Robinson, "In the Year 1915: D.W. Griffiths and the Whitening of America," in *The Black Studies Reader*, eds. Jacqueline Bobo, Cynthia Hudley, and Claudine Michel. (New York: Routledge, 2004), 229–253. In this piece, a powerful analysis of the use of the film industry to enhance the power of White supremacy, Robinson begins with an equally powerful epigraph quoting Otis Madison: "The purpose of

racism is to control the behavior of white people, not Black people. For Blacks guns and tanks are sufficient."

340 Southern, *The Music of Black Americans*, 505–510.

341 See William Barlow, "Black Music on Radio During the Jazz Age," *African American Review*, vol. 29, no. 2, 1995, 325–328, and *Voice Over: The Making of Black Radio* (Philadelphia: Temple University, 1999).

342 For more on this, see the powerful film *Scandalize My Name: Stories From the Blacklist* by Dick Campbell IV (Urban Works Entertainment, 2004).

343 Bruce Dixon, "How Corporate Dollars Dominate the Black and Latino Conversation on Network Neutrality," *BlackAgendaReport.com,* February 3, 2010. Available online at: http://blackagendareport.com/?q=content/how-corporate-dollars-dominate-black-and-latino-conversation-network-neutrality.

344 Bruce Cosby, *African and the Challenge of Western Technology: Understanding the Role of Technologies in History* (Buffalo, N.Y.: People Printing, 2005).

345 For instance, as Kevin Phillips has explained in his chapter "Technology and the Uncertain Foundations of Anglo-American Wealth," the "early stages of major innovations have generated rising social and economic inequality almost as a matter of course.... In short, technology, like finance, is the arena of an elite." *Wealth and Democracy: A Political History of the American Rich* (New York: Broadway Books, 2002), 250.

346 This analogy again appears in Robert McChesney's statement in the PBS documentary *Merchants of Cool* (PBS, 2001) where he says, "[Corporations] look at the teen market as part of this massive empire that they're colonizing. *Teens are like Africa*" (emphasis added). Transcript available online at: http://www.pbs.org/wgbh/pages/frontline/shows/cool/etc/script.html.

347 The destruction of Black Wall Street in Tulsa, Okla., is but one part of this. For more on this history and its particular and lasting psychological impact on African America see our interview with Drs. Shawn Utsey and Mark Bolden about their research on the subject with the author. Available online at: http://www.voxunion.com/?p=66.

348 This point is partially made by DuBois in *Black Reconstruction in America* where not only does he outline the specifics of the economic and political backlash, but also discusses the issue of image and justification in terms of historiography that he refers to in a chapter titled "The *Propaganda* of History" (emphasis added). In a previous chapter, "Back Toward Slavery," he summarizes the point: "It must be remembered and never forgotten that the civil war in the South which overthrew Reconstruction was a determined effort to reduce Black labor as nearly as possible to a condition of unlimited exploitation and build a new class of capitalists on this foundation" (670). Later he continued explaining that this need was justified, protected by "a

determined psychology of caste [that] was built up. In every possible way it was impressed and advertised that the white was superior and the Negro an inferior race. This inferiority must be publicly acknowledged and submitted to" (695).

349 See, for example, this issue discussed in terms of an absence of a Black public sphere in the context of Black radio in Catherine R. Squires, "Black Talk Radio: Defining Community Needs and Identity," *The Black Studies Reader*, eds. Jacqueline Bobo, Cynthia Hudley, and Claudine Michel (New York: Routledge, 2004), 193–210. See also, Houston Baker, "Critical Memory and the Black Public Sphere," *The Black Public Sphere: A Public Culture Book*, eds. The Black Public Sphere Collective (Chicago: University of Chicago, 1995), 7–37.

350 Neal, in *What the Music Said,* writes, "While the show [*What's Happening?*] succeeded, however humorously, in capturing the depressed economic state of Watts, it also offered a glimpse of a highly depoliticized Watts. This is ironic given the show's link to Watts' radical political past. The show's title was borrowed from the name of a real coffeeshop that served as a focal point for the district's burgeoning activist class. The Watts Happening Coffee House" (98).

351 This "tradition" of a dissident press is described well in Lauren Kessler, *The Dissident Press: Alternative Journalism in American History* (London: Sage Publications, 1984).

352 One example is of the press coverage of the "Mau Mau" (Kenyan Land and Freedom Movement) that needed to be negative not only to save British colonialism in East Africa but also colonialism in general throughout the continent as positive spin of one revolutionary movement might encourage more elsewhere. See Hawk, *Africa's Media Image*. See also, Allimadi, *The Heart of Darkness*.

353 Altschull, *Agents of Power*.

354 See Baffour Ankomah, "The Role of the African Media in Promoting African Integration," in ed. Mammo Munchie, *The Making of the Africa-Nation: Pan-Africanism and the African Renaissance* (London: Adonis and Abbey Publishers, 2003) 169–207.

355 Allimadi, *The Heart of Darkness*.

356 This is actually the deepest aspect discussed somewhat implicitly in Common's *The Corner* (2005) where The Last Poets (and Common himself) describe the importance of the ghetto corner as a Black public sphere. See also *The Black Public Sphere: A Public Culture Book,* The Black Public Sphere Collective, eds. (Chicago: University of Chicago, 1995). It is also important also to note that attempts like that of Booker T. Washington to combat the imagery set in films such as *Birth of a Nation* (Washington's response was to make *Birth of a Race*) failed as not only were such films enormously popular, but the rights garnered by MGM to re-issue that film launched the wealth and power of that particular movie house, further cementing the negative imagery of Black people to the rise and establishment of the

film industry and mass media in general. For more on that, see the brilliant essay by Cedric J. Robinson, "In The Year 1915," 229–253.

357 The recording of live DJ mixes at parties or those created specially for distribution in local communities was done in direct contradiction to the kinds of spaces developed around commercial or mainstream media, which made new room for hip-hop or varying forms of rap music mixes. This was particularly so at the time (early 1970s) when there were no rap radio or video outlets and a subaltern cultural expression was emerging.

358 Herbert Gans quoted in David Armstrong's *A Trumpet to Arms: Alternative Media in America* (Boston: South End Press, 1981), 18. Armstrong's work is another among the ignored great histories of this tradition of underground press and demonstrates in great detail both the historical need, function, and subsequent suppression of such media work that continues to inspire *FreeMix Radio* and, of course, many others were they to get wind of it.

359 Again, a point raised and often ignored by Harold Innis within "conventional" media studies. *The Bias of Communication* traces world history through the use of media technology as mechanisms of control. And similar to an earlier point made about DuBois and his discussion of the use of historiography to suit this mission, so too does Innis make the case at the end of his work about the negative impact of education on the study of media and society in general.

360 "The phrase 'invisible class empire' refers to hidden class structures and processes through which superclass leaders, along with their credentialed-class allies, penetrate and dominate the American political system. It refers to the processes used to disguise this reality and the concealed political, economic, and cultural dimensions of superclass power." Robert Perrucci and Earl Wysong, *The New Class Society: Goodbye American Dream?* (Lanham: Rowman and Littlefield, 2003), 120. Hence the problem even "insider" Jamie Johnson had in making his two documentaries on this modern-day elite, *Born Rich* and *The One Percent*, where in each case there was tremendous hesitancy among his interviewees.

361 Which themselves have been the subject of a good deal of study, concluding, in at least one instance, that board interlocks—where corporations share the same director—have an "overwhelming" influence on the "strategic choices of firms." Mark Mizruchi, "What Do Interlocks Do? An Analysis, Critique, and Assessment of Research on Interlocking Directorates," *Annual Review of Sociology*, no. 22, 1996, 271–298, 292. In other words, interlocking boards of directorates do extend the influence of a small number of the elite over a great number of corporations who then greatly impact the lives of most in this society and around the world.

362 It is important to note that the Chief Executive Officer, while a top executive, is still an employee in the service of the corporation's board of directors and top stockholders.

They are hired and fired (albeit often with lovely "Golden Parachutes"), and the face of a company is not necessarily the most powerful. In other words, as former CEO of Time Warner Richard Parsons—a Black man—said in his response to a "Call to Action" (produced at a Black Corporate Directors Conference, which challenged directors to do more to diversify the corporations for which they worked), "Do I think that somehow we need to come together collectively to validate this initiative? No, because each director's obligations and responsibilities are to the shareholders of the entity that he or she is serving." *Black Enterprise,* February 2008, 122.

363 Glenn Greenwald, speaking on *Democracy Now!,* July 24, 2008, referring to those who finance both major electoral political parties so as to ensure their interests are served regardless of who is elected. Available online at: http://www.democracynow.org.

364 Parenti, *Democracy for the Few,* 8.

365 Mark Achbar, dir., *The Corporation* [Film] (Big Picture Media, 2003). However, unlike this documentary, the argument here is that their primary goal goes beyond simple profit accumulation for profit's sake. Corporations, by seeking profit, seek further control over the behavior of the populace as this is, as stated above, the primary role of money—the control over the behavior of those without it. By determining levels of poverty, a society's elite manages behavior. It is no different than when in class students are asked who would immediately take off their clothes and run naked across campus. No hands rise. But when the idea of a promise of money (ten thousand, one-hundred thousand, a million dollars, and so on) is made as an exercise, many more hands go up. Even those who resist out of pride admit at least considering it as money levels go up. Or even more simply, the question is then asked, "How many of you would even be here to hear this lecture were it not for a promise of a grade, which leads to a promise of a degree, which leads to a promise of money?" Few if any ever say "me!"

366 These are now Universal Music Group, Sony Music, and Warner Music Group. EMI is a distant fourth.

367 Palast, *The Best Democracy Money Can Buy,* 65.

368 According to the trade website *FMQB* on July 9, 2010, "Universal Music has led the major labels with a 30.3 percent share of the market, while Sony Music scored second with 28.3 percent." Available online at: http://fmqb.com/article.asp?id=1870158.

369 For more on this, see Jared A. Ball, "Hip-Hop and the 'Anti-Blackness Antagonism'," *BlackAgendaReport.com,* July 6, 2010. Available online at: http://blackagendareport.com/?q=content/hip-hop-and-%E2%80%9Canti-blackness-antagonism%E2%80%9D.

370 And also consider these interlocks in the context of the statement made by Jeff Immelt on September 11, 2001: "My second day as chairman [of General Electric], a plane

that I lease, flying with engines I built, crashed into a building that I insure, and it was covered with a network I own." Quoted in Perrucci and Wysong, *The New Class Society: Goodbye American Dream?*, ix.

371 It is worth raising as a question what this means to have Bronfman—as representing a particular racial, class, and gendered elite—with this much influence over the popularity of Black expression. In his book *The Holocaust Industry* (New York: Verso Books, 2000), Norman Finkelstein details Bronfman's major role as president of the World Jewish Congress and self-proclaimed spokesperson of "the Jewish people" in bilking billions of dollars due rightfully to the survivors of the Nazi Holocaust (90). Finkelstein has also referred to Bronfman plainly as "a crook" (December 17, 2008). Available online at: http://www.youtube.com/watch?v=HxMkavCbums&feature= related). This perhaps says much about what kinds of expression Bronfman would prefer be made popular.

372 Defended, shared, promulgated through alliances such as the Business Roundtable, whose website is quite clear: "Business Roundtable is an association of chief executive officers of leading U.S. companies with $4.5 trillion in annual revenues and more than 10 million employees. Member companies comprise nearly a third of the total value of the U.S. stock markets and represent over 40 percent of all corporate income taxes paid. Collectively, they returned $112 billion in dividends to shareholders and the economy in 2005.... Roundtable companies give more than $7 billion a year in combined charitable contributions, representing nearly 60 percent of total corporate giving. They are technology innovation leaders, with $90 billion in annual research and development spending—nearly half of the total private R&D spending in the U.S.... The Roundtable is committed to advocating public policies that ensure vigorous economic growth, a dynamic global economy, and the well-trained and productive U.S. workforce essential for future competitiveness. Business Roundtable believes that its potential for effectiveness is based on the fact that it draws on CEOs directly and personally, *and presents government with reasoned alternatives and positive suggestions.... The Roundtable believes that the basic interests of business closely parallel the interests of the American people*, who are directly involved as consumers, employees, shareholders, and suppliers.... In general, the Roundtable focuses on issues it believes will have an effect on the economic well-being of the nation" (emphasis added). Available online at: http://www.businessroundtable.org.

373 McChesney, *The Political Economy of Media*, 308.

374 *Vivendi Annual Report 2009*. Available online at: http://www.vivendi.com/vivendi/ Annual-Reports, 4975.

375 *Sony Music Entertainment Annual Report 2009*. Available online at: http://www.sony. net/SonyInfo/IR/financial/ar/8ido180000023g2o-att/SonyAR09-E.pdf.

376 *Warner Music Group Annual Report 2009*. Available online at: http://investors.wmg.

com/phoenix.zhtml?c=182480&p=irol-reportsannual. WMG's primary investors are three private equity groups: Thomas H. Lee Partners L.P., Bain Capital, and Providence Equity Partners, who combined manage more than $110 billion and invest in hundreds of businesses.

377 Adam Satariano, "Music Sales to Rise After 'Turning Point' in 2013, Report Says," *Bloomberg Business Week*, June 15, 2010. Available online at: http://www. businessweek.com/news/2010-06-15/music-sales-to-rise-after-turning-point-in-2013-report-says.html.

378 TheyRule.net has recently been massively updated allowing users to map out the latest boards of directors and interlocks in what is at once fun, fascinating, and appropriately infuriating.

379 Regarding media, the FCC is notorious for this kind of revolving door between the industry and the very agency nominally there to oversee those companies. See Joe Ciarallo, "Burson-Marsteller EVP Leaves to Join FCC as Senior Counselor to Chairman," which talks about the recent hiring of Josh Gottheimer as Senior Counselor to the FCC Chairman. A top executive from a leading public relations (propaganda) firm whose job it is to promote the voice of the corporations they are hired by is now a "senior counselor" to the head of the Federal Communications Commission (June 23, 2010). Available online at: http://www.mediabistro.com/ prnewser/prs_revolving_door/bursonmarsteller_evp_leaves_to_join_fcc_as_ senior_counselor_to_chairman_165571.asp. Consider also the recent report from *Democracy Now!* (July 23, 2010), which discussed that fact that "three out of every four lobbyists who represent oil and gas companies previously worked in the federal government, according to a new analysis by the *Washington Post*. That's a rate that is more than double revolving-door standards on Capitol Hill." Available online at: http://www.democracynow.org/2010/7/23/three_of_every_four_oil_gas.

380 Bagdikian, *The New Media Monopoly*, 27. And very similar to the point made in the affirmative by Brzezinski, *The Grand Chessboard*.

381 "With a growing list of radio, newspaper, and television assets on the auction block, some new players are on the verge of assembling the conglomerate of the 21st century: *the private-equity media empire*." D. Berman and S. McBride, "Private Equity May Face Snags in Media Hunt," *Wall Street Journal*, October 27, 2006, emphasis added.

382 Advertising drives the entire media industry, largely determining its content. Ownership becomes irrelevant when it is the major advertisers who wield the necessary money required for sustainability. This weakens all arguments popular within "media reform" circles, which call for "ownership diversity" as a core value or component in substantial change in media content. Again, the issue is the reach that those in power have: for example, according to TheyRule.net, and based on

2004 SEC filings, Proctor and Gamble, the number one spender of advertising dollars in 2007 ("Marketer Tree 2008" from Advertising Age, available online at: http://adage.com/marketertrees08/) was (is?) connected to General Electric (owner of NBC Universal though ownership may be sold to Comcast) through Alan Lafley who sat on both boards and to Time Warner via connections through common boards of directors with AMR and General Motors, all of whom have a common ideological and political set of interests, which must include suppression of dissent, however it might be expressed.

383 Max Horkheimer and Theodor Adorno, *Dialectic of Enlightenment* (New York: Continuum, 1944), 131.

384 Lippmann again is important here. As a friend to the elite, as council to those who rule, he was clear: "Stereotypes may be the core of our personal tradition, the defenses of our position in society" (*Public Opinion*, 63).

385 Sandoval, *Methodology of the Oppressed,* 81.

386 For more on these myths, see Peck and Street, *Barack Obama and the Future of American Politics.* See also the writings of Glen Ford and Bruce Dixon of *BlackAgendaReport.com* or Larry Pinkney of *BlackCommentator.com.* Hear also our interview with Adolph Reed on "Obamaism," in which Reed describes Obama as a "neo-liberal fraud," (July 21, 2008). Available online at: http://www.voxunion.com/?p=83.

387 Ibid.

388 Kwame Ture, Speech delivered to the Patrice Lumumba Coalition in New York City, July 1996.

389 Bernays, *Propaganda*, 161.

390 Which, as accurately described by Huey P. Newton, are, "Technological advancements…gained through expropriation from the people, including slavery proper but also chattel slavery followed by wage slavery. With this expropriation, a reservoir of information was created so that Americans could produce the kinds of experimental agencies and universities that created the information explosion," in Hilliard, *The Huey P. Newton Reader*, 256.

391 Wynter, *American Skin.* This is, again, similar to the statement made by Lippmann that stereotyping is essential to maintaining power. See note 261.

392 Wynter, *American Skin,* 16.

393 Ibid., 11–39.

394 Ibid., 20.

395 Lippmann, *Public Opinion*, 63.

396 Wynter, *American Skin,* 23, emphasis added.

397 Barlow, 2.

398 Wynter, *American Skin,* 24.

399 For example, Poison Pen's "Message to the Industry Coon," from Immortal Technique's *The 3rd World* (2008) and Aaron McGruder's censored episodes of *The Boondocks* demonstrate the desire among many in African America to battle against this perpetuation of such myths. And NYOIL said "Ya'll Should All Get Lynched" (2008). Available online at: http://www.youtube.com/watch?v=diKUyMNgj_s.

400 Chancellor Williams, *Destruction of Black Civilization,* (Chicago: Third World Press, 1987), 310.

401 C. Wright Mills, *The Power Elite,* 402. See also George, *The Death of R&B,* 8, and Wynter, *American Skin,* 51.

403 Southern, *The Music of Black Americans,* 505–510.

404 Neal, *What the Music Said,* 17, 27.

405 Wynter, *American Skin,* 52, emphasis added.

406 Ibid., 52.

407 Michael O. Grafton, "Hip Hop Ain't Nothing but the Young People's Blues," *MyBrotha.com,* April 26, 2007. Available online at: http://www.mybrotha.com/hip-hop-blues.asp.

408 (1964), 37.

409 The number of companies referenced regarding the music industry change from source to source and due to the constant flux of official ownership, mergers, and so on. However, by "Big 4" I refer to the three companies (UMG, WMG, Sony and EMI) that today supply 100 percent of the songs with most spins or airplay nationally. In fact, UMG and Sony regularly from week to week provide 90 to 100 percent of all Top 10 songs spun on radio nationally.

410 Important detail involved in this process can be found in Rose, "Contracting Rap…," but suffice it to say that artists sign away rights to the ownership and the lion's share of the wealth produced from the promotion and sale of that art in exchange for pennies on the dollar and an often brief fifteen minutes of fame.

411 Jenny Toomey of the Future of Music Coalition in her interview with *CounterSpin,* December 22–December 26, 2006. Available online at: http://www.fair.org/index.php?page=3025.

412 Kofksy, 12.

413 Thall, ix

414 McChesney, Newman, Scott, *The Future of Media,* 244.

415 Thall, ix.

416 Ross, 1.

417 Ronald V. Bettig, *Copyright Culture: The Political Economy of Intellectual Property* (Boulder, Co.: Westview Press, 1996), 103.

418 Ibid., 226.

419 McChesney, *The Problem of the Media,* 232–233.

420 McChesney, Newman, and Scott, *The Future of Media*, 245.

421 McChesney, *The Problem of the Media*, 234–235.

422 Jasci, personal communication with the author, 2005.

423 Krasilovsky and Shemel (2000).

424 Thall, 133.

425 Dannen; Krasilovsky and Shemel; Rose.

426 Rose, 548.

427 McLeod.

428 Bettig, *Copyright Culture*, 2.

429 "Consciousness-industry" comes from Sut Jhally who is quoted with Karl Marx in Bettig, *Copyright Culture*, 35.

430 Oligopoly Watch, "*The Latest Maneuvers of the New Oligopolies and What They Mean*," June 19, 2008, emphasis added. Available online at: http://oligopolywatch.com.

431 David Kravets, "Copyright Czar Backs IP Enforcement, 'Fair Use,'" *Wired.com*, June 22, 2010, emphasis added. Available online at: http://www.wired.com/threatlevel/2010/06/copyright-czar-report/#more-17033.

432 Wendy Day of the Rap Coalition can be found online at: WendyDay.com.

433 This section was originally published as a book review in *The Global Journal of Hip-Hop Culture*. *See* Adam Haupt, "Stealing Empire: P2P, Intellectual Property, and Hip-Hop Subversion" [Book Review], *The Global Journal of Hip-Hop Culture*, vol. 4, no. 1, June 2009. And hear our interview and discussion of the book and related issues online at: http://www.voxunion.com/?p=864.

434 Haupt *Stealing Empire*, xv.

435 Ibid., 220.

436 Ibid., 43.

437 Ibid., 141.

438 Ibid., 1. Taken from Hardt and Negri's conception of "Empire."

439 Ibid., 31.

440 Ibid., 9.

441 Ibid., 26.

442 Ibid., 8.

443 Ibid., 36.

444 Ibid., 27.

445 Ibid., 158.

446 Discussed in Žižek, *In Defense of Lost Causes*, 157–210, in the chapter discussion titled "Revolutionary Terror." Žižek's point summarized seems to be that if there is a claim against Empire, abuse, colonialism, and so on, that those challenging those forces can and should engage in the violent defense of their causes, as opposed to engaging in the "bullshit" of contradictory claims of Empire and the room that

Empire leaves for the agency of the individual to overthrow it by means acceptable to Empire.

447 Haupt, *Stealing Empire,* 219.

448 "The Corporate Music Industry Is Dead," December 31, 2007. Available online at: http://www.downhillbattle.org/?p=601.

449 Madhava Prashad quoted in Cedric Robinson, "The Appropriation of Frantz Fanon," *Race and Class,* vol. 35, no. 79, 1993.

450 Eric Boehlert quoted in Eric Klinenberg, *Fighting for Air: The Battle to Control America's Media* (New York: Metropolitan Books, 2007), 72. Recent mergers bring this number closer to the dominant three (UMG, Sony, WMG).

451 For example, "In 1916, the Music Publishers Protective Association (MPPA) noted that publishers were paying as much as $400,000 a year to artists for their songs" in exchange for the exclusive rights to both own and promote or resell that music. Krasilovsky and Shemel, 408.

452 Klinenberg, *Fighting for Air,* 73.

453 Rose.

454 Klinenberg, *Fighting for Air,* 73.

455 The immensely powerful, talented, and political all-Black rock/hip-hop/funk band quartet fronted by the "Mayor of D.C. Hip-Hop," Head-Roc aka OMV ("Old Man Vance"). Find him online at: http://head-roc.com.

456 Not to mention that all three companies are owned by Viacom, which also owns Infinity Broadcasting, a major "urban" radio company.

457 Golding and Murdock, 23.

458 Kirk.

459 Even when the location of this performance is hip-hop parties, and even when they are hip-hop parties whose expressed goal is to "Kill Whitey!.... Kill the whiteness inside." These all-white-hosted, mostly white-attended hip-hop gatherings, where free entry can be gained with buckets of chicken, are perfect examples of the desire to transcend Whiteness without the risks involved with actually leaving white people or environments. As one such party attendee was described, "A regular Kill Whitie partygoer, she tried the conventional hip-hop clubs but found the men 'really hard-core.' In this vastly whiter scene, Casady said that "it's a safe environment to be freaky." Michelle Garcia, "Deejay's Appeal: 'Kill the Whiteness Inside!' In Brooklyn, a Club Following Feels the Irony," *The Washington Post,* August 26, 2005.

460 Barlow, *Voice Over.*

461 The words of Mel Watkins in Barlow, *Voice Over,* 1.

462 For instance, both Alan Freed and Dick Clark were enormously popular personalities in radio and television. Both took money to play certain records and, for Clark, who owned stock in the artists that he was paid to play, made a ton of money. But Clark

also followed the laws of the social order and never played Black records and never allowed for his *American Bandstand* crowds to be mixed. Freed, on the other hand, broke those social mores. He played Black music and organized major concerts that would play to mixed audiences. As the 1960s began and the old payola scheme of payment to disc-jockeys was exposed followed by Congressional investigations and the punishment of those found guilty, it was Freed not Clark who paid the price. He lost jobs and money, and eventually drank himself to death. Ventriloquism requires separation for the re-imaged image to have the intended effect. People in proximity to one another, intimately exchanging space and culture are far too impervious to such efforts. Substantive exchange among groups targeted for separation is anathema to a society dependent on such stratification. Freed, not Clark, broke that basic principle and paid for it. And Clark? When not running from Michael Moore's attempt to question him about poor relations with and treatment of his workers in *Bowling for Columbine* (Dog Eat Dog, 2002), he could for years be seen annually during New Year's Eve specials. For more, including Clark's "formidable business empire," whose vast use of payola had even *The Washington Post* calling for it to be called "Clarkola," see Barlow, *Voice Over*, 191–193.

463 Glen Ford, "GOP Bullies on Vouchers: No Democracy for Black City," *BlackCommentator.com,* July 3, 2003. Available online at: http://www.black commentator.com/49/49_dc.html.

464 Jaze Zara, "Statehood for America's Last Colony," *Green Party*, March 3, 2009. Available online at: http://www.gp.org/first100/?p=140. Also, Parisa Norouzi of Empower D.C. speaks to VFP Convention attendees, Washington, D.C., August 8, 2009. Available online at: http://www.youtube.com/watch?v=4jGNOS097KI.

465 "I would think that at 2 a.m. on the streets of Georgetown, a group of three people, one of whom is 15 years old, one of whom is a bald chunky fat guy, are going to stand out. They were Black. *This is not a racial thing to say that Black people are unusual in Georgetown.* This is a fact of life." Andy Solberg, Washington, D.C. Second District Police Commander. Quoted in "Commander Issues Apology After Controversial Comments," *WTOP.com,* July 13, 2006, emphasis added. Available online at: http://www.wtop.com/?nid=25&sid=844185. And for more on the colonial structure of the city itself, see our June 4, 2010 interview with community activist Kwasi Seitu which is available online at: http://www.voxunion.com/?p=2707.

466 Juanita Darling, *"Re-Imaging the Nation: Revolutionary Media and Historiography in Mesoamerica," Journalism History*, vol. 32, no.4, Winter 2007.

467 Richard Prince, "Whiteness at the Top," *Richard Prince's Journal-isms*, July 25, 2008. Available online at: http://www.mije.org/richardprince/Whiteness-at-the-top. See also Richard Prince, "Whiteness at the Top, Part II," *Richard Prince's Journal-isms*, July 30, 2008. Available online at: http://www.mije.org/richardprince/Whiteness-

top-part-ii. While these Prince columns focus on "diversity" among top executives working in mainstream television (twenty-one of twenty-four network executives are White), ownership of Black radio nationally is only 1.6 percent, according to *CounterSpin* from Fairness and Accuracy in Reporting (FAIR), August 15, 2008. And as argued above, ownership is itself irrelevant in terms of determining content in mainstream commercial media.

468 DaveyD, *Facing the Music: A Report on Radio Reform Campaigns*, March 24, 2006. Available online at: http://daveyd.com.

469 Carolyn Weiner, "Educational Reform Risks Creation of Conceptual Ghettos for Young Children of Poverty," August 2001. "The concern is raised that, without attention to language learning needs, classes for young children from poverty homes will become, 'conceptual ghettos where children, walled off from newer teaching strategies, are relentlessly confronted with what they don't know, can't do, and don't care about.'" Available online at: http://www.bookflash.com/releases/100459.html.

470 According to Ben Bagdikian, who has described the five CEOs currently heading up companies as owning today the amount of mass media owned twenty years ago by fifty corporations, "No imperial ruler in past history had multiple media channels that included television and satellite channels that can permeate entire societies with controlled sights and sounds." *The New Media Monopoly*, 27.

471 (2008). Available online at: http://www.stateofthemedia.org/2008/narrative_yearinnews_intro.php?media=2

472 Who, in Jamie Johnson's documentary *The One Percent* (Jamie Johnson, 2006), can be seen disowning his granddaughter for talking publicly about being born wealthy.

473 Doug Henwood, "The Washington Post: The Establishment Paper," Fairness and Accuracy in Reporting (FAIR), January/February 1990. Available online at: http://www.fair.org/index.php?page=1195.

474 Clear Channel Branded Cities. Available online at: http://www.brandedcities.com/.

475 Thomas Franks interviewed about his book *The Wrecking Crew: How Conservatives Rule* on "Media Matters with Robert McChesney," August 10, 2008.

476 Which include the Brookings Institution, Council of Foreign Relations, the American Enterprise Institute, and even Black conservative gatherings such as the Booker T. Washington Conference, where White conservative ideals are given Black face for apparent legitimacy. However, and not discounting other means of disseminating a true minority's ideology, according to a recent report by Fairness and Accuracy in Reporting, it has been noted that there was a 17 percent drop in 2007 of references to these think tanks in mainstream presses. *Extra!* March/April 2008.

477 Wilson, *Blueprint for Black Power*.

478 *FreeMix Radio: The Original Mixtape Radio Show* has been freely distributed in and around Washington, D.C., since 2004. The mixtape CD is itself used and formatted

into a kind of radio program on CD exposing listeners to music and ideas that are intentionally excluded from mainstream media. More information can be found online at: www.voxunion.com.

479 *"Washington Post* circulation decline continues, *USA Today* circulation increases." *Washington Business Journal,* November 5, 2007. Available online at: http://www. bizjournals.com/washington/stories/2007/11/05/daily9.html.

480 According to *Echo Media,* Washington, D.C.'s *Afro-American Newspaper* has a daily circulation of 12,500 with "100,000 loyal readers." Available online at: http:// www.echo-media.com/MediaDetailNP.asp?IDNumber=10083. It is likely that this "daily" number is truly weekly since the paper is only distributed once a week on Thursday.

481 Louise Story, "Higher Value of Eyeballs," *The New York Times,* November 5, 2007, C6.

482 McChesney, *The Political Economy of Media: Enduring Issues, Emerging Dilemmas,* 257.

483 See note 452.

484 For example, there is no metro train service to Georgetown.

485 Consider the well-hidden upper northwest hideaway that is Dumbarton Oaks as an example of beautiful "public" space not intended to be easily found or reached by those not intended to be there.

486 The Trinidad section of Northeast D.C. where the neighborhood has several times been barricaded off to "unauthorized" vehicular traffic.

487 Antonio Gramsci, "Ideological Material," in *The Antonio Gramsci Reader* (New York: New York University, 2000), 380–381.

488 U.S. Census Bureau. Available online at: http://quickfacts.census.gov/qfd/states /24/24033.html.

489 Glen Ford, on an in-house, never-aired panel on Black Radio History hosted by National Public Radio, March 24, 2007. See also Arbitron's *Black Radio Today 2008* report: "Well over 90 percent of Black consumers aged 12 years and over listen to the radio each week—a higher penetration than television, magazines, newspapers, or the Internet. Radio reaches Black audiences everywhere they are: at home, at work and in the car; in stores and restaurants; online; and, more recently, via cell phones. Regardless of age, time of day or geography, radio is the true media companion of Black consumers."

490 As exemplified in the recent and first-ever report produced on ad revenue spent on Black-targeted media, radio is used "more than any other medium" to reach Black audiences. Eight hundred and five million dollars was spent between October 1, 2006 and September, 30, 2007 on Black-targeted radio, or 35 percent of the total $2.3 billion spent on Black-targeted media during that same timeframe. Available

online at: http://www.insidebrandedentertainment.com/bep/article_display.jsp?JS ESSIONID=2v0jHLkhpvwnxny2wTVtY1S382l9JSLNTbXsyTTLzRYTGHL32W nl!1158789824&vnu_content_id=1003703403.

491 Point 5 of the 1966 FBI COINTELPRO (Counter Intelligence Program) document specifically targets Black youth as potential threats and calls for special efforts to protect against their radicalization. "A final goal should be to prevent the long-range growth of militant Black nationalist organizations *especially among youth*. Specific tactics to prevent these groups from converting young people must be developed." Ward Churchill, and Jim Vander Wall, *The COINTELPRO Papers: Documents from the FBI's Secret War Against Domestic Dissent* (Boulder, Co.: South End Press, 1990), 111, emphasis added.

492 The most recent (Winter 2007) combined ratings (9.5) of WPGC (5.5) and WKYS (4.0) trump that of WHUR's (6.9). Available online at: http://www.arbitron.com/ home/content.stm.

493 Glen Ford, "Who Killed Black Radio News?" *BlackCommentator.com*, May 29, 2003, emphasis added. Available online at: http://www.blackcommentator.com/44/44_ cover.html. Glen Ford is now editor-in-chief of *BlackAgendaReport.com*.

494 Radio One, after some recent sell-offs, owns fifty-three stations in sixteen urban markets, according to its website. Available online at: http://www.radio-one.com/ properties/radio.asp.

495 Interviews conducted and videotaped by Leah Tayor, former student intern with the author while at Morgan State University, Fall 2007.

496 Comments made during the aforementioned NPR panel on Black Radio History, March 24, 2007.

497 See Barlow, *Voice Over*, for a full account of the repeated claims of such portrayal by those concerned with such negative imagery. The point is that these images have and continue to persist despite any apparent government oversight.

498 McChesney, *The Political Economy of Media*, 418. And today, President Obama's newly forming FCC shows no sign of breaking this pattern. Matthew Lasar, *Ars Techna,* July 1, 2009. "Last year Stanford Law Professor Lawrence Lessig ran a rant in *Newsweek* calling for the White House to 'shut down' the FCC and replace it with a new entity—something with personnel 'absolutely barred from industry ties,' Lessig wrote. Well, it doesn't appear that the Obama administration has heeded this advice. Last Ars checked (about three seconds ago), the agency was still around. As for the industry ties—sorry Larry, they're still there in Genachowski's picks." Available online at: http://arstechnica.com/tech-policy/news/2009/07/meet-the- genachowskis-a-in-depth-look-at-the-new-fcc.ars.

499 "Top Online Companies." Available online at: http://www.stateofthemedia. org/2010/media-ownership/sector_online.php?s=4&so=-1&compare=.

500 Jaron Lanier, author of *You Are Not a Gadget* (New York: Knopf, 2010), interviewed on *Media Matters with Bob McChesney,* Sunday March 28, 2010. Available online at: http://will.illinois.edu/mediamatters/show/march-28th-2010/.

501 Matthew Hindman, "The More Things Change, the More They Stay the Same: Online Audiences and the Paradox of Web Traffic" [Online lecture], March 11, 2009. Available online at: http://www.youtube.com/watch?v=p9kV8QLpYC8. Hindman is also author of *The Myth of Digital Democracy* (Princeton, N.J.: Princeton University, 2008).

502 "Hip-Hop Bloggers: If I Ruled the Blogosphere," April 21, 2010. Available online at: http://www.rappersiknow.com/2010/04/21/hip-hop-bloggers-if-i-ruled-the-blogo sphere-part-i/.

503 "Radio, Radio: FMC and the 2010 Media Ownership Review," *The Future of Music Coalition.* Available online at: http://www.futureofmusic.org/blog/2010/07/14/ radio-radio-fmc-and-2010-media-ownership-review.

504 "Nielsen: Radio Listening Shows Stability," *FMQB.com,* June 22, 2010. Available online at: http://fmqb.com/article.asp?id=1885932.

505 Jared A. Ball, "The Titans of Technology."

506 The 1996 Telecommunications Act allowed by 2001 for "Clear Channel and Viacom alone [to control] 42 percent of radio listeners and 45 percent of industry revenues," according to, "Radio, Radio: FMC and the 2010 Media Ownership Review." The report also concludes that "the restructuring of radio has led to a severe reduction in competition and the homogenization of radio formats—changes which plainly undermine the FCC's primary goals of competition, localism, and diversity."

507 A Chicago University study on the subject shows upwards of 60 percent of Black youth dislike and want change to the popular hip-hop and R&B that they are forced to hear due to the herein described process of popularization and apparent lack of awareness of alternatives (February 2007). Available online at: blackyouthproject. com.

508 Hence Theodor Adorno's point that "like and dislike are inappropriate to the situation.... Familiarity is a surrogate for the quality ascribed to it."

509 Fall, Winter, Spring, and Summer sessions from 2005 to 2006 at the University of Maryland at College Park. The projects were designed to create awareness through detailed monitoring of content, precisely the kinds of images, stereotypes, and imbalances between substantive political content in music or "news." Students kept diaries and charts, and sent written and phoned-in complaints to the FCC when they thought necessary and then made end-of-the-semester presentations on their findings.

510 Palast, *The Best Democracy Money Can Buy.*

511 Achbar, *Manufacturing Consent.*

512 Lippmann, *Public Opinion*, 19, emphasis added. In other words, for the news to make sense or to have the desired impact of limiting the thought of its audience or targets, general opinions of what is covered must already have been set. The news can never raise, discuss, or spend too much time illuminating various topics, as it only exists to reify or amplify existing views.

513 Speech given to Black radio DJs in Atlanta, 1967. Available online at: http://odeo.com/audio/5430283/view.

514 Donna Lamb, "Disappearing Voices in Black Radio," *BlackStarNews.com*, July 7, 2008.

515 Speech given during COINTELPRO panel convened by Cynthia McKinney in Washington, D.C., September 2005. Available online at: http://voxunion.com/realaudio/coupradio/DaveyDonCOINTELPRO.mov.

516 U-Saviour, dir., *Disappearing Voices: The Decline of Black Radio* [Film] (Black Waxx Multimedia, 2009). Available online at: http://www.disappearingvoices.com/.

517 Comments made by Iyanna Jones during her interview on *CounterSpin*, August 15, 2008. Arbitron also recently settled a law suit in New York City where they had not sought Black recipients of the Portable People Meter (PPM) used in calculating audience.

518 David Segal, "Where Have All The Protests Gone?" *The Washington Post*, September 24, 2008. Available online at: http://www.washingtonpost.com/wp-dyn/content/article/2008/09/23/AR2008092303283_pf.html.

519 "'Talk,' in the Past Tense: Why There Are No More Petey Greenes on Local Radio," *The Washington Post,* July 22, 2007. Available online at: http://www.washingtonpost.com/wp-dyn/content/article/2007/07/20/AR2007072000478.html.

520 Janet Shan, "Two Top Executives, Alejandro Claiborne, Lee Michaels, Leave Black-Owned Radio One," *The Hinterland Gazette*, May 12, 2008. Available online at: http://blackpoliticalthought.blogspot.com/2008/05/two-top-executives-alejandro-claiborne.html.

521 "With a growing list of radio, newspaper, and television assets on the auction block, some new players are on the verge of assembling *the conglomerate of the 21st century*: the private-equity media empire." Berman and McBride, "Street Sleuth," C1, emphasis added.

522 Fanon, *Toward the African Revolution*, 34

523 Mike Boyer, "Oprah's Cosby Moment," *Foreign Policy*, January 9, 2007. Available online at: http://blog.foreignpolicy.com/node/3007.

524 For a powerful insight into Winfrey's function, see Daphne Brooks' "The Other Side of Paradise: Feminist Pedagogy, Toni Morrison Iconography, and Oprah's Book Club Phenomenon," in *Step into a World: A Global Anthology of the New Black Literature*, ed. Kevin Powell (New York: John Wiley and Sons, 2000), 163–172. Here Winfrey

comes only to play a role of "comforting and converting the upper-class white female subject" and portraying the "nineteenth century cult of domesticity... offering her viewers a fantasy of leisure and comfort."

525 Bell (2004); Kozol, *Shame of the Nation.*

526 McChesney, *The Political Economy of Media*, 277–278.

527 Lucian James, "American Brandstand Report 2008," *AgendaInc.com*. Available online at: http://www.agendainc.com/media/ambr08.pdf. This trend seems to be dying out as lyrics focus less on brands than on simple thoughtlessness or general sex-related content. In this most recent report, James writes, "All brand mentions in lyrics in 2008 fell sharply. Overall, the amount of brand mentions fell to 584 mentions in 2008, compared with 793 in 2007 and a high of 837 in 2006." Nike won with only 40 mentions in 2008.

528 Theodor Adorno, "On the Fetish-Character in Music and the Regression in Listening," in *The Essential Frankfurt School Reader*, eds. Amdrew Arato and Eike Gebhardt (New York: Continuum, 2002), 271.

529 The credit for the correctness of this connection or comparison between Radio-Alger and NPR goes entirely to Dr. Chris Tinson of TRGGR Radio who mentioned it during our interview (September 18, 2008).

530 Noam Chomsky lecture, "Authors @ Google," April 25, 2008. Available online at: http://www.youtube.com/watch?v=rnLWSC5p1XE. Chomsky refers to and explains further his idea that "the U.S. is the one country founded as an empire."

531 Bond's *Fanon's Warning* looks at the neo-colonialism in contemporary struggles of the African continent and international capital where Fanon's warnings against the incompleteness of revolutionary efforts would lead to just these kinds of arrangements with colonial puppets as "African leaders."

532 (1965), 69–97.

533 (1965), 71.

534 79.

535 *Marketplace* is produced by American Public Media (APM). APM and Public Radio International (PRI) are America's main syndicators of public radio programming outside of NPR. Both APM and PRI, not surprisingly, represent the same interests as NPR.

536 Deborah Bolling, "Tavis Smiley," *The Philadelphia City Paper*, November 21–27, 2002. Available online at: http://www.citypaper.net/articles/2002–11–21/om. shtml. His comments could also apply to his current nationally syndicated weekend radio program, "The Tavis Smiley Show," distributed by PRI and aired on public radio stations across the nation.

537 Jhally, *bell hooks: Cultural Criticism and Transformation*, 1996.

538 (1965), 73.

539 Ibid., 73.

540 Quoted from information provided in 2006 by KWMU in St. Louis. Formerly available online at: http://www.kwmu.org/Support/Underwriting/demographics.html.

541 "NPR Audience Profile," retrieved January 11, 2010 from: http://www.wqub.org/media/NPR%20Profile%20stats%202009/NPR%20demographics.pdf.

542 Steve Rendell and Daniel Butterworth, "How Public is Public Radio?" *Extra! Fairness and Accuracy in Reporting,* May/June 2004.

543 Ibid.

544 Interview conducted during the author's radio program, *Jazz and Justice,* on WPFW 89.3 FM, May 10, 2008.

545 Personal communication with the author, August 10, 2007.

546 Zein Elamine of Save Our Neighborhood Schools Coalition has spoken very highly of the support that his organization has received from DJ and host EZ Street from WPGC (March 9, 2008).

547 Interview for *Jazz and Justice,* WPFW 89.3 FM, Pacifica, Washington, D.C., September 15, 2008.

548 Churchill spoke of the rise of Alan Pinkerton who, in the early 1860s, convinced the federal government of a need to protect the incoming President Lincoln from a threat that no one to this day can verify ever existed. The purpose being to create the problem that he could then prevent in order to assure his own rise in the field of police work but that, according to Churchill, began the official relationship between private contracting and state power (a la Blackwater mercenaries today), which were designed to assure national state elite power (September 2005). Available online at: http://www.youtube.com/watch?v=MWYeZxSAwJ8.

549 Churchill and Vander Wall, *The COINTELPRO Papers,* 92.

550 Ibid., 110.

551 Ibid., 111, emphasis added.

552 George Jackson, *Soledad Brother: The Prison Letters of George Jackson* (Chicago: Lawrence Hill Books, 2004), April 4, 1970, 237, emphasis added.

553 For an updated discussion of the current state of such high childhood commercialization, see Robert McChesney's interview with Susan Linn on June 28, 2009. "Our guest this week is Susan Linn. Linn is Associate Director of the Media Center of the Judge Baker Children's Center and an Instructor in Psychiatry at Harvard Medical School. Dr. Linn is a co-founder of the national coalition Campaign for a Commercial-Free Childhood. She is the author of *The Case for Make Believe* and *Consuming Kids.*"

554 Bill Cosby and Alvin Poussaint on "victimization" where their arguments mirror the neo-liberal ones made by Oprah Winfrey and John McWhorter. Their new book,

Come On People!, given full-segment air time on NBC's *Meet the Press* and even more room on that show's website, seeks to deny structured denial of Black uplift by describing continued inequality as the result of Black behavior itself divorced from societal influence. "Their new book hopes to address the crises of people who are stuck because of feelings of low self-esteem, abandonment, anger, fearfulness, sadness, and feelings of being used, undefended, and unprotected. *These feelings often impede their ability to move forward*" (emphasis added). Available online at: http://www.msnbc.msn.com/id/21279731/.

555 Alex Constantine, *The Covert War Against Rock: What You Don't Know About the Deaths of Jim Morrison, Tupac Shakur, Michael Hutchence, Brian Jones, Jimi Hendrix, Phil Ochs, Bob Marley, Peter Tosh, John Lennon, and The Notorious B.I.G.* (Port Townsend, Wash.: Feral House, 2000), 9. Parenthetically, Constantine—returning to our previous discussion of copyright as colonial theft—notes how "[c]rushing musical voices of dissent was proving to be an immensely profitable enterprise because a dead rocker leaves behind a fortune of publishing rights and royalties" (64). The industry and those who control it do quite well and suffer not at all like the families and supporters of radical artists whose lives and careers are destroyed as the owners of their art continue to profit from that property regardless of the condition of the artists themselves.

556 Constantine, *The Covert War Against Rock*, 15. Here Constantine is quoting Donna Demac, an instructor of "interactive telecommunications" at New York University.

557 Armstrong, *A Trumpet to Arms*, 138–159. "In 1970, Senator Thomas Dodd attempted to write press suppression into law, introducing what he termed the 'Urban Terrorism Prevention Bill.'" See also Paul Samberg's *Fire! Reports from the Underground Press* (Boston: E. P. Dutton, 1970) to see the specific kinds of journalism targeted for suppression.

558 The idea simplified is that political organizations, particularly in Black America, form coalitions to put public pressure on Black-targeted radio challenging them to hire local reporters and develop newsrooms. Without this, radio can never again be expected to serve the needs of the people as opposed to corporate power and selected members of a neo-colonial Black elite. To hear more on this idea and the details of developing community pressure on local Black-targeted radio for the inclusion of locally produced news, listen to Bruce Dixon and Glen Ford describe the project in the 2008 Free Press National Conference on Media Reform panel "News for the People: Can Black Radio Provide the News We Need?" Available online at: http://www.voxunion.com/?p=67.

559 In response to the statement of Kanye West that the media offer an inaccurate portrayal of Black people and that George Bush doesn't care about Black people, NBC Universal issued the following as part of their statement: "Kanye West

departed from the scripted comments that were prepared for him, and his opinions in no way represent the views of the networks. It would be most unfortunate if the efforts of the artists who participated tonight and the generosity of millions of Americans who are helping those in need are overshadowed by one person's opinion" (emphasis added). Lisa de Moraes, "Kanye West's Torrent of Criticism, Live on NBC," *The Washington Post,* September 3, 2005. In other words, no one, particularly representatives of the colonized, is allowed to say what they do on air without it being scripted or sanctioned from above. This also points to the fact that whatever is on air that is dehumanizing is perfectly acceptable to those in power.

560 Achbar, *Manufacturing Consent.*

561 Jhally, *bell hooks: Cultural Criticism and Transformation,* 1996.

562 Amos Wilson, "The Impact of Media on the African Psyche." Speech aired on *Democracy Now!,* February 5, 1999. Available online at: http://www.democracynow. org/1999/2/5/amos_wilson_the_impact_of_the.

563 Armand Mattelart and Michele Mattelart, *Theories of Communication: A Short Introduction* (London: Sage, 1999).

564 Hanno Hardt, *Critical Communications Studies: Communication, History and Theory in America* (New York: Routledge, 1992).

565 Simpson, *Science of Coercion,* 8, emphasis added.

566 Wilson.

567 George Ciccariello Maher, "Brechtian Hip-Hop: Didactics and Self-Production in Post-Gangsta Political Mixtapes," *Journal of Black Studies,* vol. 36, no. 1, 2005, 129–160.

568 Shah, "Modernization, Marginalization, and Emancipation," 143–166.

569 Juanita Darling in "Re-Imagining the Nation" quotes Harva Hatchen as defining revolutionary media as "illegal and subversive mass communication utilizing the press and broadcasting to over-throw a government or wrest control from alien rulers."

570 Personal communication with the author, interview for *Jazz and Justice,* WPFW 89.3 FM, July 14, 2008.

571 The work of Fairness and Accuracy in Reporting (FAIR) is of value here. As they reported in their May/June 2002 edition of *Extra!* titled "*Power Sources: On Party, Gender, Race and Class, TV News Looks to the Most Powerful Groups,*" "Instead of a liberal bias, the study found, source selection favored the elite interests that the corporate owners of these shows depend on for advertising revenue, regulatory support and access to information. Network news demonstrated a clear tendency to showcase the opinions of the most powerful political and economic actors, while giving limited access to those voices that would be most likely to challenge them."

572 Shah, "Modernization, Marginalization, and Emancipation," 144.

573 Ibid., 143.

574 Rose.

575 For more, see the reporting and writing of Gary Webb, whose work on *The Dark Alliance* (New York: Seven Stories, 1998) between U.S. intelligence agency involvement in the flooding of Black communities with illegal drugs is under-discussed and underappreciated.

576 As attested to in personal communication with an unidentified New York City police officer after unsuccessfully chasing teenage street vendors on July 24, 2004.

577 R.I.P. Justo, whose work and dedication to the mixtape form is unmatched and essential to the sub-culture. It is, however, an unfortunate part of the pattern of colonialism that his work for and love of the mixtape has unwittingly aided the processes of co-optation.

578 Spirer's documentary also exposes a contemporary RAPINTELPRO, or modern-day COINTELPRO, targeting *only* Black rappers and their associates. For more, see Greg Thomas' unpublished 2010 essay, "Mi Say WAR: Hip-Hop vs. the Bourgeois West... and 'Hip-Hop' Studies?" Available online at: http://www.voxunion.com/?p=2736.

579 "The Recording Industry Association of America (RIAA) is the trade group that represents most of the recording industry in the US.... The RIAA's members include more than 500 record companies and "90% of all legitimate sound recordings produced and sold in the United States." (*The Computer Internet Lawyer*, February 2003.)

580 See, among other sources, *The Larry Davis Story* [Film] (Mvd Visual, 2003) by Troy Davis for a most famous example of this. Available online at: http://www.blackstarvideo.com/videos2/The-Larry-Davis-Story.html.

581 All the following interviews regarding use and function of mixtapes can be seen or heard at the FreeMix Radio blog: http://mixtapeliberation.blogspot.com.

582 Founding Chair of the Africana Studies and Research Center at Cornell University.

583 Fairness and Accuracy in Reporting (FAIR), "*Finding Fault on Both Sides Can Be False Balance,*" *Action Alert!*, September, 30, 2004. "While fact-checking is an essential media function, particularly during an election year, it's a hollow exercise if journalists start with the assumption that both sides must be found equally guilty of falsehoods. It is, in fact, not always the case that both campaigns are responsible for deceptive claims to the same degree; coverage that insists on a false even-handedness, while pretending to expose political mendacity, actually gives cover for it by neutralizing criticism with the 'they all do it' defense. Such coverage may protect news outlets from charges of bias, but it does a disservice to voters."

584 William J. Harris, ed., *The Leroi Jones/Amiri Baraka Reader* (New York: Thunder's Mouth Press, 1991), 463.

585 "A new FAIR study of NPR's guest list shows the radio service relies on the same elite and influential sources that dominate mainstream commercial news, and falls short of reflecting the diversity of the American public." *How Public is Public Radio? A Study of NPR's [National Public Radio] Guest List.* Fairness and Accuracy in Reporting, June 2004. See also Achbar, *Manufacturing Consent.*

586 Hemant Shah, personal communication with the author, July 14, 2008.

587 Hemant Shah, *Journalism in an Age of Mass Media Globalization,* June 2007. Available online at: http://www.idsnet.org/Papers/Communications/HEMANT_SHAH.HTM.

588 A point with which Shah himself agrees, stating that while it had not occurred to him that mixtapes could be put to such use, the idea is a good one. Locally produced, consumed, and focused is precisely what EJ calls for. Personal communication with the author, July 14, 2008.

589 A terrific overview of this history exists in the chapter "Rise of the Underground Press" in Armstrong's *A Trumpet to Arms.* Armstrong extends this history so as to incorporate the origins of the Black, Indigenous, Latino, and radical White presses, demonstrating them as emancipatory in that they also "participated in the events they covered" (50).

590 Altschull, *Agents of Power,* 148–149.

591 This issue, the struggle over "desettlerizing the media," is also highlighted in what remains a strong overview of mass media in "post"-colonial Africa. Dhyana Ziegler and Molefi K. Asante, *Thunder and Silence: The Mass Media in Africa* (Trenton, N.J.: Africa World Press, 1992), 109.

592 Baffour Ankomah, "The Role of the African Media in Promoting African Integration," 173.

593 Ibid., 176.

594 Altschull, *Agents of Power,* 150.

595 Sally Lehman, "The Danger of Losing the Ethnic Media," *The Boston Globe,* March 5, 2009. Available online at: http://www.boston.com/bostonglobe/editorial_opinion/oped/articles/2009/03/05/the_danger_of_losing_the_ethnic_media/.

596 Personal communication with the author, March 13, 2010. Dr. Mark Bolden was part of our small crew conducting interviews on the historical relationship between mixtapes, or "PA tapes," and Go-Go music.

597 For more on this minus this particular political lens or focus on the communicative aspect of mixtapes and P.A. tapes, see Natalie Hopkinson, "Go-Go Music Is the Soul of Washington, But It's Slipping Away," *The Washington Post,* April 11, 2010. Available online at: http://www.washingtonpost.com/wp-dyn/content/article/2010/04/09/AR2010040903257.html?referrer=emailarticle. See also Kip Lornell and Charles C. Stephenson, Jr., *The Beat: Go-Go Music from Washington,*

D.C. (Jackson, Miss: University Press of Mississippi, 2009).

598 The iconic character, neighborhood disc-jockey, played by Samuel Jackson in Spike Lee's *Do The Right Thing* [Film] (40 Acres and a Mule, 1989).

599 See Appendix A for details on the legality of mixtape radio.

600 Donn C. Worgs, "'BEWARE OF THE FRUSTRATED...'

The Fantasy and Reality of African American Violent Revolt," *Journal of Black Studies*, vol. 37, no. 1, September 2006, 20–45.

601 An undying love and respect for the founding comrades in this first attempt at grassroots organizing, whose names are mentioned for that reason alone and not necessarily to suggest a continuing agreement with the arguments made herein. Suzette Gardner, Ciatta Baysah, Maleena Lawrence, Mark Bowen, and Roxanne Lawson.

602 Here, again, this is not meant to implicate these artists in the politics of this document or even to suggest total agreement. Rather, their willingness to lend their expertise to such a project is born more out of their adherence to hip-hop communal values of love, respect, and support for similar-minded folks in the community. Special thanks again to such as Head-Roc, DJ Eurok, DJ RBI, DJ Underdog, 2-Tone Jones, Bush Head Ed, Asheru, and DJs Soyo and Earth 1NE.

603 See Appendix A for details.

604 Ibid.

605 The 1955 conference of the "Non-Aligned" nations of the so-called "Third World." Hear more about this historic conference and its legacy in 2010 in "The Continued Importance of Bandung and Non-Alignment," *Voxunion.com,* April 26, 2010. Available online at: http://www.voxunion.com/?p=2606.

606 An inspirational media activist who continues his work...

607 U.S.-based artist Wise Intelligent reported that another artist, Young Buck, described in an interview on Hot97 in New York that his song would be kept of his upcoming Interscope (UMG) release because CEO Jimmy Iovine and his "lyrics committee" found the content offensive (April 19, 2007). Available online at: http://www.hiphopcongress.com/2007/04/the-story-behind-interscope-records-lyric-committee/#more-284.

608 For instance, in his coverage of the recent entombment of Black Power within the Smithsonian, Richard Prince of *Journal-isms* wrote that "the [Black Power] activists didn't always feel so alienated [from mainstream mass media], according to playwright Amiri Baraka, formerly LeRoi Jones. The media 'were a little naive earlier,' he told *Journal-isms.* 'But they got wise. You used to be able to hear Dr. King, Malcolm X, and Stokely Carmichael'.... But those voices soon disappeared. Today, 'they only put fools' on the air. (And too many, [Askia Muhammad] Toure added, are happy to go on.)" (March 30, 2009). Available online at: http://mije.org/

richardprince/black-power-and-mainstream-media.

609 As opposed to more routine and serious attention paid these issues in the journalism of more progressive, radical, and revolutionary presses, for instance, the Socialist Worker's Party's *The Militant* or the Revolutionary Communist Party's *Revolution*. Even the online Independent Media network offers a more open forum of these issues.

610 The other is a piece on cutting welfare. And again, this is not to discount the value in their studies or their overall diversity. Readers will get pieces about Africa, India, the Middle East, and so on. It is simply that when it comes to those colonized at "home" (though there is one story in their 2008 study of the Indigenous) there is very little to no attention paid.

611 The late long-time Washington, D.C.-based activist, friend, and mentor. Smith is founder of Black Voices for Peace and had worked tirelessly despite his having been diagnosed with cancer.

612 Jared A. Ball, "Diversity Schmifersity: When It Comes to Black Even the Left Ain't Right," *BlackAgendaReport.com*, March 20, 2010. The study examined the 261 episodes spanning January 2009 to January 2010.

613 Noam Chomsky, "The Center Cannot Hold: Rekindling the Radical Imagination," *DemocracyNow.org*, May 31, 2010, emphasis added. Available online at: http://www.democracynow.org/2010/5/31/noam_chomsky_the_center_cannot_hold.

614 Formerly with BlackCommentator.com and now executive editor at BlackAgendaReport.com.

615 Interview conducted in January of 2007 during the Free Press Media Reform Conference in Memphis, Tenn.

616 Hardt, *Critical Communications Studies*, emphasis added.

617 Aptheker, *American Negro Slave Revolts*. This is in reference to the ways in which forms of communication have always been seen as part of a protection of what Aptheker calls the "American slaveocracy," which had always the need to "develop numerous psychological, social, juridical, economic, and militaristic methods of suppression and oppression" (53). He also describes what was thought important among "intelligent masters," the need for "*communication* of sound religious instruction [to their slaves] as the *truest economy* and the most efficient police," (58, emphasis added). He also notes how the "machinery of control" necessitated the planting of "secret agents to pervade the black community" so as to ascertain whether or not David Walker's *Appeal*, that "revolutionary pamphlet," was in circulation (61–62). Communication and the press had/have very specific purposes in any given society no less now than then.

618 Perkins, "The Defense of Slavery in the Northern Press on the Eve of the Civil War," 501–531. See also Saxton, "Problems of Class and Race in the Origins of the Mass

Circulation Press," 211–234. See also Hale, *Making Whiteness.*

619 Slavoj Žižek, *Violence* (New York: Picador, 2008), 189.

620 *Democracy Now!* issues of post-Katrina/levees New Orleans are discussed only within the context of Ensler's work (April 11, 2008). Available online at: http://www.democracynow.org/2008/4/11/v_to_the_tenth_thousands_of.

621 Dan Berger, "Defining Democracy: Coalition Politics and the Struggle for Media Reform," *International Journal of Communication* 3, 2009, 3–22.

622 C. Riley Snorton, "New Beginning: Racing Histories, Democracy, and Media Reform," *International Journal of Communication 3,* 2009, 23–41, 36, 38, emphasis added. See also McChesney's response to these criticisms, "Understanding the Media Reform Movement," *International Journal of Communication* 3 (2009), 47–53.

623 To her/their credit, Laura Flanders and her *GritTv* (grittv.org) do a far greater job at being diverse racially, ethnically, and in terms of sexual orientation, though more could be done there, too, to include further Left politics in the program. And for more on the pirate radio movement see the film by Mary Jones and Jeff Pearson, *Pirate Radio USA* (Deface the Nation Films, 2006) which can be found online at: http://www.pirateradiousa.com/.

624 Bill Moyers, "Interview with James Cone," *Bill Moyers Journal,* November 23, 2007. Available online at: http://www.pbs.org/moyers/journal/11232007/profile.html.

625 John Henrik Clarke, "Christopher Columbus and the Afrikan Holocaust," 1992. Available online at: http://www.youtube.com/watch?v=4oN4PQLfteg.

626 Darling, *"Re-Imaging the Nation."*

627 Roger Streitmatter, *Voices of Revolution: The Dissident Press in America* (New York: Columbia University, 2001), xi, 279, original emphasis.

628 Gabriel Weimann, "The Psychology of Mass-Mediated Terrorism," *American Behavioral Scientist*, vol. 52, no. 1, September 2008, 69–86.

629 Again, the existence of talk radio and popular national Black radio such as Tom Joyner, Tavis Smiley, Michael Baidsen, Joe Madison, and so on does not in anyway change this.

630 Klein, *The Shock Doctrine.* However, unless otherwise specified, this summary of her work comes from her own summary video produced as a companion to the book with Alfonso Cuaron. Available online at: http://www.youtube.com/watch?v=aSF0e6oO_tw.

631 Wunyabari Maloba, "The Media and Mau Mau: Kenyan Nationalism and Colonial Propaganda," in *Africa's Media Image,* ed. Beverly G. Hawk (Westport, Conn.: Praeger Publishers 1992), 59.

632 Ward Churchill, *Kill the Indian and Save the Man*, 5, emphasis added.

633 Ibid., 6.

634 Todd Williams, dir., *The N-Word* [Film] (Trio Film, 2004).

635 L. Timmeran, et al., "A Review and Meta-Analysis Examining the Relationship of Music Content with Sex, Race, Priming, and Attitudes," *Communication Quarterly*, vol. 56, no. 3, August 2008, 303–324.

636 Jared Ball, "Barack Obama, 'Connected Distance,' Race and 21st Century Neo-Colonialism."

637 "To be black is literally abnormal. The effect, Fanon observed, that to be black is never to be a man or a woman. It is to be, under this collapse into pathogenic reality, locked in underdevelopment, frozen, in other words, in perpetual childhood." Lewis Gordon, "Grown Folks' Business" in *Hip-Hop and Philosophy: Rhyme 2 Reason,* eds. Derrick Darby and Tommie Shelby (Chicago: Open Court, 2005), 108.

638 Mark Bolden, et al, "Beyond Health Disparities: Examining Power Disparities and Industrial Complexes from the Views of Frantz Fanon (Part 1)," *The Journal of Pan-African Studies*, vol. 3, no. 8, June 2010. Co-authored with The Fanon Project: Drs. Mark Bolden, Chante DeLoach, Alex Pieterse, Otis Williams, Sirein Awadalla, and Jared Ball.

639 *Yo TV!* California State Conference: 19th Annual NAACP State Convention FCC Forum Oakland, Ca., October 26–29, 2006. Available online at: http://www.youtube.com/watch?v=mR8CHfxgQ-I.

640 Panel convened by the Patrice Lumumba Coalition, New York, N.Y., 1991.

641 Simpson, "U.S. Mass Communication Research, Counterinsurgency, and Scientific 'Reality,'" 314–319, emphasis added.

642 Ibid., 315, emphasis added.

643 Simpson; Streitmatter, *Voices of Revolution*.

644 DuBois, *Black Reconstruction in America*, 727.

645 This view may be reinforced by both the derivative status of the book in relation to the show containing the copyrighted material and the proximity of the hyperlink for sale to the hyperlinks for streaming and downloading the show.

ABOUT THE AUTHOR: JARED BALL

Dr. Jared A. Ball is the father of two brilliant and adorable daughters, Maisi and Marley, and the fortunate husband of Nelisbeth Y. Ball.

After that he is an associate professor of communication studies at Morgan State University, where his research interests include the interaction between colonialism, mass media theory and history, as well as, the development of alternative/underground journalism and cultural expression as mechanisms of social movements and political organization.

Ball is a columnist with, and produces a weekly radio column for, BlackAgendaReport.com. He is producer and host of the Legacy Edition of We Ourselves which airs on Washington, D.C.'s WPFW 89.3 FM Pacifica Radio, and is the founder and producer of FreeMix Radio: The Original Mixtape Radio Show, an emancipatory journalistic political mixtape.

He is a former editor of and current peer reviewer for the first academic journal dedicated to hip-hop, *The Global Journal of Hip-Hop Culture* from Words. Beats. Life., and has been a board member of the International Association for Hip-Hop Education, as well as a Communications Fellow for the Green Institute.

I Mix What I Like! A Mixtape Manifesto is his first book. He can be found online at voxunion.com.

SUPPORT AK PRESS!

AK Press is one of the world's largest and most productive anarchist pub

lishing houses. We're entirely worker run and democratically managed. W operate without a corporate structure— no boss, no managers, no bullshit. W publish close to twenty books every yea and distribute thousands of other title published by other like-minded inde pendent presses from around the globe.

The Friends of AK program is a way tha you can directly contribute to the con tinued existence of AK Press, and ensur

that we're able to keep publishing great books just like this one! Friend pay a minimum of $25 per month, for a minimum three month period into our publishing account. In return, Friends automatically receive (fo the duration of their membership), as they appear, one free copy of ever new AK Press title. They're also entitled to a 20% discount on everythin featured in the AK Press Distribution catalog and on the website, on an and every order. You or your organization can even sponsor an entir book if you should so choose!

There's great stuff in the works—so sign up now to become a Friend c AK Press, and let the presses roll!

Won't you be our friend? Email friendsofak@akpress.org for more info, o visit the Friends of AK Press website:
http://www.akpress.org/programs/friendsofak